MEDICAL SCIENCE

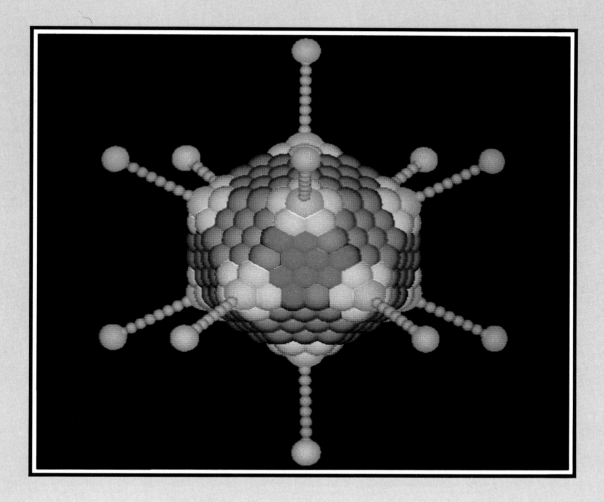

Southside

Editor Peter Furtado
Art Editor John Ridgeway
Designer Ayala Kingsley
Picture Editor Linda Proud

Project Director Lawrence Clarke

Advisors
Professor Donald Henderson,
Johns Hopkins University
Sir Peter Medawar, Nobel Laureate
Professor Norman Shumway,
Stanford University
Dr William Brock, University of
Leicester
Professor John Humphrey, Royal
Postgraduate Medical School
Dr Jean Ross, Charing Cross
Hospital Medical School

Contributing Editor Bernard Dixon

Contributors
Jenny Bryan (1, 9)
Bernard Dixon (1, 9, 11, 14, 16, 19)
Richard Fifield (6)
Caroline Richmond (2, 3, 4, 5, 7)
Martin Sherwood (8, 10, 12, 13, 15,
17, 18)

AN EQUINOX BOOK

Planned and produced by:
Equinox (Oxford) Ltd
Musterlin House,
Jordan Hill Road
Oxford OX2 8DP

Published by:
Southside (Publishers) Ltd.
an imprint of
Canongate Publishing Ltd.
17 Jeffrey St.
Edinburgh EH1 1DR

Copyright © Equinox (Oxford) Ltd
1989

ISBN 90002526 3

Printed in Spain by H. Fournier, S.A.

Contents

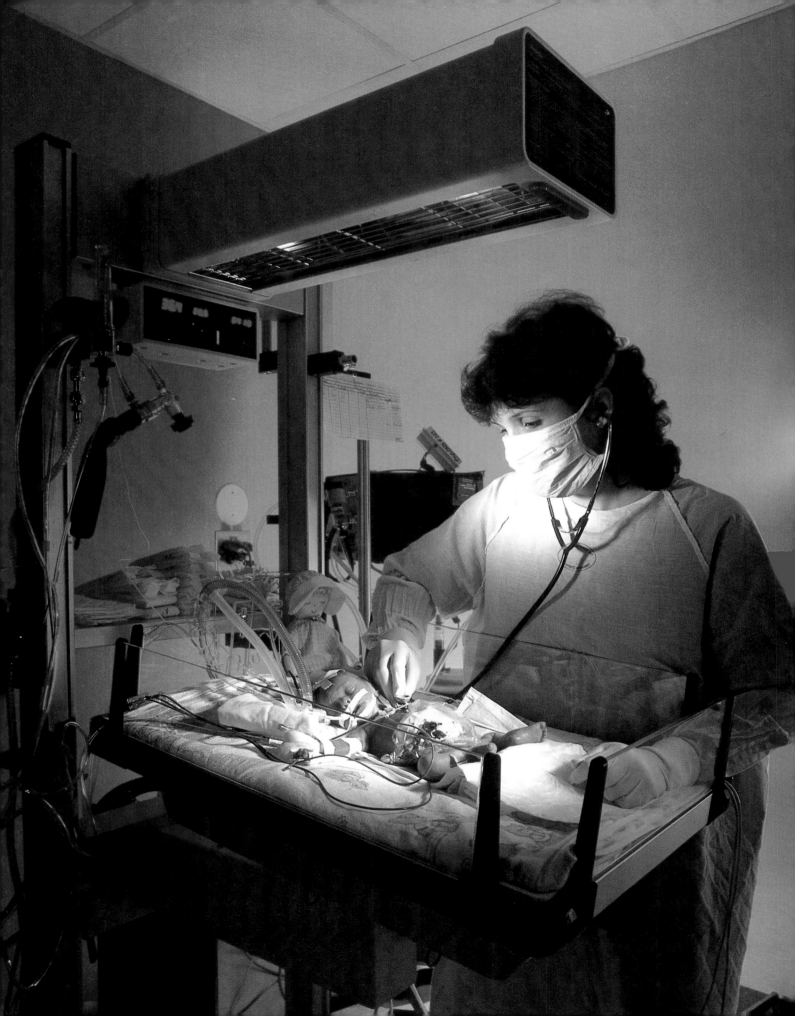

Medicine, Doctors and Health

1

The multiple causes of illness...The challenge to medicine...Health for rich and poor...The development of modern medicine...PERSPECTIVE...Ancient medicine... Medieval and Renaissance medicine...Medicine and science...Identifying microbes...Medicine in the 17th century...Seeing into the body...Paying for medicine

From earliest times, efforts to understand how the body is constructed and how it works have gone hand-in-hand with attempts to comprehend and treat ill health. Whether by probing human anatomy or by charting physiological processes, investigators have provided insights not only into normality but also into the abnormality that we call disease. Erratically at first, and with many false trails, this rational approach led to modern medical science, whose spectacular triumphs range from the global eradication of smallpox to the transplantation of ailing organs and the exquisite intricacies of brain surgery. Today, recognition of these achievements is tempered by two cautions. First the benefits of science-based medicine have been applied inequitably, leaving appalling imbalances in the burden of disease between countries of the North and the South. Second, mechanistic methods have been so successful that they may have obscured the subtle interplay between mind and body, and eclipsed healing as an art.

Health and illness

The achievements of medical science in this century, and the possible limitations of those achievements, both derive from the idea that particular diseases have particular causes (◗ page 9). In recent years scientists have found that, for a number of reasons (◗ page 12), people vary considerably in their innate susceptibility to many illnesses, including infections. A prime example is coronary heart disease. While arguments continue about their relative weight, many different factors influence the condition's onset and course (◗ page 57). For this reason, and because personality and mental attitude are also relevant, coronary heart disease is one of those which critics of wholly materialistic medicine have highlighted as needing a holistic approach. While not repudiating medical science, holistic practitioners advocate a return to the Hippocratic approach of treating the whole person rather than tinkering with specific malfunctioning parts.

The multifactorial nature of disease is the principal explanation for the contrasts in health between and within different societies. Thus many of the conditions responsible for mass mortality in the Third World are not exotic tropical diseases confined to those regions by accidents of geography. They are infections like measles, made more virulent by poverty and malnutrition. "Diseases of civilization", on the other hand, are those (like coronary heart disease) which are associated with overeating and other aspects of the affluent lifestyle. Even within developed countries, different socio-economic groups show persistent disparities in measures such as perinatal mortality rate (stillbirths and deaths in the first four weeks). There are, in turn, several causes of these contrasts, including differences in nutrition, living conditions, and access to and use of medical services.

▲ *Asclepius, the Greek god of medicine, mentioned by Homer in the "Iliad" as a physician, but later deified as the god of medicine and son of Apollo, was killed by Zeus in case he passed his knowledge on to humankind. His cult was celebrated at temples at Epidavros and Kos, where a ritualistic form of treatment was offered for many diseases, involving interpretation of dreams and purification.*

The origins of scientific medicine

Knowledge of anatomy, physiology and pathology as we now understand them began to emerge with the Greeks. They were also the first to recognize the distinction between internal and external causes of illness, which became a vital strand in the emergence of scientific medicine.

Hippocrates (c.460-c.377 BC) was a blend of scientist and artist, who examined his patients at the temple-hospital on the island of Kos with both empathy and rationality. He believed that disease occurred when four humors – blood from the heart, yellow bile from the liver, black bile from the spleen and phlegm from the brain – became out of balance. Although long discredited, this theory was important in combining a picture of the body as a machine, subject to adjustment when it malfunctioned, with an awareness that the whole person was much more than the sum of the individual parts, and should be given treatment accordingly. In this, Hippocratic medicine paralleled the even older Chinese tradition, founded on the complementary principles of yin (female principle) and yang (male), whose correct proportions were essential for health.

The scientific identification of the causes of illness began in the 17th century

Egyptian medicine
The ancient Egyptians seem to have been the first to realize the possibility of rational therapy, albeit through attempts to placate evil spirits. Many of their drugs were foul substances, given in the belief that they would be unwelcome to the demons possessing patients' bodies. Gradually, however, cause and effect became apparent as practitioners noted the difference between poisonous, ineffective and genuinely potent preparations. The Egyptians also anticipated the scientific stance in another sense, with doctors specializing in eyes, bellies, heads and other parts of the body.

The authorities of medieval medicine
Although more often remembered for his erroneous ideas about the physical world, Aristotle (384-322 BC) was a prime figure in the history of Greek medicine. By dissecting small animals and describing their internal anatomy, he laid the foundations for the later scrutiny of the human body. The person who took the next major step was Galen of Pergamon (AD 129-199), who dissected rhesus monkeys and possibly also human bodies. He described the arteries and veins, itemized tendons and muscles, classified bones, and even revealed the working of the nervous system by severing a pig's spinal cord at different points and demonstrating that corresponding parts of the body became paralyzed. After Galen's death, however, anatomical research ceased and his work was considered infallible for 1200 years.

Challenging Galen
It was only with the work of Andreas Vesalius (1514-1564) that Galen's ideas were challenged. Vesalius became professor of anatomy and surgery at Padua immediatey after graduating in 1537, and began a lifetime of scrupulous dissection of the human body. In his "De Humani Corporis Fabrica" he illustrated not just what bodily parts looked like, but how they worked.

▲ **Temperaments associated with the four humors** – phlegmatic, sanguine, choleric and melancholic. The humors were said to govern character as well as health.

▼ **A medieval illustration of collecting and preparing herbs.** In the 16th and 17th centuries this skill formed the essence of pharmacy and was based on empirical knowledge and on folklore.

► **The ancient and obscure art of trepanning, drilling a hole in the head,** seen here in a 16th-century engraving.

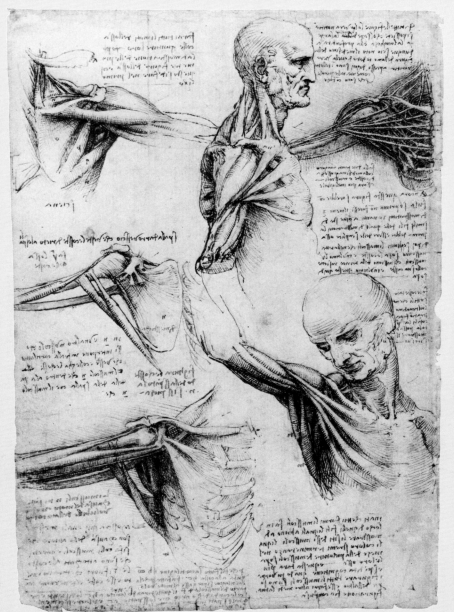

Renaissance medicine

The tradition established by Vesalius was continued by a succession of researchers at Padua including Gabriello Fallopio (1523-1562), discoverer of the Fallopian tubes, and Sanctorio Sanctorius (1561-1636) who initiated the serious study of body chemistry. A remarkable phase of conquest was completed when William Harvey demonstrated the circulation of the blood in the early 17th century and Marcello Malpighi revealed the blood capillaries as the link between arteries and veins.

Such efforts were greeted with skepticism by vitalists, who believed that the body's workings could never be fully understood in material terms. Similar opposition confronted the physicians and biologists who were increasingly successful in understanding living creatures as machines. It was Thomas Sydenham (1624-1689), an English physician with little interest in anatomy, who took the next rational step, by trying to specify and classify different illnesses. Distinguishing diseases from their victims, he also suggested that at least some were due to particular agents fighting against the healing powers of the body. This led to a spate of accurate descriptions of diseases – notably by Bernardino Ramazzini (1633-1714), an Italian physician who founded occupational medicine by listing the conditions associated with 40 trades.

The increasingly close liaison between medicine and science was furthered in the 18th century by such figures as Stephen Hales, the first person to measure blood pressure; Albert von Haller, pioneer in the study of nerves and muscles; and Claude Bernard, who began to delineate the process of digestion and founded experimental medicine.

◀ *The muscles of the shoulder, by Leonardo da Vinci (1452-1519). Leonardo's very detailed anatomical studies were in advance of any in his time, but they were never published and his knowledge was lost or ignored at the time. Only very occasionally, as in a drawing of the circulation of the blood through the heart, did his work show any reliance on Galenic ideas rather than on individual observation.*

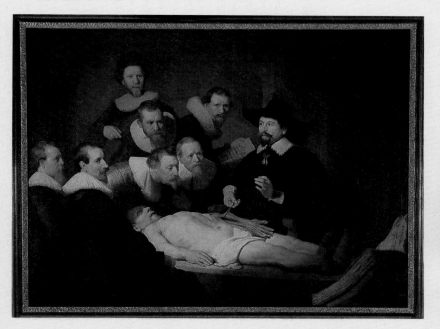

◀ *"The Anatomy Lesson", (1632) by Rembrandt in which the students intently observe dissection.*

▲ *Ambroise Paré (c. 1510-1590), the French military surgeon who introduced more humane surgery.*

Bacteria were discovered a century before they were known to cause illnesses

▶ *Louis Pasteur (1822-1895), seen here testing a vaccine on himself; his observations of the exact relationships between microbes and diseases revolutionized medical science.*

▼ *Florence Nightingale (1820-1910), the English woman who established the first professional nursing service, for British soldiers in the Crimean War (1853-1856). On her return she helped to lay the foundations for a new style of health care, with well-run and hygienic wards in airy hospitals.*

Discovering microbes

The marriage between medicine and science was consummated in the late 19th century by a group of scientists who finally showed that unseen micro-organisms caused epidemics and other diseases now known as infections. This idea was a venerable one, supported by the efficacy of measures such as the quarantine which kept bubonic plague out of Venice between 1370 and 1374. Yet there was no proof – not even when Anton van Leeuwenhoek (1632-1723) used his finely-ground lenses to discover "animalcules" (which we would now recognize as microbes such as bacteria) in the late 17th century. The Dutch linen draper was well ahead of his time – further investigations of the microbial world, and of its relationship to health had to await technical improvements in the microscope, which did not come for over 100 years.

Even when micro-organisms were more widely recognized, proof that they are transmitted from person to person, causing particular diseases, was not possible until the idea of spontaneous generation had been discredited. In 1688 the Italian physician Francesco Redi (1626-1697) had demonstrated that maggots did not develop in decaying meat when it was protected from contamination by flies. But it was not until the mid-19th century that the French chemist Louis Pasteur (1822-1895) confirmed that "animalcules" too did not appear, unless introduced from the outside, in food materials that had been sterilized by boiling.

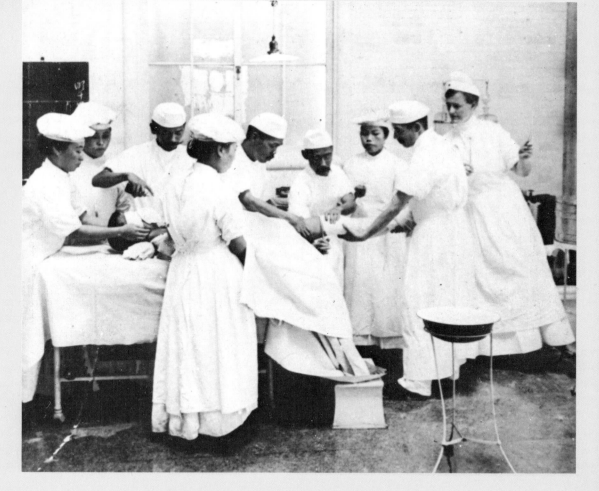

▲ The first microscope, made by Anton van Leeuwenhoek (1632-1723), with a single, powerful lens set within a brass plate.

▶ The introduction of ether and chloroform as anesthetics revolutionized surgery for surgeons as well as patients.

Medicine in the 19th century

Pasteur made a second discovery that was to transform the practise of medicine. Asked to investigate occasional irregularities in wine and vinegar making, he found that each was promoted by a particular sort of microbe and that when the processes went awry a different organism was present. Undrinkable "ropey" or "oily" wine, for example, always resulted from contamination with specific, atypical types of microbe. It was a short but brilliant step from these "diseases" of wine to the idea that human and other animal maladies might also be produced by specific, characteristic sorts of micro-organism. But so it proved. Beginning with chicken cholera, and anthrax in sheep, Pasteur found that they too were caused by corresponding bacterial species. This led him to highly successful efforts to weaken the organisms by aging them so that when injected into healthy animals they no longer triggered the disease but did elicit specific immunity. Although Edward Jenner had pioneered vaccination against smallpox nearly a century before, Pasteur's was the demonstration that established the feasibility of immunization in general and led to the conquest of conditions such as diphtheria and poliomyelitis.

Another result of Pasteur's earliest experiments was that the English surgeon Joseph Lister (1827-1912) devised a method of overcoming a severe problem created by the very success of another branch of medicine. In the mid-19th century, the American dentist Thomas Morton (1819-1868) and the Scottish physician James Simpson (1811-1870) pioneered the use of ether as an anesthetic. Chloroform was introduced shortly afterwards.

These developments were a great boon to practitioners of surgery – transforming amputation, for example, from a maneuver that was agonizing for patients and required unrealistically speedy dexterity from surgeons. They had also made it possible to contemplate sophisticated and time-consuming operations deep inside the body. By facilitating surgery, however, the availability of anesthesia had focused more attention on one of its complications: vile, suppurating wounds. It was Lister, shortly after Pasteur had shown that suppuration too was caused by micro-organisms, who began using a carbolic spray to play over the operation site. By reducing postoperative infection dramatically, antiseptic surgery (soon superseded by aseptic methods in which all materials and dressings were sterilized) transformed the work of surgeons. Together with the later introduction of blood transfusion, it also encouraged further innovation in operations.

The German bacteriologist Robert Koch (1843-1910) took Pasteur's work further and established the supreme importance of specific etiology – the idea that particular diseases have particular causes. Between 1879 and 1900, the causative agents of at least 22 infections were confirmed using Koch's approach. In turn this prompted the idea of a specific therapy, the use of drugs targeted like magic bullets to seek out and kill "pathogens" without harming the tissues of the body. The founder of the science of chemotherapy, based on this hope, was the German bacteriologist Paul Ehrlich (1854-1915). Ehrlich's greatest triumph came in treating human syphilis with an arsenic compound, Salvarsan, in 1911.

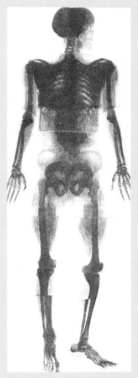

▲ An X-ray of the late 1890s, by Wilhelm Röntgen (1845-1923); his work brought a new era of non-invasive study of the body in sickness and health.

Imaging the Body

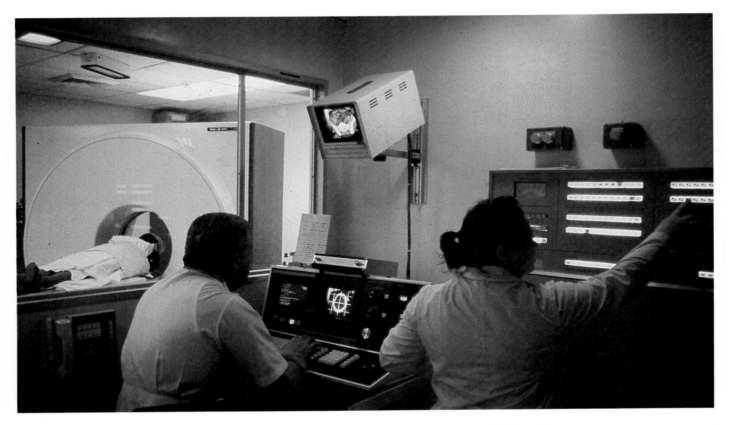

Seeing into the body

Ever since X-rays were first used in 1895 to capture a likeness of the bones of the human hand, scientists have been looking for better and safer ways of monitoring the internal workings of the body. The X-ray remains the most frequently used diagnostic imaging test. For routine screening for lung disease and detection of simple fractures, it is quick, cheap and effective. But it does have limitations in detecting abnormalities deep inside the body, and its risk of damaging the fetus makes it unsuitable for monitoring pregnant women.

Three developments in imaging which have occurred since the 1950s – two of them since 1970 – have enabled doctors to get a better view of the body than ever before. In the first of these, ultrasonography, sound waves inaudible to the human ear are bounced off the internal structures of the body. The "echoes" which are picked up as the sounds leave the body vary according to the density of the tissues through which they have passed. Ultrasound is especially useful in detecting objects lying in a watery environment, a fact that makes it perfect for monitoring the growth of the fetus. Recent developments with the technique give moving pictures of the baby.

Ultrasound is frequently used to detect fetal abnormalities such as spina bifida, as well as to check for normal growth; and some of the most skilled technicians can recognize abnormalities inside the heart of the fetus.

Ultrasound is also useful in imaging some other organs such as the gall bladder which are difficult to pick up with other techniques because of their position in the body.

In computerized axial tomography (CAT, or CT) scanning, X-rays are passed through the body and a computer converts data on the amount of X-ray absorbed by each tissue into a picture of the internal structures. Each picture is made up of thousands of tiny dots, and can differentiate between bone, fat, muscle and water because of the variations in the amount of X-rays absorbed by these tissues. "Slices" of tissues are examined to detect tumors, blood clots and other abnormalities which would be invisible to normal X-ray machines.

CT scanning is increasingly used in hospitals, but it too has limitations; and the risks which accompany exposure to X-rays from regular CT scans cannot be ignored. These problems may be avoided if the newest technique, nuclear magnetic resonance (NMR), fulfills its initial promise.

NMR does not use X-rays. Instead, radio waves of a known frequency are passed through the body in a huge magnetic field. When the magnet is switched on, the atoms in the body are excited by the radio waves and move into a high-energy state. As they lose this energy they give off weak radio signals which can be picked up and converted into a picture of tissues. The frequency of the radio waves can be tailored according to elements most common in the particular tissues to be investigated. So if doctors wish to check the pattern of hydrogen (most common in watery tissues), carbon (bone), phosphorus (muscle) or other elements in a tissue, they can choose the appropriate frequency.

Although NMR is safer and more effective it is too expensive and experimental to take over from CT scanning and ultrasound in the near future.

▲ A CT scan computer detects differences between radiation emitted and the rays detected after passing through the body.

▼ Thermography detects variations in the heat given off by parts of the body; it is particularly useful in detecting cancers.

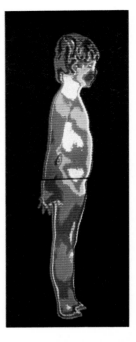

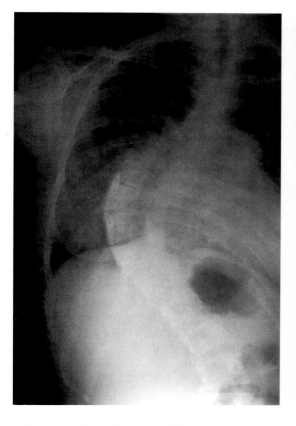

▲ X-ray of a malformed vertebral column. X-rays remain the most common diagnostic aid used for skeletal and lung disorders.

▼ Ultrasound offers an opportunity to study pregnancy, without the dangers of X-rays. Here the head of the fetus is visible.

► CT scans allow doctors to investigate the relative position of the organs. This is a slice through the base of the skull and eyeballs

► NMR scans, as of this slice through a chest, can detect subtle changes in tissue composition, and are completely non-invasive.

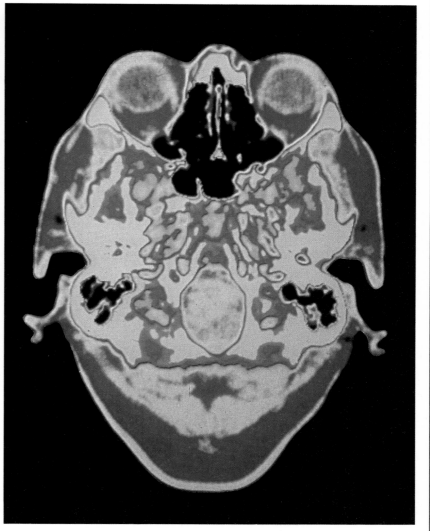

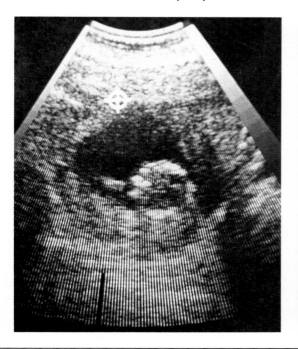

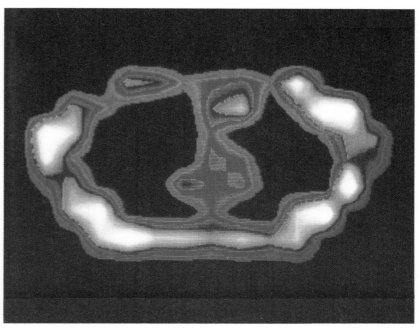

See also
Intestinal Infections 49-56
Respiratory Infections 65-72

Towards the modern age

During the early 20th century, many drugs were discovered to destroy infections without harming the patient. In 1932, German physician Gerhard Domagk (1895-1964) introduced the first of the sulfa drugs, which produced near-miraculous cures for scarlet fever, meningitis, gonorrhea and several other infections. During the Second World War, the Australian pathologist Howard Florey (1898-1968) and the German biochemist Ernst Chain (1906-1979) developed penicillin on the basis of observations made ten years earlier by the Scots bacteriologist Alexander Fleming (1881-1955), thereby launching the golden age of antibiotics – substances produced by one organism which destroy or inhibit the growth of others. Penicillin was even more effective than the sulfa drugs, had virtually no side-effects and acted against a wide range of bacteria. Together with the wide-spectrum tetracyclines and streptomycin, the anti-tuberculosis antibiotic isolated in the USA during 1944 by emigré Ukrainian Selman Waksman (1888-1973), later semi-synthetic versions of penicillin have transformed the treatment of infectious disease.

The idea that diseases have particular causes did not just apply to infections; it was underlined by the discovery early this century of vitamins – specific chemicals whose absence created characteristic patterns of symptoms. Around the same time an English physician, Archibald Garrod (1857-1936), described several hereditary defects such as phenylketonuria, the end-results of particular defective genes. Specific etiology gained further support when a lack of insulin was found to be the cause of diabetes, and when certain forms of anemia proved to be attributable to irregularities in the hemoglobin molecule. During very recent years the theory has been strengthened further with the detection of oncogenes – particular fragments of the DNA double-helix which are thought to be the basic causes of certain types of cancer. There are also suggestions that some forms of mental illness are caused by certain associated aberrations in the chemistry of the brain.

The complex causes of disease

Despite this succession of triumphs in accounting for disease, specific etiology has had its critics. At the outset, two skeptics (◗ page 49) demonstrated their disbelief over the alleged discovery of the cholera bacillus by consuming large amounts of it with impunity. This led to a recognition that an encounter with a pathogenic microbe is rarely sufficient for it to produce its relevant illness. Although the tubercle bacillus, for example, is necessary for tuberculosis to develop, and is in one sense therefore the cause of the disease, other factors such as malnutrition and fatigue play an important part in determining the outcome of infection. A healthy, well-nourished body may respond vigorously by repelling the invaders and becoming immune, without the individual concerned even being aware of the fact. But someone whose diet has been inadequate to sustain those defenses may succumb to what used to be called consumption and die an early death. Such discoveries, plus those of the HL antigens which are genetically determined markers on our tissues but are apparently related to the likelihood of contracting particular diseases, and the knowledge that the state of mind can influence one's susceptibility to diseases (including cancer) and chances of recovering from them, have made the medical profession increasingly aware in recent years that understanding the causes of disease is not simplistic.

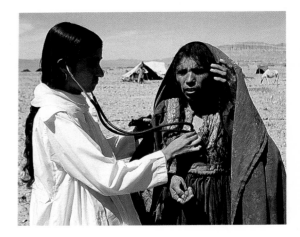

▲ ▼ *A "barefoot doctor" in Pakistan, trained in simple techniques of recognizing and treating diseases. The number of patients to each doctor in different countries underlines the problem of aiming at "health for all" by AD 2000.*

Population per physician

East Africa		
Central Africa		
West Africa		
South-East Asia		
South Central Asia		
North Africa		
Southern Africa		
East Asia		
South West Asia		
Caribbean		
Central America		
South America		
Oceania		
Europe and North America		

0   2,500   5,000   7,500   10,000   12,500   15,000   17,500

Paying for health

Modern medicine is too expensive for most individuals, even in wealthy areas, and many countries run health insurance schemes. Germany was the first nation to institute health insurance when, in 1883, the government launched a plan by which employers and workers in certain industries contributed payments towards a fund covering medical care in the event of illness. Since then, many other public and private schemes have come into being, providing full or partial settlement of physicians' and hospital fees, drug bills, and ancillary expenses. Britain's National Health Service, inaugurated by the post-war Labour administration in 1946, was designed to ensure that medical attention was free at the time of need, all working persons and employers making compulsory contributions. At the other extreme, American schemes such as Blue Cross are entirely private and optional, with gradations of dues and benefits. Some governments subsidize private insurance plans of this sort. Cover for hospital charges is the commonest form of private medical insurance, particularly in countries like the USA where medical expenses can be cripplingly severe.

Disorders of the Senses

2

Short-, long- and farsightedness...Blindness and partial blindness...Color blindness...Astigmatism... Cataracts... Conduction and nerve deafness... PERSPECTIVE...Contact lenses...Lazy eye and squints... Failures of balance

Anatomy of the eye

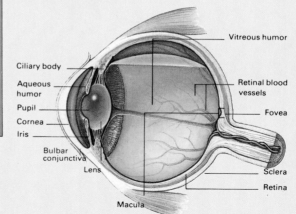

When the sense organs are damaged or destroyed, either through disease, injury or the normal processes of aging, their functions are impaired. We lose some of our sense of smell and taste when we get older, but the most noticeable changes are in our sight and hearing.

Correcting poor vision

Normal vision, once called 20/20 but now 6/6 vision, is the ability to see a standard chart from a distance of 6m (20ft) with either eye. A 6/5 eye can see at 6m what a normal eye must be within 5m to see, and is therefore better; a 6/9 eye is worse. Near-sightedness (myopia) is the inability to focus on distant things. The eye's lens bends the light rays too far inwards, so they meet before they get to the retina, and diverge again. Longsightedness (hyperopia) is the inability to focus on close things. The eye's lens does not bend light rays sufficiently to converge them on the retina. Farsightedness (presbyopia) is decline of the near-focusing muscles. Astigmatism is imperfect vision in particular planes caused by uneven curvature of the cornea or lens.

The need for glasses indicates faulty focus; it cannot be improved by exercises. Wearing glasses of the wrong strength is harmless, as is reading. Shortsighted people need concave lenses; longsighted and farsighted people need convex lenses. In spectacles both types of lense distort vision – concave lenses make objects (and the wearer's eyes) look smaller; convex lenses make them look larger. Lenses for astigmatism differ in thickness vertically and horizontally.

Contact lenses fit directly over the cornea and give better correction than spectacles, as they do not enlarge or reduce the size of objects. Hard contact lenses present an optically even surface, correcting astigmatism. In the USSR nearsightedness has been cured by making tiny radial scars in the cornea to change its shape.

▲ *The earliest recorded use of spectacles was by a Dominican friar in Italy in the mid-14th century; by the 16th century, when this engraving was done, various forms were available, including a pinhole design to assist with myopia.*

► *In myopia, or short sightedness, the image forms in front of the retina, usually because the eyeball is lengthened; presbyopia, the weakening of the lens-focusing muscles, has a similar effect. A concave lens is used to correct this, by making the light rays diverge before entering the eye. In hyperopia, or long sightedness, the opposite is true, and a convex lens is used to converge the light rays so that they can focus exactly on the retina. Some conditions require bifocal or trifocal lenses, offering the wearer a variety of focusing options through various parts of the lens.*

Short sight

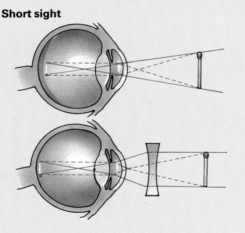

Long sight

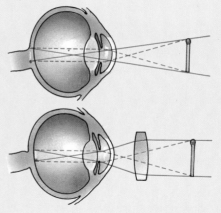

General visual defects

Vision is impaired if the retina becomes detached from the choroid behind it or the vitreous matter in front, and is worst when the detachment is near the center or over the macula. Though painless, this produces spots and flashes before the eyes and loss of part of the visual field. Causes include a general tendency to poor adhesion, blows to the eye, cysts, tumors, scar tissue, bleeding or retinal tearing. Detached retinal tissue tends to tear, and torn retinal tissue to detach. Treatment is by sealing around the tear and re-attaching it to the choroid, using an ice probe or laser beam.

Spots before the eyes are usually caused by floaters, small cell clusters released from the eyeball's lining. They are untreatable but disappear spontaneously. Bloodshot eyes, from burst blood vessels on the eye's surface, occur spontaneously or after injury. They are harmless and disappear within 10 to 14 days.

Color blindness is an untreatable, retinal condition commoner in men but inherited through both parents. Usually the sufferer cannot distinguish between red and green; occasionally the confusion is between blue and yellow.

Night-blindness is the inability, usually inherited, to see in dim light. It is occasionally caused by deficiency of Vitamin A or can be an early sign of retinitis pigmentosa, an inherited disease in which the retinal pigment degenerates, causing eventual blindness.

Cataract – clouding of the lens – occurs with aging but may also be congenital, or caused by injury, infection, metabolic disorders or some drugs. It cannot be made better or worse by reading or lighting levels. Treatment is by removing the lens under local or general anesthetic. Healing and permanent adjustment takes three months. Lack of a lens to focus light entering the eye is overcome by using glasses or contact lenses.

Blindness

Total blindness occurs only when eyes or their nerves are lost through injury. Ordinary blindness – absence of useful sight – is caused by degeneration in old age, diabetes, trachoma (◗ page 117), glaucoma, detached retina or corneal scarring. In degeneration or diabetes, the blood vessels in the retina or macula burst and then heal to form an overgrowth of new vessels which interferes with vision. Lasers or xenon arcs can be used to arrest their growth and partly remove them; these potent light rays can be focused onto an area of one micrometer.

Glaucoma, high pressure within the eyeball, damages and gradually kills nerve fibers and blood vessels. Treatment is by eyedrops that widen the pupil's drainage channel, tablets that reduce the eye's fluid production, or an operation to widen or make new drainage channels. Early stages of glaucoma, and damage from diabetes and high blood pressure, can be detected by inspecting the retina for bleeding or fluid exudates, descriptively called "cotton wool patches".

Corneal scars can be caused by diseases including ulcers and glaucoma, and may lead to blindness because they are opaque. Removing the damaged cornea and replacing it by a graft is successful in 85 percent of cases. The grafted cornea is removed from the donor within ten hours of death and can be stored for up to 20 days before use. Grafted corneas are not rejected by the body's immune system because they require no blood supply and do not provoke the body to produce antibodies (◗ page 97). Corneal ulcers heal slowly and with difficulty because there is no blood supply.

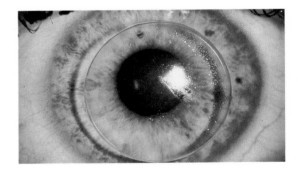

▲ *Hard contact lenses automatically correct astigmatism, as do some soft lenses. These are made thicker and heavier at the bottom, and thus orient themselves correctly in the eye. Bifocal contact lenses similarly orient themselves by gravity.*

Contact lenses

The first glass contact lens was made in 1887 by A.E. Fick, a Swiss physician. Today, of the two types of lens, hard lenses are made of perspex or oxygen-permeable plastic. Because they are rigid they present an optically even surface to the world, correcting astigmatism. They remain in the eye because of the capillary action of tears, which provide a form of suction. They may fall out if the eyes become dry and they become uncomfortable if tiny particles of dust slip underneath them.

Soft lenses are made of thin plastic, and contain water. They have the texture, thinness and appearance of cellophane and cover a larger area of the eye than hard lenses. Without this extra size they would be difficult to insert and remove. Their flexibility means that they cannot correct astigmatism, but they do allow a more intimate fit over the cornea, so dust does not get under them. Because they are permeable to water and tears they can hold bacteria, which breed in them if they are not kept very clean. Contact lenses cannot slip behind the eye because the junction of the conjunctiva and eyelid prevents them.

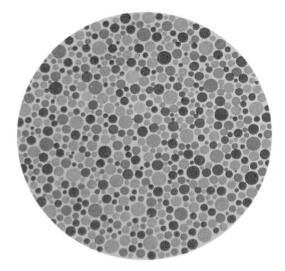

▲ *Color blindness, tested with charts in which images are concealed in a random network of dots, is usually caused by a defect in one of the three groups of primary-color-sensitive cone cells of the retina. It cannot be corrected.*

Laser therapy

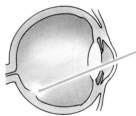

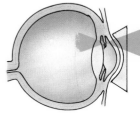

▲ ◄ A diseased retina, often found in diabetes, can result in the profuse growth of new blood vessels. These may grow over the macula and cause the retina to detach. A recent treatment uses an argon laser to fuse the blood vessels, thus preventing further growth. Lasers are also used to correct defects to the iris.

▼ When a cataract develops, the lens grows steadily more opaque; the operation to remove the lens with the cataract is relatively simple. Since some of the focusing work of the eye is done by the cornea, the patient is able to see with the help of spectacles.

"Lazy eye", cross-eyes and squints

Better known as amblyopia, "lazy eye" is not lazy at all. It is caused by focusing defects that prevent the brain from combining information from both eyes. In an adult this can cause double vision but in children the brain simply ignores information from one eye. It must be corrected by the age of six; after that age, the brain cannot learn to interpret information from the "lazy" eye.

Strabismus – squint or cross-eyes – results from faulty alignment of the six muscles that surround the eye. One or both eyes may be affected. It has a number of causes including attempts to overcome focusing defects. Children do not spontaneously "grow out" of strabismus, which is usually cured by glasses. If not, an operation to reduce the length of some external eye muscles can produce improvement if done before the age 5-6. Corrective therapy such as eye exercise rarely helps.

Half-closing the eyes, which is sometimes also called squint, is an attempt to improve short sight. Like reducing the aperture of a camera, it increases depth of field. Short sight can be corrected by either glasses or contact lenses.

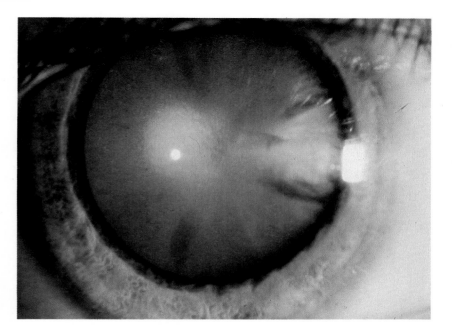

Hearing failure

Deafness is caused by a selective lack of perception or by loss of conduction. Conduction deafness is due to ear or nose infections, which can inflict long-term damage, or otosclerosis, where new bone growth fixes the stirrup (one of the three bones of the middle ear), so it cannot vibrate and transmit sound. The stirrup can be freed, or replaced with a plastic substitute, by an operation. People with conduction deafness speak quietly because they hear their own voices amplified through their skull bones (a similar effect is produced by talking with hands over the ears). One way of detecting this type of deafness is to place a ticking watch near the ear; the watch sounds louder when touching the head.

People with perceptual (nerve) deafness speak loudly as they hear their own voices faintly. They cannot hear high-pitched noises or sounds like s, f, p, k, t and hard g. Nerve deafness may be congenital or caused by noise pollution, degeneration in old age (presbyacusis), head injuries, and some drugs and poisons. It is often compounded by tinnitus, an intermittent ringing or buzzing in the ears, and by an inability to select certain sounds while disregarding others.

Hearing aids consist of a miniature microphone, amplifier and loudspeaker. They are a great help in conduction deafness but less so in nerve deafness, as it is difficult to amplify some sounds selectively without others. Each person with nerve deafness has a different loss of perception for pitch, loudness and selectivity, so hearing aids must be tailored to individual needs.

The eardrum can rupture when subjected to pressure from within (pus from infections) or outside (poking with hard objects, head injuries, diving or a slap on the ear with a hollowed palm). It is accompanied by great pain, deafness and nausea. Small perforations heal spontaneously if kept free from infection, but larger ones may need surgical repair or a graft, usually from the wall of a vein.

Failure of balance

Menière's disease consists of giddy attacks, often during sleep, with nausea and vomiting. It can be preceded by tinnitus and usually begins with mild fluctuating deafness on one or both sides. It is caused by excess fluid in the inner ear, brought on by hereditary factors, stress, disease or high doses of quinine or aspirin. Treatment includes restricting fluid intake, diuretics, seasickness remedies, antihistamines or blood-vessel dilator drugs. Motion sickness is provoked by fluid movement in the semicircular canals, which have nerve receptors. Drugs prevent or relieve it.

Hearing in old age

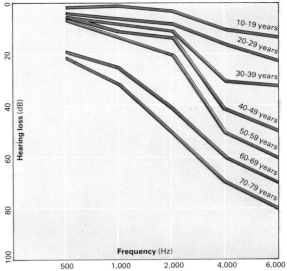

▲ The ability to hear declines steadily with age, starting from the late teens. The highest pitch disappears most quickly.

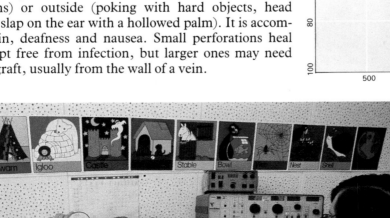

◄ Testing the auditory evoked response in a child.

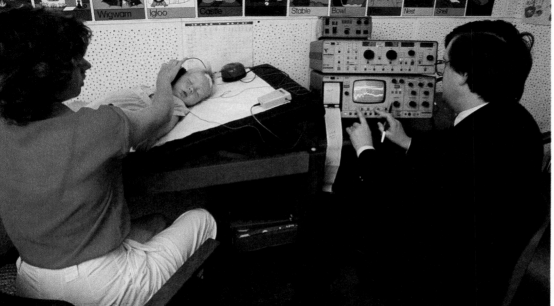

Epilepsy...Motor neuron disease...Parkinsonism, multiple sclerosis and other disorders of the brain... Headaches and migraine...Fainting and stupor... Neuritis, neuralgia and diseases of the nerves... PERSPECTIVE...Famous neurologists...Boxing and brain damage...Brain cell transplants?

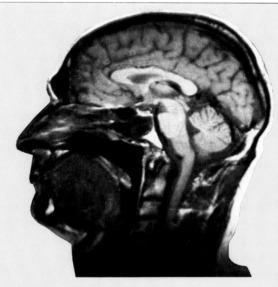

▲ NMR section through the brain.

The two parts of the nervous system vary greatly in their reaction to damage and disease. The cells of the peripheral nervous system can regenerate; those of the central nervous system – the brain and spinal cord – are susceptible to damage, and once lost are irreplaceable.

Epileptic fits

Violent electrical activity in the brain produces epilepsy (fits). Fits can also be induced by brain infections, strokes, heatstroke, drugs, poisons and drug withdrawal. Only 25 percent of chronic sufferers have an obvious cause such as brain tumors (◆ page 18). Most sufferers are mentally and physically normal between fits, and their EEG may show no abnormalities. There are three kinds of epileptic fit. In *grand mal*, which is preceded by a premonition ("aura"), the sufferer shouts and falls down unconscious with muscles tensed, and then twitches and writhes, salivating, incontinent, and with eyeballs rolling. After two to five minutes movements cease and the patient regains consciousness, feeling tired, dazed, with aching head and sore muscles. *Petit mal* begins and ends abruptly. The patient becomes pale and normal activitites are suspended for 5 to 30 seconds as the eyes stare or blink rapidly. In focal epilepsy, the patient undergoes muscle spasms for several minutes, starting at the mouth, thumb, or big toe and moving over the body. There is a temporary loss of awareness, sometimes followed by hallucinations. Nothing can cut short any kind of epileptic fit but recurrences may be controlled by drugs.

EEGs – recording the brain's activity

The electrical activity of the brain's surface can be recorded from the scalp. The technique, electroencephalography and the recording made, an electroencephalogram, are both called EEGs.

Electrodes, usually 16, are placed in standard positions on or just under the scalp, and the electrical differences between them are chaneled through the encephalograph, which converts the impulses into the vertical movement of a pen over a sheet of paper. The resultant encephalogram takes about 30 minutes to record.

Most normal adults have an alpha rhythm, which is abolished by thinking or opening the eyes. Beta rhythms, which are fast, are found in anxious people and can be induced by drugs. Theta waves, slower than alpha, are found in many normal adults, probably arising from the temporal lobes. Delta waves, which are very slow, are often found between epileptic fits.

Normal EEGs vary between individuals, and with age, emotions, metabolic changes, drugs and state of consciousness, including sleep. Despite these variables, EEGs reveal a lot about many brain and metabolic diseases, from epilepsy and dementia to myxedema (◆ page 29) and liver disorders. EEGs alone are not a good measure of brain death – patients have recovered from barbiturate coma and hypothermia although their EEGs recorded no brain activity.

Other methods of comparable, non-invasive brain investigations include ultrasound and scanning (◆ page 10), which can show cerebral blood flow and the site of blood vessel and brain tissue damage and tumors. The brain is also investigated by injecting into arteries dye that shows on X-ray, and radioactive chemicals, including some that penetrate the blood-brain barrier only where there is disease.

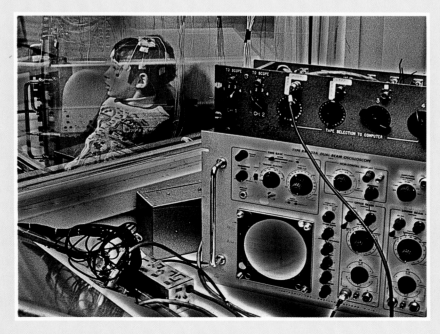

◀ *Taking the EEG of a child. The electrical activity of the brain was first demonstrated by the German psychiatrist Hans Berger in 1929, when he identified alpha waves. It was many years before the value of his work was generally appreciated.*

Invariably, serious brain damage cannot be treated

Wasting diseases, tumors, concussion, migraines...

Motor neuron disease, which often runs in families, is a wasting disease starting in tongue, hand and arm, with intermittent cramp. The disease gradually spreads over the body and death, usually from pneumonia (◗ page 68), takes place within three years. Its cause is unknown and there is no treatment. It was first described in 1865 by French neurologist Jean-Martin Charcot (1825-1893), Freud's teacher; Charcot also made the first distinction between Parkinson's disease (parkinsonism) and multiple sclerosis.

Senile dementia and Alzheimer's disease, severe insanity caused by brain degeneration, are related conditions starting in mid- or later life. A few cases are caused by poisoning, liver disease, tumors or alcoholism. Early symptoms are mental deterioration and apathy. Death takes place within five to ten years, but some sufferers benefit from an operation to drain the cerebrospinal fluid.

Multiple sclerosis results from progressive loss of the myelin sheath covering nerves in the brain and those leading around the body, resulting in visual disturbances, abnormal movement, and loss of coordination, strength and stamina. The sufferer may also experience emotional upsets, apathy and an inability to concentrate. Onset is usually in early adult life, and the disease goes through cycles of improving and relapsing. Patients survive for an average of 20 years.

Parkinsonism, caused by cell death in the substantia nigra, starts in late middle age. It may be caused by drugs, follow encephalitis or arise spontaneously. Patients suffer tremor and apathy, and have difficulty starting to move and stopping once they are moving. Unlike multiple sclerosis, for which there is no treatment (◗ page 124), parkinsonism can be treated with the drug L-dopa and physiotherapy.

Brain tumors vary in effect depending on their site and which brain structures they compress. There may be loss of senses, movement or speech; or sustained headache, nausea and mental deterioration.

Boxing and brain damage

"It started two years ago and it's been getting more acute. I'm always tired. I go to bed and sleep eight, ten hours, but two hours after I get up I'm tired and drowsy again...for 33 years I've been taking punches." These were the words of Muhammad Ali (b. 1942), former world heavyweight boxing champion, when brain damage was diagnosed in September 1984. Ali has been slurring his speech and repeating himself – symptoms of damage to the brain – since 1980.

Boxers occasionally get brain hemorrhages in the ring, and often suffer the accumulated effects of thousands of blows. Frequently these lead to "punch-drunkenness" – slurred speech, unsteady gait, poor memory and clumsiness. Ex-boxers may be impotent, insomniac and have deteriorating vision. Most of the damage is in the substantia nigra, a key part of the brain's motor system; other damage is to the cortex and cerebellum. There is often retinal detachment and dementia.

Shortly before Ali's condition was known, both the American and British Medical Associations published reports on boxing and brain damage and adopted policies in favor of banning professional boxing. Those who support professional boxing point out that the number of known injuries, serious or otherwise, is small in proportion to the number of contests.

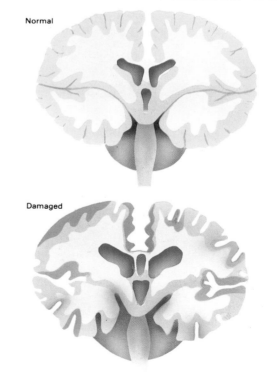

Normal

Damaged

▲ ◀ **Muhammad Ali and Leon Spinks** in the ring, fighting for the heavyweight championship of the world. When a boxer is hit on the head his brain is slammed against his skull. This may result in internal bleeding. In the long run this can cause brain damage and even death; a boxer's brain in section may appear shrunken, with enlarged spaces and separated tissues.

Ventricle

Separated tissue

Bleeding

Patients are frequently cured, and usually improved, by surgery. Stroke, loss of blood supply to part of the brain (◆ page 64) and brain damage can cause paralysis, or loss of speech or vision, depending on their location.

Fainting is loss of consciousness because insufficient blood is reaching the brain. Sufferers must be allowed to remain with their heads low until they recover. Narcolepsy, abnormal desire for sleep and repeated daytime sleeping attacks and paralysis, is a rare disease running in families; it is treated by stimulation drugs. Concussion is temporary loss of consciousness, lasting a few minutes, after head injuries. Stupor is partial loss of consciousness and has a variety of causes. Concussion and stupor often indicate brain damage or bleeding, and medical help should be sought promptly, even though there are usually no lasting effects. Coma, prolonged unconsciousness, is a sign of serious damage or disease.

Frequent ordinary headaches are usually a sign of tension or worry. They occasionally indicate eye strain but are almost never a sign of a brain tumor. Migraine (sick headache) is found in children and adults, and usually fades after 60. It is often preceded about 20 minutes earlier by a premonition ("aura") including numbness, nausea, dizziness or speechlessness. An attack consists of throbbing head pain, often with vomiting, chill, tremor, dizziness and an aversion to lights and sounds. It affects five women to every two men, and is commoner in people who live stressful lives. It is often precipitated by allergies to food such as red wine, cheese, chocolate and onions. It can be reduced in frequency by avoiding foods to which the sufferers know they are allergic, and by regular meals, rest and relaxation. Attacks can be cut short if medicines (including ergotamine) are taken when the aura first appears. People suffering frequent attacks can prevent many recurrences by taking beta-blocker drugs (◆ page 52).

Stroke

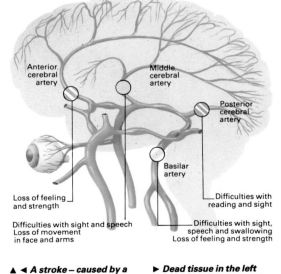

Anterior cerebral artery

Middle cerebral artery

Posterior cerebral artery

Basilar artery

Loss of feeling and strength

Difficulties with sight and speech
Loss of movement in face and arms

Difficulties with reading and sight

Difficulties with sight, speech and swallowing
Loss of feeling and strength

▲ ◄ *A stroke – caused by a blood clot in or damage to the arteries of the brain – may cause paralysis in different parts of the body depending on which region of the brain has its blood supply cut off. A blockage in the anterior artery is the most common (◆ page 58).*

► *Dead tissue in the left side of the brain, caused by a stroke, with a number of smaller areas of damage on the right side. Such NMR scans, which show up abnormalities undetectable with X-rays, have greatly improved diagnosis of brain diseases and tumors.*

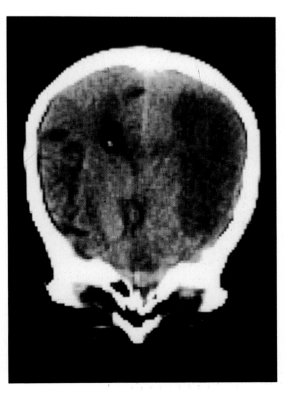

Neuralgia, sciatica, tics, tremors...

Inflammation of the nerves is called neuritis. Degeneration and other diseases in the nerves is neuropathy. Their effects are similiar and each can be caused by pressure, oxygen shortage, infection, poisons, diabetes, gout or vitamin B1 deficiency. There is prolonged numbness, tingling or paralysis as the nerve loses its sensory or motor function, and the area it innervates becomes acutely painful for some days. Bell's palsy is a neuropathy of the nerve controlling facial expression and eyelid closure on one side of the face. Paralysis is complete after two days, but 85 percent of cases recover over a few weeks; other cases recover slowly and incompletely regenerate. Neuralgia – nerve pain, found in older people – can occur anywhere in the body but is commonest in the trigeminal nerve. Carpal tunnel syndrome, compression of the nerve at the wrist, is commonest in people who work with their hands. Minor surgery can relieve the compression. Sciatica is inflammation and pain in the sciatic nerve. Commoner in men, it can start around 40.

Tics are involuntary nervous twitches such as blinking, grimacing or shaking the head. Commonest in teenagers, they are a sign of stress and neurosis. Choreas are diseases with involuntary tremors, tics and jerks. Some cause only mild disability; others, like Huntington's chorea, are fatal. Torticollis, muscle spasm turning the head to one side, is a lifelong disease. The cause is unknown. Restless legs syndrome consists of tingling or pain in the legs when they are still, so that the sufferer feels obliged to walk or move. It can be associated with iron deficiency, and is often relieved by iron or sedatives.

Brain transplants

In recent years, scientists have been able to make a brain graft "take" in animals. Pieces of implanted fetal brain, or brain cells separated and injected as a suspension, will grow fibers into the host brain. The host brain is less good at growing fibers into the graft. British biologist Steve Dunnett has used grafts to restore lost agility and memory to aged rats. Scientists in New York and Oxford have used grafts to cure rats with inherited absence of brain-secreted hormones. Swedish biologist Anders Bjorklund has cured rats with experimentally-produced parkinsonism, by grafting fetal substantia nigra neurons into their brains. He achieved the same result by transplanting adrenal medulla cells. These are derived from the spinal cord and have the same transmitter chemical, dopamine, as the substantia nigra. Swedish neurologist Erik-Olof Backlund has transplanted adrenal medulla cells into two severely ill parkinsonism patients, in 1982 and 1983. The first showed marginal improvement; the second was unchanged. In the future, despite such disappointing results, transplants are likely to help patients with diseased or damaged brains.

▼ *Paraplegic athletics. Paraplegia, paralysis of the legs, and tetraplegia, paralysis of all four limbs, occur when the spinal cord is partially or wholly severed. The limbs affected lose all sensation and voluntary movement. Despite recent experimentation on regenerating severed spinal cords in animals, human paraplegia and tetraplegia remain incurable, but rehabilitation may improve the quality of life.*

Mental Disorders

4

*The definition of mental illness...Neurosis...
Personality disorders...Psychosis...The treatment of
mental disorders...PERSPECTIVE...Freud and Jung...
Other founders of modern psychology...Munchausen's
syndrome...Redefining psychiatry*

Sigmund Freud   **Carl Jung**

Disorders of the mind, as opposed to disorders of the brain which have indisputably physical origins, are usually broken down into three main categories: neuroses, personality disorders and psychoses. Such disorders are, however, notoriously difficult to categorize, and behavior that is considered normal in some situations and at some periods may be regarded as abnormal in others.

Medical interest in mental illness developed in the 19th century, and the best-known attempt to explain the origins of mental disorders was that of Sigmund Freud, whose work as a psychoanalyst in Vienna at the turn of the 20th century led him to formulate the view that all such disorders were related to infant sexuality. Freud's view was challenged at the time, not least by Carl Jung and Alfred Adler, and is today generally considered to be too simplistic, failing to take other factors, including the social origins of psychological stress and society's expectations of normality, into account.

Mental illness is usually caused by a combination of factors, including the person's emotional disposition, emotional stress and sometimes physical stress. The symptoms may include disorders of perception, thought, memory, emotion, consciousness and the awareness of self. Neuroses, unlike psychoses, do not involve sharp breaks with reality or hallucinations; personality disorders involve set patterns of behavior that range from mild to behavior severe enough to resemble the pyschotic. Treatment of mental disorders may involve psychotherapy, group or art therapy, behavior therapy or treatment with drugs to alleviate the symptoms.

Freud – the founder of psychoanalysis
Sigmund Freud (1856-1939) developed the technique of free association – saying everything that enters the mind without attempting to make it logical or socially appropriate. This brings to consciousness repressed memories and drives. From this he formed the theory that human beings are controlled by powerful unconscious forces which frequently conflict with the demands of the conscious mind and are rarely subject to conscious control. He also realized that the whims and the desires of the unconscious are revealed in dreams.

Psychoanalysis, his system for understanding the mind and correcting its disorders, is based on the notion that the libido, the driving force present from birth, expresses itself as sexual energy and the will to live. If this is blocked or misdirected, however, it leads to conflicts later in life. He introduced the distinction between the id (that part of the mind concerned with instinctive desires), ego (conscious self) and superego (restraining forces).

Freud introduced the idea of the Oedipus complex (based on the mythical Greek king Oedipus who unwittingly killed his father and married his mother). The son becomes jealous of the place his father holds in his mother's affections and is consumed by feelings of aggression and hatred, which smoulder indefinitely. The tension between father and son is eradicated if the son marries someone (often physically like his mother).

Jung and the collective unconscious
Carl Gustav Jung (1875-1961), one of Freud's early colleagues, organized the first Psychoanalytic Congress in Salzburg in 1908 and was the first president of the International Psychoanalytic Association. He broke away from Freud in 1913 to form the school of "analytic psychology".

His ideas of a collective unconscious have been widely misunderstood. He was not proposing a "group mind", but saying that human behavior, conscious and unconscious, is affected by our evolutionary past and racial experience; that instincts are more subtle and fundamental than mere eyeblinks and knee jerks; and that evidence of these "intellectual instincts" is seen in the imagery of art and dreams.

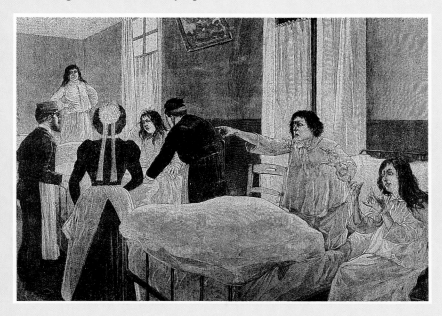

◄ *The French Hospice of St Anne for the mentally ill in 1901.*

Adler argued that the drive for power was a fundamental urge, expressed neurotically as the inferiority complex

Neurosis

The mildest psychological disorder is neurosis. All of us have reacted to stressful situations and felt depressed, anxious or fearful at some time. The neurotic person has similar feelings, the difference being that these feelings are central to their life and the conflicts arising from stress remain unresolved. The neurotic typically feels helpless and useless and acts in such a way as to lessen discomfort rather than strive for positive accomplishment. Unlike psychotics (◆ page 24), sufferers are fully in touch with reality but are handicapped by excessive emotional reactions. Classification of neurosis into various categories is fairly arbitrary but is based on the major symptom. The main neurotic states are hysteria, depression, anxiety and obsession.

Treatment for neuroses (◆ page 28) can involve psychotherapy or drugs, or both. Since many neuroses disappear spontaneously, psychotherapy (a scarce resource in most countries) is reserved for those cases in which the underlying cause is unlikely to heal itself. Phobias are treated with tranquillizers or desensitization – a form of behavior therapy where the patient is gradually exposed to the threatening situation or object. Anxiety and insomnia are usually treated with minor tranquillizers, and depression with antidepressives.

Hysteria
The condition of hysteria is one where subconscious motives produce physical symptoms that have psychological advantage or symbolic value. These include "conversion" symptoms such as paralysis, tremor, blindness, deafness or multiple allergy; and "dissociative" symptoms such as partial (and selective) amnesia, wandering around in a wraith-like state (fugue), madness (or rather the patient's idea of madness) and multiple personality. Frequently such symptoms vanish after a dramatic event.

Charcot – the founder of modern psychiatry
Modern ideas of diagnosis and treatment start with French neurologist Jean-Martin Charcot (1825-1923), a flamboyant character, who founded the Paris school of psychotherapy at the Salpetrière Hospital. The first to describe many neurological diseases, he wrongly believed that hypnosis was a symptom of hysteria, but correctly believed that hypnosis resulted from suggestion and described its stages (lethargy, catalepsy and sleep-walking) in neurological terms. Freud was one of his pupils.

Adler and the inferiority complex
Alfred Adler (1887-1937), one of Freud's earliest supporters, was the first major disciple to break from him. Disagreeing with Freud's view that sexual conflicts lay at the root of all neuroses, Adler left the Viennese Psychoanalytic Society in 1911. He emigrated to the USA and founded the school of "individual psychology", convinced that the fundamental driving force was a desire for power, expressed neurotically as the inferiority complex. He also believed that men and women are fundamentally alike, differences being determined by social and cultural factors. Thus, in a male society, the female attempts to assert herself; her protest takes many forms and, where conflict arises, results in emotional disturbance.

Moniz and surgery on the mind
Egas Moniz (1874-1955), professor of neurology at Lisbon, is remembered for two major innovations, cerebral angiography and lobotomy. In 1935, at a neurological conference in London he learned that neuroses had been induced in normal healthy apes but could not be induced in apes whose frontal lobes were removed. Believing that mental illnesses had physical roots, he theorized that by severing the frontothalamic fibers, anxiety would be reduced. The first frontal lobotomies were performed in 1935. Of 20 patients, all survived; seven were declared cured and eight improved.

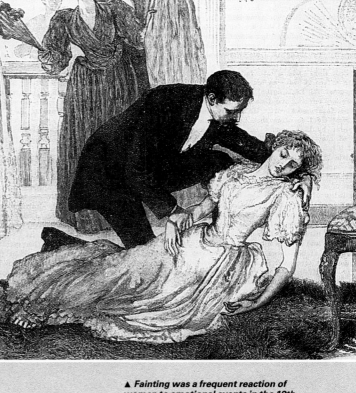

▲ *Fainting was a frequent reaction of women to emotional events in the 19th century. It was partly caused by tight corsetting impairing blood flow, but it was also a form of hysteria, made fashionable by the ethos of the day.*

STRESS

Depression
Neurotic depression is usually an overreaction or prolonged reaction to events, but may occur with little or no stimulus. Sufferers are preoccupied with the event that triggered the depression, and feel weighed down, inactive and unable to think rapidly. Depression is often mixed with anxiety.

▼ A Polish child, emotionally disturbed and depressed during the Second World War, scrawling wildly on the wall when requested to draw a picture of her home.

Anxiety
Neurotic anxiety develops when there is an overreaction to stressful events. Occurring in attacks or as a persisting state, its psychological symptoms include worry, dread and panic, and bodily symptoms include palpitations, shaking and diarrhea.

Obsession
In obsessive-compulsive disorders, sufferers feel subjectively compelled to perform an action or dwell on an idea, despite their own attempt to resist it. They recognize the compulsion as coming from within themselves but as being alien to their personality; attempts to dispel the unwanted thoughts or urges may lead to a severe inner struggle, with intense anxiety.

▲ Anorexia nervosa is an eating disorder classically found in emotionally immature girls with overprotective parents. Sufferers perceive themselves as fatter than they are, and starve or induce vomiting to stay thin. Bulimia nervosa, compulsive overeating found in young adult women, may be caused by ambivalence or aversion to male sexual advances.

Neurasthenia
Fatigue with irritability, headache, depression, insomnia or inability to concentrate on or enjoy things is called neurasthenia. It often follows infections, exhaustion or stress.

Phobia
Phobias are intense dread of things, frequently spiders and snakes, or situations, particularly crowds, enclosed spaces (claustrophobia), or open spaces (agoraphobia).

Hypochondria
Excessive concern with general health or some part of the body is hypochondria. Concern over mental health is rare in hypochondriacs, who usually feel mentally sound.

Münchausen patients may mutilate themselves to gain the attentions of the medical profession

Personality disorders

Maladaptive behaviors, which usually appear around adolescence and persist throughout life, can be personality disorders. They often resemble psychoses except that there are no delusions. The sufferer is less "ill" than abnormally developed – in the same way that a physically handicapped individual is not ill but has an abnormal physical constitution. Personality disorders can be categorized into two main areas. The first, known as organic, relates to disorders caused by some physical ailment, such as faulty brain development resulting from genetic make-up, infection or drug poisoning. The second, known as functional, relates to a breakdown in behavior resulting from environmental factors, such as childhood deprivation. Specific categories of functional disorder range from the paranoid to the psychopathic, and can include sexual deviations. Treatment often involves behavior therapy and major tranquillizers.

◄ *Baron von Münchausen in a classic portrait depicting his duelling scars.*

▼ *The view that the individual psyche is essentially social led to the development of group analytic psychotherapy. The theory builds on the Freudian theory and is therapy of the group, by the group, through the group, including the conductor as a member of the group.*

Affective disorders
Paranoid personalities take offence and defend their personal rights readily, never see themselves as being in the wrong but blame conspirators, and may be jealous and self-important. People with affective personality disorders may be elated, with enhanced zest and activity; or depressed, worried and pessimistic; or alternate between the two. Schizoid personalities are cold, hold back from social contact and affection, and avoid competitive situations. Explosive personalities are subject to outbursts of intense hate, anger, violence or affection. Anankastic personalities are meticulous perfectionists, rigid and cautious. Hysterical personalities are shallow, labile, dependent, suggestible and theatrical, needing constant attention and appreciation. Asthenic personalities appear passive, complying with the wishes of others and lacking intellectual or emotional vigor.
The most serious personality disorder is that of psychopaths, who disregard their social obligation, show impetuous violence or callous unconcern, and are cold, aggressive or irresponsible. They are often highly intelligent, do not respond to punishment, and are often adept at concealing or rationalizing their actions.

Münchausen's syndrome

Heironymus Karl Friedrich, Baron von Münchausen (1720-1797), a Hanoverian soldier, fought in the Russian army against the Turks and became notorious for his exaggerated accounts of his exploits. His name now is used to describe the uncommon syndrome of exaggerating or inventing symptoms.

Typically, Münchausen patients collapse outside police stations or doctors' offices, are pathological liars, have a "grid-iron" abdomen from operation scars, and are clingingly dependent on hospital staff, whom they thank profusely. Men slightly outnumber women; many have had extensive medical experience as patients, failed medical students, or in occupations such as nursing and radiography.

Examples include one patient with fictitious chest pain, who diverted an aeroplane to an unscheduled city; another injected feces into his joints to induce inflammation; others induced seizures or gynecological disease; eight patients are known to have had amputations after minor injuries – they seemed able to dictate their wishes for surgery to their doctors. Others have falsely claimed the death of a loved one in order to assume the role of distraught and suicidal bereavement. Often a mother has fabricated symptoms in her child; usually she chooses fits, though ex-nurses opt for more exotic disorders.

FUNCTIONAL

ORGANIC

Deviations of sexuality

Sexual activities are regarded as deviations when sexual gratification is derived in abnormal or unusual circumstances. Hence "deviation" is an ill-defined term. Sexual deviation usually is understood to include bestiality (intercourse with animals), pedophilia (sexual desire for children), sadism (desire to inflict pain or punishment during intercourse), masochism (desire to be hurt or punished during intercourse) and fetishism (sexual gratification from non-sexual objects, which frequently includes articles of clothing).

Exhibitionism is a compulsion to reveal the sex organs. In men this tends to be due to self-hatred or aggression to women; in women to emotional immaturity or hysteria.

Transsexuality is a fixed belief of having the wrong sex of body; transsexuals are not biologically of mixed or "wrong" sex. The only treatments are cross-dressing or a sex-change operation. Transvestism is pleasure, not necessarily sexual, from masquerading as the opposite sex. Transsexuals and transvestites are rarely homosexual.

Drugs

Regular consumption of alcohol, tobacco, glue vapor or certain drugs can lead to mental dependence (craving for the drug and compulsion to take it), and physical dependence (physical symptoms if the specific drug is withdrawn). Drugs causing dependence include narcotics (morphine, codeine, heroin and methadone), hypnotics and sedatives (barbiturates and tranquillizers), hallucinogens (LSD, mescaline and psilocybin) and stimulants (amphetamine and cocaine). Withdrawal of stimulant drugs causes lethargy, insomnia and restlessness; withdrawal of alcohol, or narcotic and sedative drugs, can cause excitement, tremor, insomnia and fits.

The mental symptoms of withdrawal are reduced by tranquillizers and the physical symptoms by beta-blockers. There is no treatment that reduces the craving, which eventually fades but is readily reinstated if the habit is resumed. The most common addiction is to tobacco, but its seriousness is often disregarded because cigarettes can be bought legally and the habit is still relatively inexpensive and socially acceptable.

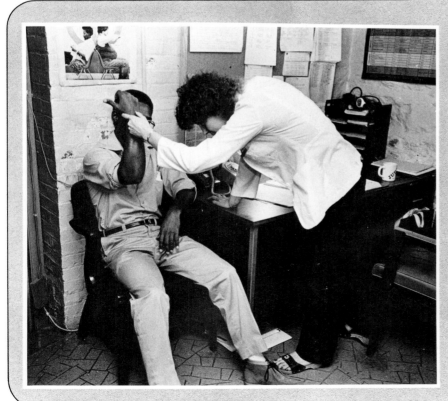

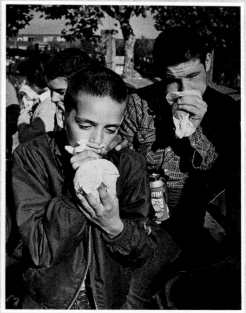

◀ ▲ *Drug addiction, from glue to heroin, can cause physical as well as mental disorders and requires treatment on both levels.*

Psychosis

A psychosis is not simply an extension of a neurotic illness or personality disorder – although some cases are indistinct, for the most part the difference is stark and dramatic. Psychotics lose touch with reality completely as they act out their fantasies in life. Like personality disorders, pyschoses can be divided between organic, caused by some physical ailment, and functional, which include two well known states – schizophrenic and affective reactions. Swiss psychiatrist Emil Kraepelin (1856-1926) devised the first classification of psychoses, dividing them into manic-depressive psychosis, paranoia and "dementia praecox" – renamed schizophrenia by his colleague Eugen Bleuler (1857-1939). Bleuler saw the essence of the condition as a splitting of the mind, not into two parts but into fragments; ideas are disconnected, emotions are inappropriate to thought and behavior to reality.

Schizophrenics often feel that their most intimate thoughts are known to others, and see themselves as the pivot of all that happens. Voices may address them, or comment on their behavior. Everyday objects may possess a special, often sinister, meaning, intended solely for the patient. Schizophrenics show little sign of holding to a train of thought, and may sit still in odd positions (catatonia) for hours.

Treatment for psychoses includes major tranquillizers, psychotherapy, or both. Mania or manic-depression is treated with the antidepressant lithium carbonate. Extreme cases of mood and behavior including catatonia, mania and paranoia are treated with electroconvulsive therapy (ECT).

ORGANIC
(◀ page 17)

▼ *The definition of schizophrenia varies enormously from one country to another; proportionately the diagnosis is twice as common in the USA as in Britain. In the USSR and South Africa the boundaries between penal and health-care systems are blurred. "Schizophrenia" is used as an excuse to denigrate intellectuals (such as Andrei Sakharov, below), who criticize the regime, and to deprive them of their liberty. Having committed no crime, they cannot be imprisoned; instead they are incarcerated in hospitals until they are "cured".*

Comparable cases are discovered from time to time elsewhere – in England in the 1970s, three elderly women were found languishing in mental hospitals 50 years after being sent there for having illegitimate babies, and two "mad" patients (a man and a woman) in Irish mental hospitals were found to have been committed on the say-so of their spouses, who wanted them removed.

Szasz and Laing — rethinking psychiatry
Thomas Szasz (b. 1920), psychiatry professor at the State University of New York, argues that since psychiatrists cannot agree on the causes, diagnosis or course of schizophrenia, it must be a bogus disease. Hence, psychiatrists are bogus doctors who think they are practising medicine but in fact are agents of social control, just as much in the West as in the Soviet Union. Szasz accepts that people have mental problems but does not regard these as diseases, and will only treat patients who come to him voluntarily. He also argues that, since mental illness is a myth, it also follows that insanity cannot be used as a defense in criminal actions. Only 10 percent of patients in British mental hospitals are detained compulsorily, compared with 90 percent in the USA. However, in Britain, "voluntary" detention can easily be replaced by compulsion if the patient does not cooperate and, in the USA, voluntary patients usually pay for themselves while compulsory patients need not. Szasz argues that, whatever the percentage, detention reflects an attitude; he condemns societies that lock up an individual who has broken no law.

British psychiatrist R.D. Laing (b. 1927) regards madness as a reasonable protective reaction against the stresses of the world in general, and family life in particular. He argues that families find an individual's withdrawal intolerable, calling the sufferer "disturbed", and that psychiatrists collude with the family.

FUNCTIONAL

Schizophrenia

In hebephrenic schizophrenia the person's mood is variable and often inappropriate. They may be giggling, lofty, grimacing or smiling, making hypochondriacal complaints or continuously talking repetitively. Catatonic schizophrenics alternate between overactivity and stupor, or automatic obedience and negativism. Paranoid schizophrenics have long-lasting delusions and hallucinations, usually of persecution but sometimes of jealousy, exalted birth or Messianic mission. In acute schizophrenic episodes, a previously normal person experiences a dream-like state and a slight clouding of consciousness, with bewilderment; people, objects or things may become charged with personal significance. The condition usually remits spontaneously after a few weeks or months. Usually the cause is unknown; sometimes it is brought on by hallucinogenic drugs.

Autism

The form of schizophrenia beginning in infancy known as autism appears before 30 months. Autistic children respond abnormally to sounds and images, and have problems understanding speech. Their own speech is delayed, and is often a mere echo of what is said to them. Their grammar is immature and they cannot use abstract terms. The social problems of autistic children include poor eye-to-eye contact and cooperative play, and they may spend hours in repetitive or ritualistic behavior. Intelligence is usually low, and all but the brightest (about 15 percent) spend their entire lives in institutions.

Manic-depression

Affective disorders are recurrent psychoses consisting of either mania or depression, or alternating cycles of both. In manic psychosis (or the manic phase of manic-depressive psychosis), patients are excessively cheerful and active, speaking rapidly, shifting from one idea to another, teasing and joking. They may be overconfident, overoptimistic and overimportant, running up debts or endangering their social position by embarrassing behavior. In depressive psychosis (or the depressive phase of manic-depressive psychosis), patients feel their depression as a heavy physical blanket wrapped around them. They are unhappy with no apparent cause, find meeting people an ordeal, wake in the night, think slowly and indecisively, and feel unworthiness and guilt.

◄ ▲ *Mental hospitals aim to provide an environment in which the patient can feel secure from external threats and from the danger of self-inflicted injury.*

See also
Nervous System Disorders 17-20
Hormonal Imbalance 29-32

The treatment of mental disorders

Drugs treat the symptoms of mental disorder. Psychotherapy and group therapy aim to deal with the underlying cause. Psychotherapy encourages the patient to express spontaneous thoughts so that previous forgotten experiences and repressed feelings are brought to consciousness, giving insight into present behavior and feelings. Behavior therapy consists of rewards for desirable behavior.

"Major" tranquillizers include chlorpromazine (Largactil), and prochlorperazine (Stemetil). They impair aggression, fear responses, mania, paranoia, delusions and hallucinations, and halt the loss of self-care. "Minor" tranquillizers, such as diazepam (Valium), calm anxiety. They produce dependence if taken over a long period. Beta-blockers are also used to treat anxiety when symptoms are mainly physical, such as palpitations and tremor.

Antidepressives, which include dothiepen (Prothiaden) and trimipramine (Surmontil) work by gradually building up levels of certain brain chemicals. They do not produce a "high", and their effect is not felt until they have been taken for several days. Lithium carbonate is thought to work by replacing body sodium, which is involved in chemical reactions during mood changes. Adverse effects include fine tremor, which is relieved by a beta-blocker, and frequent urination.

With electroconvulsive therapy (ECT) the patient is anesthetized and given a muscle relaxant; then a small electrical current is briefly applied through terminals placed on each temple. Usually given in a three-week course of six treatments, it causes temporary memory loss.

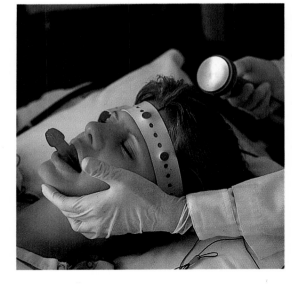

▲ *Electric shock therapy involves passing a 100 volt current across the patient's head. Although its effect is still not fully understood, results show that it may prove life-saving for sufferers of affective psychoses and may help schizophrenics.*

▼ *The lunatic asylum of the 18th century, as seen by William Hogarth in his series of paintings the "Rake's Progress", was a place in which disturbed people were abandoned; whatever treatment they received was more sadistic than helpful.*

Hormonal Imbalance

5

The origins of hormonal disorders...Thyroid and parathyroid disorders...Growth hormone imbalance – gigantism and dwarfism...Addison's disease...Gout... Diabetes...PERSPECTIVE...Studying adrenal glands... The search for a cure for diabetes

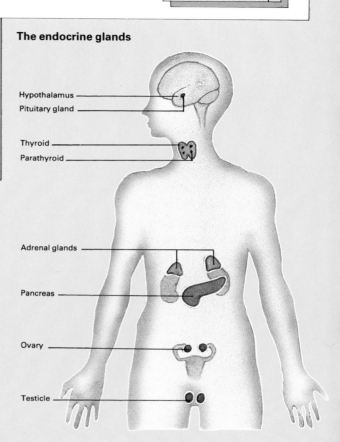

The endocrine glands

Hypothalamus

Pituitary gland

Thyroid

Parathyroid

Adrenal glands

Pancreas

Ovary

Testicle

When the body produces insufficient quantities of a particular hormone or enzyme, diseases result which doctors can usually treat successfully, normally by replacing the deficient substance. When a hormone is over-produced by a tumor, this can generally be found and reduced by operation or radiation.

Disorders of the thyroid gland

Hyperthyroidism, the excessive secretion of thyroid hormones (also known as thyrotoxicosis or Graves' disease), affects eight times as many women as men. Sufferers have increased appetite and anxiety, palpitations, sweaty hands and an inability to relax physically or mentally as they produce too much adrenaline. Often they have diarrhea, tremor, wasted limb muscles and (for reasons that are not understood) protruding eyeballs. In extreme cases this leads to thyrotoxic crisis – mental and physical exhaustion, delirium, fever, mania or delusions, and fast heartbeat. Immediate treatment is with cooling, sedatives and beta-blockers (◆ page 60). The disease sometimes ceases spontaneously. Longterm treatment is by antithyroid drugs, radioactive iodine to destroy part of the thyroid, or partial removal of the gland. Sometimes the remaining thyroid tissue diminishes some years after the operation, so patients are checked annually.

Hypothyroidism (myxedema) causes slow mental and physical acitivity, usually more obvious to relatives than to the patient. Its symptoms are often mistaken for aging. The sufferer is forgetful, tired and hypersensitive to cold, puts on weight, has dry skin and coarse hair. If the disease progresses, further symptoms may develop, including swollen face, puffy eyelids, thick skin and lips, large tongue, decreased sweating, slow monotonous nasal speech, and, occasionally, delusions. Children with thyroid deficiency are mentally retarded and babies become cretins with permanent mental impairment unless it is diagnosed and treated quickly. Treatment is with hormone replacement (thyroxine).

A goiter is an enlargement of the thyroid, usually from iodine deficiency, or very hard water which can interfere with iodine absorption. Goiters are common in mountainous areas because of the lack of fish – the main dietary source of iodine.

Hyperparathyroidism, overactivity of the parathyroid gland, removes calcium from bones, causing backache. The resulting high levels of calcium in the bloodstream cause weakness, loss of appetite, tiredness, and nausea. The kidney's attempts to excrete it can cause calcium stones. Treatment is by removing part of the overactive gland. Hypoparathyroidism – insufficiency of parathyroid hormone – causes tetany (spasm of hands, feet and glottis), convulsions and, sometimes, psychoses (◆ page 26). Treatment is with calcium injections in the acute phase, followed by Vitamin D.

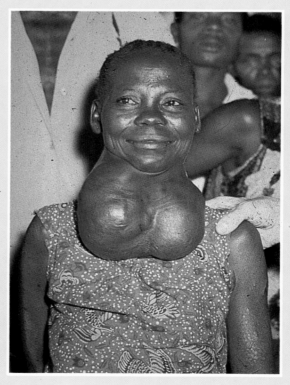

▲ *The swollen neck typical of goiter is a symptom of various thyroid disorders, often thyroid under-activity caused by lack of iodine in the diet. Iodine consumption may also be affected by exposure to cold, and a high fat and protein diet.*

The over-secretion of growth hormone can result in giants more than 2.5m tall

Growth hormone disorders

Oversecretion of growth hormone by the pituitary's secreting cells (hyperpituitarism) causes gigantism in children and acromegaly in adults. A patient with acromegaly has enlarged hands, jaw, sinuses, eyebrow ridges, tongue, lips, nose, ears, thyroid, heart and liver; thick, coarse skin; and sweats heavily. This condition is treated by a course of the drug bromocriptine; this has the same effect as dopamine, a neurotransmitter that reduces the output of the pituitary gland. Low output of growth hormone – known as hypopituitarism – causes dwarfism in children. In adults the effects are headache, partial loss of vision from pressure on optic fibers, loss of body hair, pallor from vasoconstriction, low blood sugar, low body temperature, and eventual coma and death from respiratory failure.

People whose pituitary produces insufficient vasopressin suffer from diabetes insipidus, a rare disease whose symptoms are thirst and excessive watery urine – 5 to 20 liters daily. Both hypopituitarism and diabetes insipidus are treated by hormone replacement.

Three to four percent of people over 40 suffer from Paget's disease. Increased formation and destruction of bone tissue enlarges affected bones but makes them painful, fragile and bendy. Increased blood supply to the bones makes them acutally feel warm. The pelvis, spine, tibia and skull are especially vulnerable. If the skull is affected headache and hearing loss occur. The cause of Paget's disease is unknown, but it may be a slow virus infection (◀ page 18). Treatment is concentrated on the symptoms: mithramycin (which slows cell division) or, if pain is severe, calcitonin.

Disorders of the adrenal glands

Overproduction of steroid hormones from the adrenal cortex may be caused by excessive adrenocorticotropic hormone (ACTH) secretion by the pituitary, and leads to Cushing's syndrome – moon face, distended abdomen, a "buffalo hump" of fat at the back of the neck, and depression. Women may produce noticeable quantities of androgen, and men of estrogen. Opinions about treatment vary, as do the symptoms. The usual methods are irradiation or partial removal of the pituitary. People suffering from over-production of aldosterone from the adrenal cortex notice constant thirst and an excessive urine production. Treatment for this is by operation or the drug spironolactone, which represses aldosterone.

The symptoms of Addison's disease – which is the shortage of adrenal cortex hormones – are weakness, weight loss and hyperpigmentation, especially in areas exposed to light or pressure, such as hands and knee creases. Athough old scars stay white, new ones go brown. Some patients, especially from dark-skinned races, develop vitiligo, in which areas of skin grow pale, while surrounded by excess pigment. There may also be hypotension, low blood sugar causing physical and mental tiredness, and loss of body hair, especially in women. Treatment is with cortisol (a glucocorticoid); some patients also need a mineralocorticoid. During periods of stress (as from a cold, injury or examinations), more cortisol is needed and any operation – even a dental extraction – needs special care.

Pheochromocytoma, a rare tumor of the cells of the adrenal medulla, causes the secretion of excess adrenaline and noradrenaline, with high blood pressure, pallor, sweating, palpitations and fear – in other words, a prolonged fight-or-flight response. Treatment is by operation or beta-blockers are given.

Wilson's disease

In 1911, Dr Samuel Wilson (1878-1937), a US-born London neurologist, described an inherited disease. Excessive accumulations of copper damages various organs, especially the brain, liver and kidneys. It often starts with tremor or rigidity, then fever, spasticity, rigidity, and drooling develop; patients may develop schizophrenia, brain damage, dementia or other mental disorders. The sensory nerves are spared. Terminal patients are bedridden, mentally impaired and physically distorted. The incidence is 30 per million, of whom perhaps two-thirds are never properly diagnosed. The disease is inherited from both parents, but is rarely noticeable before adult life.

Treatment has been developed principally by British physician Dr John Walshe (b. 1920). He began with injections of dimercaptol, which sticks to copper and is then excreted. In 1956 he developed an oral treatment, penicilline, which "decoppers" patients, causing spectacular improvement. However, it sometimes causes sensitivity reactions requiring corticosteroids, and can cause skin diseases and optic neuritis. For those who cannot take penicilline, in 1982 Walshe developed another, trien.

► *A medical illustration of around 1900 showing a giant, a man of normal height and a pituitary dwarf. Gigantism is usually caused by over-secretion of growth hormone (GH) by the pituitary gland in childhood; this makes the long bones grow to an exceptional degree. Sufferers can be more than 2·44m (8ft) tall.*

► *Dwarfism is often the result of under-activity of the pituitary in childhood. The bones grow slowly, and the epiphyseal plates close abnormally early. Sufferers may have a low production of other hormones, and often do not reach sexual maturity.*

Hormonal changes in the menopause

The menopause, cessation of menstruation, may be abrupt or extend over many years. It is always abrupt in women whose ovaries are removed, otherwise trophic hormones from the pituitary try to stimulate the deteriorating ovaries, causing a variety of symptoms in 85 percent of women. Only a quarter of women are totally free from vasomotor symptoms – hot flushes and drenching sweats. Fifty percent suffer them for two to five years, and a quarter suffer for longer. Mental symptoms include palpitations, insomnia, fatigue, irritability, depression and emotional instability; most psychological illness in women in their 50s is hormonal. A few years after the menopause, women are susceptible to pain on intercourse and genital infections from loss of secretions, elasticity and tone. This is treated with estrogen cream. The menopause also heralds the onset of osteoporosis (loss of bone matrix and mineral with susceptibility to fractures and spinal curvature ◗ page 36). It is worst in thin women and the fair-skinned. Though rare in men, some osteoporosis is suffered by 15 percent of women aged 50, 30 percent at 60, 65 percent at 70 and 85 percent at 80. At 50 a woman is three times as susceptible to osteoporotic fractures as a man. This increases to four times at 60, and 5 times at 70. Treatment for menopausal symptoms consists of a daily dose of estrogen plus some progesterone for 12 days a month. This is reduced over two years to a minimal dose to keep the patient flush-free. A few women never cease treatment. Treatment, essential if the ovaries are removed before age 40, does not reverse osteoporosis but prevents it worsening.

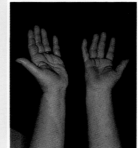

▲ Shotputters and weightlifters are prominent among athletes who have taken anabolic steriods, synthetic hormones derived from testosterone, to promote muscular growth.

◀ Vitiligo, in which areas of unusually heavy pigmentation are mixed with areas of pale skin, may be a symptom of Addison's disease, caused by the shortage of glucocorticoids.

See also
Nervous System Disorders 17-21

Gout

Usually hereditary, gout is caused by over-production of uric acid, and is more common in men and the over-40s. Uric acid accumulates in the joints, causing recurrent bouts of swelling and pain. It often attacks a big toe first, later spreading to other joints. As the attack subsides, overlying skin becomes scaly and itchy. Chronic gout brings persistent pain and deformity, and the uric acid may form kidney stones. Gout can be precipitated by drinking too much alcohol, notably wines, and overindulging in certain foods, especially offal, fatty fish and fish roe. Attacks are treated with anti-inflammatory drugs.

Failure in insulin manufacture

Diabetes mellitus is caused by shortage of insulin, which is needed so that tissues can utilize sugar. A diabetic person's blood sugar rises after meals to higher levels than the kidneys can reabsorb, so it is excreted along with water to dilute it. This causes thirst. The loss of sugar causes skin eruptions, hunger and fatigue. The body burns fat for energy, producing a rise in ketones – partially burned fatty acids. At high levels, especially after stress or infection, this causes coma, requiring urgent hospital treatment. People whose diabetes started in childhood or early adult life require injections of insulin in doses that are tailored to fit the timing and content of their meals. The patient must follow a diet that aims at reducing day-to-day variation in insulin need, not at avoiding "bad" foods. People whose diabetes starts after middle age usually suffer less severely and can be treated successfully by drugs that reduce blood sugar. Diabetics need regular checkups to assess how well they are controlling their blood sugar and check for other symptoms. In most patients diabetes thickens the blood capillary walls throughout the body, damaging kidneys, the nervous system and eyes. Low blood sugar, caused by irregular meals or sudden exercise causes hunger, nausea and giddiness. It is relieved by eating sugar.

▲ An insulin pump can be attached to a patient and maintains an even supply of insulin in the bloodstream; such pumps need be refilled only once a year.

◄ Frederick Banting and Charles Best, photographed in 1921, with one of the dogs they used to help isolate insulin.

Isolating insulin

In 1893 it was discovered that partial removal of pancreas did not cause diabetes in humans but that complete removal did. In 1889 Oscar Minkowski (1858-1931) and Baron Joseph von Mehring (1849-1902) at Strasbourg also discovered that removal of a dog's pancreas caused diabetes. Minkowski was the first of many to try giving pancreatic extracts to restore diabetic animals or humans. It is surprising therefore that it was 30 years before insulin was successfully purified and used in treatment.

In 1905 French endocrinologist Eugène Gley (1857-1930) described experiments in which he injected pancreatic extracts into diabetic dogs, causing subjective improvement. Professor John Macleod (1876-1935), at Ohio, published a book in 1913 concluding that there was a secretion from the pancreas which could never be captured. In 1915 Israel Kleiner at the Rockefeller Institute started injecting pancreatic extractions into diabetic dogs, with good results.

The cure for diabetes

A Canadian, Fred Banting (1891-1941), qualified in medicine in 1916, served as a surgeon in the First World War and became a general practitioner with a part-time teaching job at Western Reserve University. After lecturing on diabetes he wanted to research on it for three months in the summer of 1921. Macleod, without enthusiasm, allowed him laboratory space, and an assistant, Charles Best (1899-1978). Best, a graduate biochemistry student, helped Banting to remove dog pancreases.

Many of the dogs died from postoperative infection; survivors were later given extracts of pancreas from other dogs which had been killed for the purpose. As the allotted ten dogs were soon used or lost from infections in the heat of the summer, several more dogs were bought from dealers. Banting and Best induced and cured diabetes in some of their dogs. Macleod, remembering others' failure, advised caution but made many helpful suggestions. Their extracts were often ineffective or toxic. Best made unsuccessful attempts to purify the extract; success came from James Collip (1892-1965), an experienced biochemist and friend of Macleod.

The first extract to be tried on a patient was Best's. Given to the 14-year old Leonard Thompson on 11 January 1914, it failed. He received Collip's extract on 23 January; that worked. Soon the world knew that diabetes could be cured but it was several years before insulin could be made on a sufficient scale for all; patients died knowing that cure was possible but unattainable.

Banting never got on with Macleod and conducted a permanent vendetta against him. He was furious at having to share the 1923 Nobel Prize with Macleod, and gave half his prize money to his colleague Best. Macleod, following suit, gave half of his to Collip.

Macleod, Best and Collip had distinguished careers; Best trained as a doctor but stayed in research, and Collip became highly successful at extracting and purifying hormones. Banting never made another discovery of note, and died in a plane crash in the Second World War.

The history of orthopedics...X-rays, transforming diagnosis...Fractures, sprains and pulled muscles... Spinal injuries and back pain...Dentistry and orthodontics...PERSPECTIVE...Accidental injuries... New techniques of orthopedics...Arthritis...Hip replacement, major surgery

The skeletal remains of primitive Man often show signs of arthritis, bony tumours and tuberculosis. But they also show that our earliest ancestors distinguished themselves from the rest of the animal kingdom by attempting to do more than merely lick their wounds. Paleolithic Man made splints and attempted to cope with broken bones. Neolithic Man even attempted amputations and cut holes in skull bones (trepanning) with flint scrapers.

The tomb of the Egyptian King Hirkouf (2830 BC) has among the motifs at its entrance a crutch. Early Egyptian murals and pottery often depict hunchbacks, the lame, dwarfs and even such recognizable diseases as poliomyelitis. Equally, much of Hippocratic Greek medicine (*c.* 480 BC) relates to the treatment of deformities and injuries of limbs.

Nicholas André, professor of medicine in the University of Paris, coined the term "orthopedics" in the mid-18th century by taking the Greek stems orthos ("straight") and paidios ("child"). The term caught on and was soon being used to include not only children but also adults. Orthopedics is the study and treatments of diseases, deformities and injuries of the trunk and limbs. Besides bones and joints, it includes the related muscles, tendons, ligaments, bursae (the lubricating structure), nerves and blood vessels. As a subject, it became a speciality of surgery only in the last few decades of the 19th century.

An understanding of infectious disease, coupled with improved treatment, better diagnostic techniques (especially using X-rays) and the rise of chemotherapy and antibiotics, has greatly altered the pattern of orthopedics. Tuberculosis and poliomyelitis have now receded as important medical problems, to be replaced by a great increase in the number of injuries (trauma) incurred in a wide variety of ways both accidental and non-accidental, and by the untoward effects of changing diets and lifestyle.

Diagnosing and restoring broken bones

The X-rays that the German physicist Wilhelm Röntgen (1845-1923) discovered in November 1895 have completely transformed the diagnosis of broken limbs. Once the damage has been assessed it is possible to plan how best to restore a normal bone structure – the process of reduction. If there is an external wound this must first be cleansed and treated with antibiotic to prevent or halt any infection. The next step is to immobilize the limb or part of the body using splints or plaster of paris. Successful reduction requires that the broken ends of the bone be brought together. This can often be done by manipulation, but surgery may be required. Multiple breaks have to be opened usually to sort out the pieces. To achieve restoration, screws may be used, perhaps in conjunction with a metal plate.

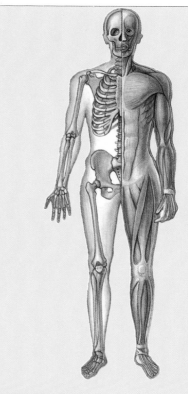

Accidental injury
After cardiovascular disease and cancer, accidental injury is now one of the greatest causes of death. Traffic accidents play a significant part in accidental injuries, and such trauma, with increasing use of the automobile, motorbike and bicycle, is now approaching epidemic proportion.

Off the road, more than half of all accidents are caused by falls, and about 90 percent of such falls involve people over 65 years of age. As we become older our bones lose mass, especially bone tissue (collagen) rather than mineral, and this causes the bones to become more porous, brittle and rarefied ("osteoporosis"). Consequently a fall for an elderly person often causes severe damage.

Leisure pursuits, such as keep-fit, sport and do-it-yourself home improvement, are becoming responsible for an increasing number of accidental injuries. Injuries may consist of torn or stretched muscles, sprained or dislocated joints, "slipped" disks, hernias, pulled tendons and bone fractures. The cause is that the tissues are suddenly stressed beyond their intrinsic strength, or consistently stressed to their limits. Certainly they become loaded in a way for which they were not adapted. A fall can cause the weight of the body to be focused on a single bone, resulting in fracture, or on a joint, causing dislocation. Over-exertion may tear a cartilage or rupture muscle fibers, as happens in tennis elbow. Fracture, swelling or sudden stretching of the various components of the chassis may cause nerve injuries. Such damage may be only ephemeral (neurapraxia), long-lasting (axonotmesis) or even irreparable (neurotmesis). Likewise, blood vessels may become contused or compressed, causing local loss of blood circulation (ischemia) which can destroy vital tissues.

In the USA alone 1 million fractures annually lose an estimated $8 billion in working time

Classifying bone injuries

Fractures of living bone come in many forms. Simple fractures are those in which the adjacent soft tissues are not broken. When the tissues overlying the broken bone become wounded, and consequently often infected, the fracture is termed compound. If the bone is broken into more than two fragments, the fracture is said to be comminuted. Sometimes a bone becomes broken on only one side and bent on the other. These greenstick fractures occur in growing children when the bones tend to be springy. When one bone component is driven forcibly into another the resulting fracture is said to be impacted. Stress fractures in bone, as in metal, occur when the material becomes fatigued due to repeated strain. Pathological fractures are caused by abnormalities that may be in origin congenital, inflammatory, neoplastic (benign and malignant growths) or metabolic.

Injuries to joints are of three main types. In sprains, the ligaments that hold the joint together may become torn. In subluxations the articular surfaces remain in contact but they become displaced from their normal positions. In dislocations, the articular surfaces become completely displaced and part of one of the bones may also be fractured. Sprains need initial rest to allow the tear to heal, and cautious exercise not to tear the damaged ligament further. Subluxations can usually be treated by applying pressure in the reverse direction to the displacement. Treatment of dislocations is similar, but an anesthetic is often given to the patients while the components of the joint are forced back into their normal position. Typical dislocations can occur to the shoulder, the elbow, the fingers, the knee and the instep. Only with considerable violence is the normal healthy hip joint likely to become dislocated. However, with elderly people whose bones are becoming brittle, a fall or a blow to the hip may sever the femoral head (ball) of the main leg bone from its shaft, which in turn may shatter the hip socket. Treatment may be to nail the femoral head to its shaft or, in extreme cases, fit a total hip replacement (▶ page 38).

Hernias

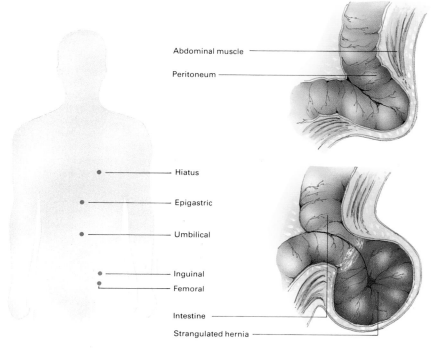

Abdominal muscle

Peritoneum

Hiatus

Epigastric

Umbilical

Inguinal

Femoral

Intestine

Strangulated hernia

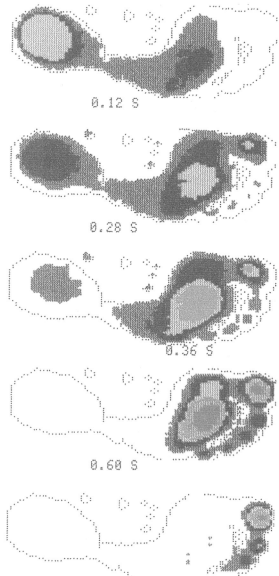

0.12 S

0.28 S

0.36 S

0.60 S

0.68 S

▲ *A pedobarograph records the pressure on each part of a foot through the stages of a single step. The foot shown here is healthy; the colors describe varying intensity in pressure. This technique, developed in the 1980s, can be used with the foot either stationary or walking to identify potential malformations at an early stage.*

Hernias

An organ or tissue may become protruded, or "herniated", from its normal cavity. The hernia may extend outside the body or between cavities within the body, as when a loop of intestine escapes from the abdominal cavity into the chest. Hernias may be congenital or acquired later in life. An acquired hernia is usually caused by overexertion. Soft tissue hernias most often occur in the groin, the thigh and the navel, and sometimes in the brain. A reducible hernia can be pushed back into its proper cavity; an irreducible hernia cannot. A strangulated hernia impedes blood circulation.

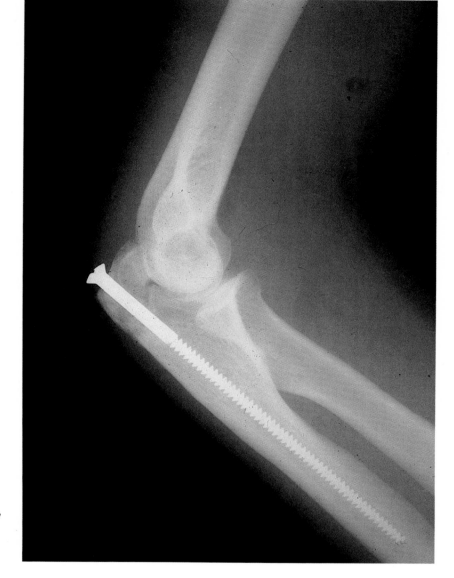

New techniques in orthopedics

Estimates suggest that the USA alone loses some $8 billion annually in working time through about one million fractures. If the disability time from these fractures could be cut by a half, the country would obviously save much money. Various physical techniques have been attempted in various countries to achieve just that.

The Russians have an ultrasonic tool which, they claim, can be used to join biological tissue, especially broken bones. To mend a broken bone, they bring the two halves together and treat them with a weak solution of acid to remove calcium salts and to make the collagen accessible. Next, they place a small plate of bone transplant over the join and bathe it in a polymerizable monomer mixed with bone shavings. The high-power, high-frequency vibrations (250 watts at a frequency of 26.5 kilohertz) cause the binder to penetrate deep into the bone parts and to harden sufficiently to hold them firm during the natural regeneration of bone tissue. German scientists have claimed similar effects using metal splints and alternating currents below 1 kilohertz.

US scientists assert that soft-tissue injuries, such as sprained ankles, strained shoulders and swollen joints, can be repaired in half the time by means of electromagnetism. They pulse the damaged tissues with high-frequency radiowaves at about 27 megahertz (just above the frequency of television). As yet there is still no satisfactory explanation as to how magnetic, electric or ultrasonic fields can actually affect living tissues.

▶ **X-ray of a broken arm with a metal pin introduced into the marrow cavity in order to strengthen the bone. Wire may also be wound around the bone to assist it to set straight, and metal plates also may assist correct healing in the case of a spiral or a comminuted fracture.**

Fractures

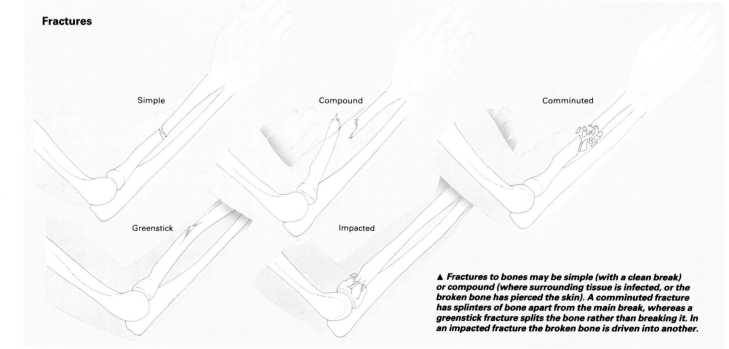

Simple

Compound

Comminuted

Greenstick

Impacted

▲ **Fractures to bones may be simple (with a clean break) or compound (where surrounding tissue is infected, or the broken bone has pierced the skin). A comminuted fracture has splinters of bone apart from the main break, whereas a greenstick fracture splits the bone rather than breaking it. In an impacted fracture the broken bone is driven into another.**

Low back pain is responsible for more lost working days in one year than all industrial strikes added together

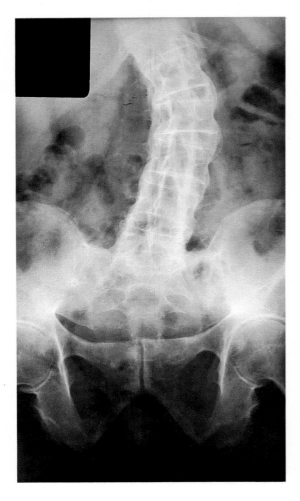

"Slipped" disks

▲ A prolapsed or slipped disk occurs when severe strain causes the pulpy nucleus pulposus of the intervertebral disk to be squeezed out and press on a nerve. The disorder may result from a flattening of the disks brought about by wear and reduction of mobility; it is cured only by lengthy rest.

◄ In the condition known as ankylosing spondylitis, the joints of the backbone become bony, and the spine grows rigid, with the patient typically locked into an extreme, forward-leaning posture.

Arthritis

Arthritis is a general term that is used to describe damaged and painful joints. The inflammation and wear responsible for arthritis can arise from a multitude of effects. Treatment consists of rest, pain-relieving drugs and the control of symptoms (by antibiotics if relevant). Osteoarthritis is a degenerative disease in which joints become damaged and limited in their movement due to changes in tissue as they age. In extreme cases, where the joint surfaces become completely degraded, it may be necessary to replace the joint or part of it with artificial components. This has been achieved for the ankle, knee, elbow and hip.

Rheumatoid arthritis (♦ page 106) is a disease of unknown origin but which seems to involve the body's own immunological system turning against components of the joints. It is accompanied by disturbance of the normal body equilibrium, loss of weight and weakness. The joints become inflamed, and may be deformed, fused and immobilized (ankylosed). Typically the disease is first observed in the fingers and wrist. When it occurs in children it is termed Still's disease. Cortisone was for long used as an anti-inflammatory drug to relieve symptoms; it has largely been superseded by other related drugs, such as prednisolone, with less undesirable side effects.

Other joint infections

Ankylosing spondylitis is a disease of the spine in which the ligaments become bony (ossified) and the lateral joints become immobilized. The condition is aptly called poker-spine although it can result in a rigid deflexion of the spine and neck. It tends to affect young male adults, although it can also affect females. Its onset is associated with persistent low back pain and stiffness. It may spread to the shoulders, hips, knees and even jaw.

New growths, or neoplasms, affect bone and the soft tissues. A range of benign growths occur in bone, including osteoma, chondroma and cysts. Giant-cell bone tumors that sometimes develop in young people can be capricious. For the most part they are innocent but occasionally they invade the lung and become malignant. The truly malignant growths are a range of various sarcomas (♦ page 97); often they are secondary deposits from growths elsewhere. Soft-tissue neoplasms can involve fatty tissues, muscle, tendon, synovial tissues, nervous tissues and blood vessels.

A range of neuromuscular disorders can be responsible for spastic paralysis, muscular weakness (dystrophies) and limited reflexes. Many are incurable and supporting appliances can be used only to control the deformities.

In healthy people muscle, bone and tendon should develop in harmony. Obesity, the excessive accumulation of fat, stresses the normal working of limbs and joints, because muscles and tendons become overloaded. The effects of wasting diseases, as in beriberi, kwashiorkor, anorexia and sickle-cell anemia, can cause an imbalance through one set of muscles being stronger than their counterparts and lead to deformities. Deficiencies in the body intake of mineral salts and vitamins can also produce deformities of the skeleton.

Injures to the spine and back

The spine not only provides a "mast" for our body but it also protects and houses the spinal cord and its associated nerves. The collagenous disks that are interposed between the vertebrae of the spine act as shock absorbers and most of the body load is transmitted through them. If for any reason a disk ruptures (prolapses), it may come to press on a nerve, causing localized pain. (A common misconception is that disks can "slip" – in fact they burst and their gelatinous content is forced through the tough outer sheath that would normally contain it.) When the prolapse happens in the region of the neck the pain is referred and is felt in the arms. When the rupture occurs lower down the spine the pain seems to come from the back or legs.

Disk prolapse is common in the lower lumbar region, especially where the mobile lumbar spine joins the rigid sacrum and pelvis. It is a common cause of low back pain – responsible for more lost working days in one year than all the industrial strikes added together. Sciatica is a painful ailment in which the sciatic nerve, the largest nerve in the body, becomes constricted in either the lumbar or sacral regions. A prolapsed disk is only one of the possible causes of sciatica.

The intervertebral disk has no blood supply and in the adult the disk's healing power is virtually nil, leading to recurring pain. Treatment varies from rest, physiotherapy and pain-relieving analgesics to various forms of traction or external support. Sometimes an operation is used to remove the ruptured disk and fuse the affected vertebrae.

The founder of modern surgery

Ambroise Paré (1510-1590) was the greatest surgeon of the Renaisssance. Following an apprenticeship to a Paris barber surgeon, Paré gained a junior post at the city's largest hospital. Subsequently he became a military surgeon.

At first Paré treated gunshot wounds, as did other surgeons, by scalding them with hot oil of elders (sambucus). In one of the Italian campaigns, he ran out of oil and was forced to apply "a digestive of eggs, oil of roses and turpentine". He found that treatment with this ointment left his patients less feverish than did cauterization; certainly, their wounds were less swollen and less painful.

Paré was a considerable innovator, designing many surgical instruments, advocating the sterilization of wounds, and designing new ways of extracting teeth, filling cavities and making dentures. He found new uses for the jointed metalwork that was being fashioned for armor – he made artificial limbs, including an iron hand.

Lifting weights

The back bone is stabilized by a series of powerful muscles attached to its sides. When one lifts a heavy load the muscles automatically contract. However, bending forwards induces the muscles to relax so that lifting a weight from the floor can easily damage the spine. This accounts for the general good advice on lifting weights to bend the knees and keep the spine upright – the muscles then contract instead of relaxing so that spinal damage is prevented.

Pressure within the intervertebral disk is least when reclining but increases on standing, leaning forward and lifting heavy objects. Surprisingly, pressures are higher when sitting than standing.

Back pain is not always involved with injury and may be caused by inefficient muscles and abnormalities in the spine causing constriction (stenosis) of the canal. Sometimes the constriction can be relieved by the removal of part of the vertebral body.

Curvature of the spine (scoliosis) can be caused by abnormal development of the vertebrae, by the legs being of unequal length, or by weakness or paralysis. It is now rare in the developed world, but was probably responsible for many of the "hunchbacks" and deformed court jesters immortalized in fiction and plays. The most common type of scoliosis is of unknown (idopathic) origin – two children in every thousand suffer to some extent from it. The suggestion that heavy shoulder bags, bad diets or unsatisfactory beds can cause curvature of the spine is unfounded. Spinal braces may be required to correct the curvature and if the deformation increases, surgery; a metal rod along the vertebral column may be necessary.

A multiplicity of lesser postural ailments are also common, including knock knees, bow legs, rigid toes, hammer toes and flat feet and their converse, "raised" arches. Many of these deformities, if caught early, can be countered or controlled by special orthopedic shoes, or by surgery. The deformities may be congenital in origin, caused by some inherent error in the fetus, or by abnormal bone growth.

Many malformations affect joints. In congenital dislocation of the hip, the ball at the top of the major leg bone fails to become secure in a shallow socket. If the dislocation can be caught before the infant tries to walk, it is possible to hold the ball against the socket and thus encourage the latter to deepen its cavity.

Tuberculosis (◆ page 72) may spread to bones and joints when the bacilli are disseminated from their primary infection in the lungs. In osteomyelitis, the interior of the bone becomes inflamed. Infection may reach a joint to cause infective arthritis by way of the bloodstream, or spread from osteomyelitis or through a wound.

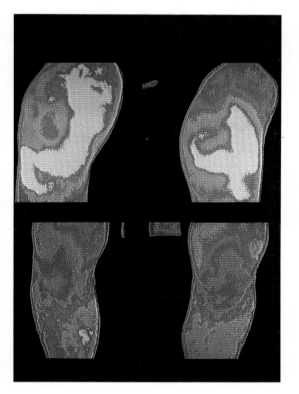

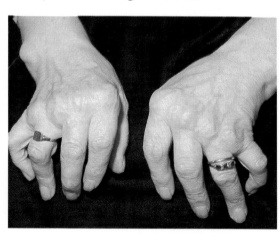

◄ *Thermograph of arthritic (top) and normal (below) knees, recording the heat difference between the healthy and infected joints. White and red areas denote unusual heat; blue and purple indicate cool skin.*

► ▼ *In rheumatoid arthritis the synovial membranes of the joints become inflamed, degenerate and stiffen; in an advanced state of the disease, the joints swell and become deformed.*

The onset of arthritis

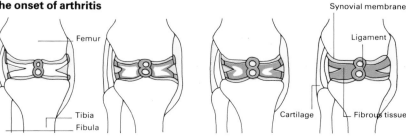

Major Surgery – Total Hip Replacement

The artificial hip

A marvel of modern surgery in the past 20 years is the replacement of arthritic and damaged hip joints with an artificial ball and socket fashioned out of metal and plastic. The procedure has freed millions of people from pain and enabled them to regain their mobility. In 1984 alone, throughout the world surgeons replaced about 425,000 hips, of which 120,000 were in the USA and 105,000 in Europe.

Such is the success of total hip replacement operations that the public views them now as run-of-the-mill. But total hip replacement, like heart surgery and kidney transplants (two other major operational successes of recent decades), depends critically on surgical technique and the general condition of the patient.

Hip surgery is major surgery. The artificial components must be made to high engineering specifications. They must be carefully inserted and aligned in their specific positions, and fixed to act normally in the human body. This they must do at 37°C in saline conditions, and with a host of biological processes and chemical materials produced by the body working against them. Few artificial materials can withstand such hostile conditions for many years, while being subjected to loadings of up to five times body weight.

Bone surgery is craft surgery; it is an art and not a science. The success of the operation depends on the skill of the surgeon to implant the artificial components correctly. It also depends on the patient's physician being able to control any adverse conditions, such as infection, even that of a tooth or of a toe, because implants are highly susceptible to infection.

Patients have to be selected carefully for this operation. Ideally the person must be free from infection, not overweight, and sufficiently fit to cope with the strain of an operation that can last between 1½ and 3 hours, or longer if there are complications. After the operation the patient must not expect to be too demanding on the joint or stress it in physical work. This favors someone of 60 upwards, in health that is otherwise reasonable. In special circumstances the operation may be performed on younger people, but with those under 20 the fact that they are still growing presents many problems.

Many surgeons take the attitude that every hip replacement is a potential problem for the years ahead and must be watched carefully and revised if necessary. Future implants could well be instrumented so that their performance under daily load can be telemetered out and monitored.

■ Antibiotic cover, aseptic techniques, careful handling of the tissues and the use of clean air operating theaters can help to reduce the infection rate to less than 2 percent (main illustration). Barrier gowns help to prevent the inadvertent flow of germs from the theater staff to the patient. Most hospitals insist that staff wear hoods in the operating theater to cover their head and hair. The surgical team consists of at least four people: the anesthetist, the surgeon, an assistant and a nurse. In teaching hospitals, there are often three surgeons – the consultant, the senior registrar and the house surgeon. It is sometimes necessary with complicated operations, to have another nurse to act as runner for special tools. The patient is positioned so as to give the surgeon the best way of approaching the hip joint. This may be from the front, the back or the side.

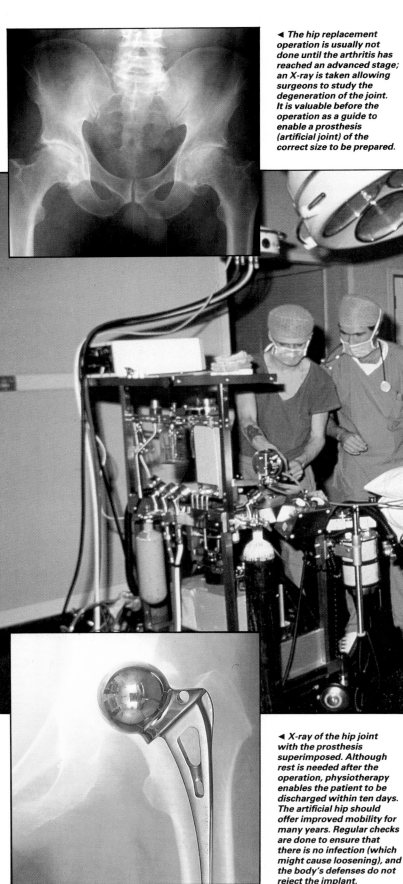

◄ The hip replacement operation is usually not done until the arthritis has reached an advanced stage; an X-ray is taken allowing surgeons to study the degeneration of the joint. It is valuable before the operation as a guide to enable a prosthesis (artificial joint) of the correct size to be prepared.

◄ X-ray of the hip joint with the prosthesis superimposed. Although rest is needed after the operation, physiotherapy enables the patient to be discharged within ten days. The artificial hip should offer improved mobility for many years. Regular checks are done to ensure that there is no infection (which might cause loosening), and the body's defenses do not reject the implant.

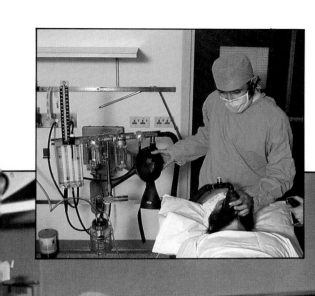

◄ **Patient monitoring is essential to anesthetics. Oxygen tension of the blood must be maintained if the patient is being kept on 40 percent oxygen with nitrous oxide or ethrane or trilene. The blood fluid volume is kept up by blood transfusion. Blood pressure is kept down to prevent blood loss during surgery.**

▼ **The artificial joint must do what the normal hip joint does when held by 27 acting muscles. Attempts have been made to fix the components by giving them a porous surface into which bone grows. The femoral section is a cobalt chrome ball set on a titanium alloy stem. The sockets are high density polyethylene.**

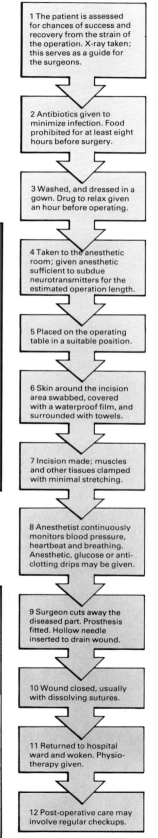

Stages in a typical operation

1 The patient is assessed for chances of success and recovery from the strain of the operation. X-ray taken; this serves as a guide for the surgeons.

2 Antibiotics given to minimize infection. Food prohibited for at least eight hours before surgery.

3 Washed, and dressed in a gown. Drug to relax given an hour before operating.

4 Taken to the anesthetic room; given anesthetic sufficient to subdue neurotransmitters for the estimated operation length.

5 Placed on the operating table in a suitable position.

6 Skin around the incision area swabbed, covered with a waterproof film, and surrounded with towels.

7 Incision made; muscles and other tissues clamped with minimal stretching.

8 Anesthetist continuously monitors blood pressure, heartbeat and breathing. Anesthetic, glucose or anti-clotting drips may be given.

9 Surgeon cuts away the diseased part. Prosthesis fitted. Hollow needle inserted to drain wound.

10 Wound closed, usually with dissolving sutures.

11 Returned to hospital ward and woken. Physio-therapy given.

12 Post-operative care may involve regular checkups.

► **Surgical tools include drains, saws, syringes, sharp spoons, broaches with sharp teeth, reamers, coagulation diathermy needles (hot needles that seal as they cut, minimizing loss of blood), scalpels, swabs, and cement guns.**

◄ **Spoons, broaches and reamers are used to cut out the diseased femoral head and socket, and cement is used to fix the prosthesis.**

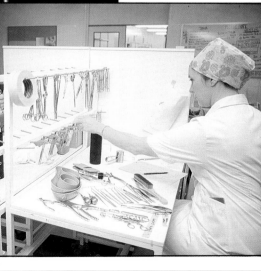

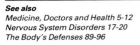

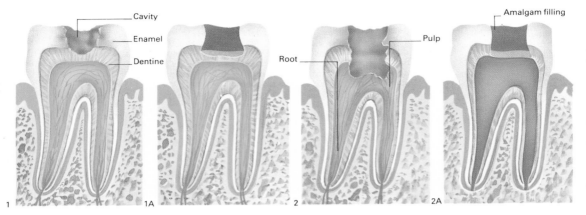

◄ *Tooth decay begins when the enamel is attacked by acid produced by plaque bacteria (1), and the decay may spread through into the softer dentine or the root, from where the infection may pass down the root canal (2) and form a painful abscess. To fill the cavity thus formed (1A, 2A), the dentist cuts away affected areas, lines the cavity and plugs the hole with a silver amalgam or a plastic filling.*

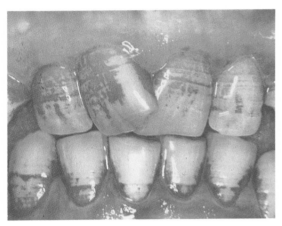

▲ *Plaque, a sticky covering of bacteria and food remains, builds up on teeth and is primarily responsible for the development of dental caries, as the acid produced by the bacteria eats into the tooth enamel. It is not usually possible to prevent plaque forming, but it can be removed by thorough brushing. Though usually hard to see, plaque can be revealed by taking a disclosing agent.*

▲ *A dentist selling dentures on the streets of Jaipur, India; dentures may be required for cosmetic purposes, or because the teeth have fallen out through widespread caries or the spread of gum infections which loosen the roots. One of the most common forms of periodontal disease is caused by toxic organic chemicals produced by plaque bacteria, in addition to the acids which attack the teeth themselves.*

Dentistry

Much knowledge of how metals, plastics and cements can be used in the body comes from dentistry. Few "living" environments are more hostile to such materials than the mouth.

For many centuries various metals and cements have been used to make good the havoc caused by tooth decay (caries). Decay usually occurs in the presence of bacteria, such as *Streptococcus mutans*, which, in the "dental plaque" that builds up on the surface of the teeth, turn sugar into acids. These acids attack the protective enamel of the teeth, dissolving away some of the minerals, and eventually the infection destroys the dentine and nerves of the teeth. Various attempts have been made to develop vaccines against such disease, and to develop chemicals that block the activity of the bacterial enzymes that help acids to form. Dental researchers are also looking for chemicals to stop bacteria sticking to the teeth in the first place.

Caries sometimes occurs in the absence of detectable numbers of bacteria and thus may have other origins. The use of fluoride ions in fluoride toothpastes (and, controversially, in the addition of fluoride to water supplies) has certainly provided a way of strengthening tooth enamel. This and other conservation approaches, including the control of diets, have led to a 40-50 percent drop in tooth cavities in the developed world over the past 25 years.

The traditional approach to dealing with tooth decay is to remove the carious part, shape the cavity, sterilize it, line it with cement and to pack it with metal amalgam. Amalgams are made from a silver, tin, copper and zinc alloy mixed on a 50:50 basis, with mercury. Inlays, based on a carefully taken cast of the cavity, may be fashioned in gold or porcelain to fit the cavity. Teeth that are hopelessly decayed or irreparably loose are normally extracted.

Since the 1970s, dentists have used an increasing range of glass and plastic materials, including various acrylates such as methyl methacrylates and cyanoacrylates, to repair teeth. These materials often prove cosmetically more acceptable than metal amalgams, but have the disadvantage that they tend not to show up on subsequent X-rays. However, the new plastics have led to a revolution in tooth coatings and claddings. Thin plastic coatings can be used to seal off the enamel. Partial tooth replacements, or crowns, which hitherto had to be fashioned in gold or porcelain and pinned in place, can now be built up in plastics and cemented onto existing teeth.

Dentures and bridges are increasingly giving way to implanted artificial teeth and tooth roots. These can be fashioned from a wide range of materials including titanium, acrylic resins, ceramic-fired alumina, carbon fibers and even lignum vitae.

Skin Disorders

7

Burns...Plastic surgery...Skin grafting...Cosmetic surgery...PERSPECTIVE...The medicinal leech... Treatments for baldness...Dermabrasion...Moles and warts...Birthmarks and tattoos...Corns and calluses

Skin disorders and abnormalities are complicated by the fact that they are usually disfiguring. The bruises, burns and other blemishes that occur as part of the skin's normal function as the body's interface with the outside world also have cosmetic implications relating to the skin's role as an organ of communication and self-expression.

Bruises and burns

Bruises – dead blood cells resulting from damaged blood vessels – are absorbed by the body. They can migrate downwards under gavity, especially in old people whose skin is lax. Scarring, the skin's method of repairing severe damage, is more permanent.

Burns may be caused by chemicals, electricity, radiation, ice, flames or contact with hot liquids (scalds) or solids. The severity of burns depends on their thickness. Superficial or first-degree burns of the epidermis only are painful for hours or days but heal without scarring. Deep dermal (second-degree) burns destroy all but the deepest dermal structures such as sweat glands. These burns lead to scarring, with poor texture skin; their blood supply is often precarious and they can progress to deep burns if they become infected or inflamed. Full thickness (third-degree) burns destroy the entire dermis including the pain receptors. Chances of survival are poor if more than 50 percent of the skin is burnt or the patient is very young or old.

The transfer of partial or full-thickness skin grafts – known as plastic surgery – is used to replace skin that is destroyed or badly scarred. Exposed surfaces are kept dry, and antiseptics are applied to skin flexures and face; dressings are applied in operating-theater conditions. Amniotic membrane may be used as a dressing. It fights infection, cuts fluid and protein losses and is readily available.

The medicinal leech

Leeches were originally collected from rivers by women who stood in the water and waited for the leeches to attach themselves. They were widely used in medicine until the late 19th century as a cure-all – it was thought they drew off "evil vapors". The medicinal leech was and still is a method of reducing bruises, inflammation and swelling.

Leeches feed by attaching themselves to the skin, making a three-sided cut. They are believed to inject an anesthetic – little pain is felt as the leech feeds – and an anticoagulant to prevent the collapse of the blood capillaries. As they suck blood, they add more anticoagulant while blood passes through their mouth. They feed rapidly, multiplying their weight eight-fold; they then dehydrate the blood and store it for long periods without putrefaction – red cells, antibodies and even bacteria can still be found six months after feeding.

Although largely superseded by new drugs, leeches are still applied today. Uses include reducing bruises around eyes that occlude vision, and encouraging blood flow in skin grafts after plastic surgery. Plastic surgeons in Nottingham, England, have now used them successfully in this way. A leech applied at once will feed for twenty minutes. Leeches live for six to twelve months without feeding and are at their best when hungry. If ravenous they start to digest themselves.

◀ A leech feeding on a human forearm.

▶ Leeches in medicinal use in the Middle Ages. At that time leeches were used indiscriminately for a wide variety of ailments, being intended to purge the system by reducing the amount of blood and so letting out noxious substances. Modern uses relate more specifically to reducing bruising or other cases where there is a build-up of blood beneath the surface of the skin.

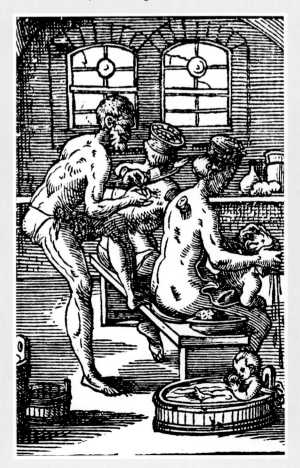

The amniotic sac in which a fetus develops is an ideal skin dressing

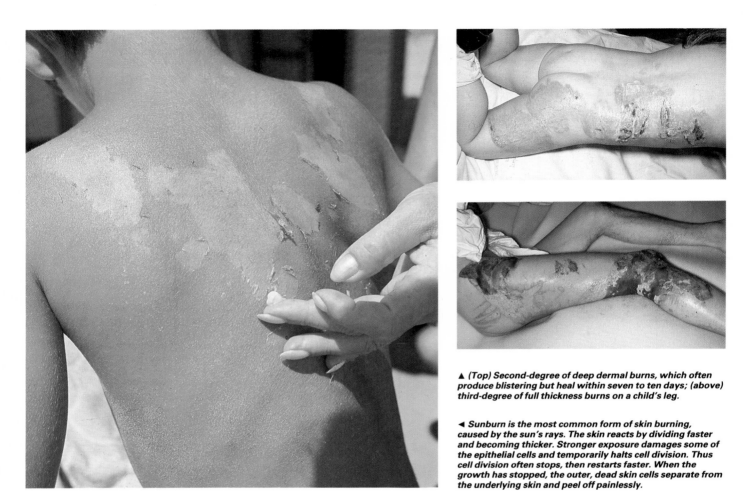

▲ (Top) Second-degree of deep dermal burns, which often produce blistering but heal within seven to ten days; (above) third-degree of full thickness burns on a child's leg.

◄ Sunburn is the most common form of skin burning, caused by the sun's rays. The skin reacts by dividing faster and becoming thicker. Stronger exposure damages some of the epithelial cells and temporarily halts cell division. Thus cell division often stops, then restarts faster. When the growth has stopped, the outer, dead skin cells separate from the underlying skin and peel off painlessly.

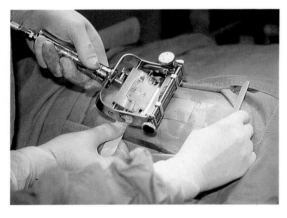

▲ Skin for grafting is removed using a special knife allowing thin layers to be taken.

◄ Human skin tissue grown in a culture. With this technique it has proved possible to grow skin to cover large areas and burns that are too extensive to be treated by grafting skin from other parts of the body may now be treated effectively in this way.

Skin is grafted by taking a partial-thickness slice, usually from the thigh or buttock. Full-thickness skin is sometimes required, usually if the underlying tissues are lost to some depth; in these cases only small areas of skin can be taken. Skin from the side of the hand is used to cover deep wounds to fingertips. If large areas of skin are lost, dehydrated pig skin is used as a temporary graft, for periods of up to ten days. It must then be replaced by another temporary layer of pig skin in large sheets, or a graft from the patient's own body. Otherwise it becomes incorporated by the body, creating an antibody response and more scarring. In 1984 American scientists reported the possibility of growing a person's own skin in tissue culture. It takes about three weeks to grow a square meter from an original two square centimeters. Meanwhile the patient's skin is covered temporarily by human amnion or dehydrated pig skin. In punch grafting, circles of skin are taken from a healthy area, dotted around the wound, and allowed to spread. Flaps of full thickness are often moved in such a way that they retain some of their original position and are pivoted onto the exposed area. These "take" better because they retain some of their original blood supply. Cross-transfer grafts of skin (finger-to-finger or leg-to-leg) have the advantage of being similar to the original skin.

Skin grafts are taken with a Humby knife, which has a roller with replaceable blades and can be adjusted for depth of cut, or with a Silver knife, which uses ordinary razor blades and is adequate for small split-skin grafts. The donor area is flattened with two boards and a thin paring taken, spread on gauze, surface up; there is no need

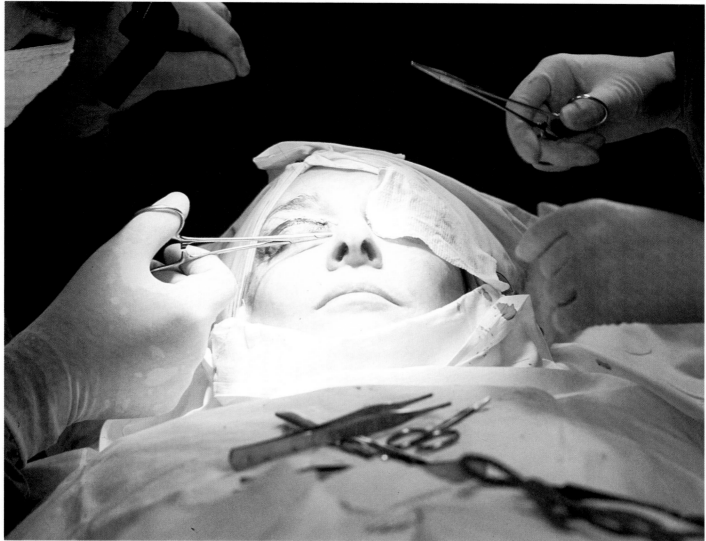

▲ *Cosmetic surgery offers the hope of restoring the youthfulness of aging skin by removing blemishes, wrinkles and bags under the eyes. This is done through stretching the skin and removing fat or excess liquid.*

to cut the graft exactly to size. The donor and graft areas are then bandaged. Skin grafts are always surrounded by a scar and generally have a different color, texture and contour from the skin they replace. Skin wounds are closed by means of nylon stitches that are subsequently removed, or subcuticular stitches using absorbable thread made of polyglycolic acid. Dirty abrasions must be cleaned as a permanent tattoo may result. They therefore may need scrubbing under general anesthetic.

Cosmetic surgery

Modern surgery has introduced a range of options for conditions of disfigurement. Noses can be straightened, made smaller or – in cases where the bridge of the nose is flat – enlarged. For enlargement, a graft of cartilage, bone or plastic is used. Chin augmentation uses rubber or bone from the nose or thigh, and is done through an incision under the chin or within the mouth. Protruding ears can be made flatter by removing some cartilage behind the ear. For face-lifts, incisions are made in front of and behind the ears, extending to the neck hairline, and the skin is pulled up and back. Eyelids can be done with the face-lift or separately. Incisions are made along crease lines of the upper lid and directly below the lower lid.

Breast reduction requires incisions below the breasts or at the side. If a lot of tissue is removed the nipples are repositioned. Breast augmentation is done by implanting soft silicone gel between the breast tissue and the muscle, so that the breast drapes over the implant.

Baldness treatments
Ordinary male baldness, an inherited condition, is the death of scalp hair follicles after exposure to male hormone. Other than by castration before puberty, baldness cannot be slowed, halted or reversed. There are three surgical treatments. Punch grafts or groups of one to 15 hair follicles are taken from elsewhere on the scalp and shared out over the bald area. Whole flaps of skin can be shifted round the scalp, leaving scars but hiding the bald areas. Finally, nylon fibers – artificial hair – can be implanted. However, this often leads to inflammation, infection and scarring.

Dermabrasion and peeling
"Sand paper" dermabrasion surgery improves the appearance of skin that has been pitted with acne. The improvement depends on the depth of pitting; about 60-80 percent of acne scars are improved. Chemical peeling is used to remove fine lines from skin. A solution of phenol and soap is applied to the face with a cotton swab. This produces a superficial burn and fibrosis. The skin then peels, removing fine lines as it goes. Pigmentation is also lost and so this is best used in pale-skinned people.

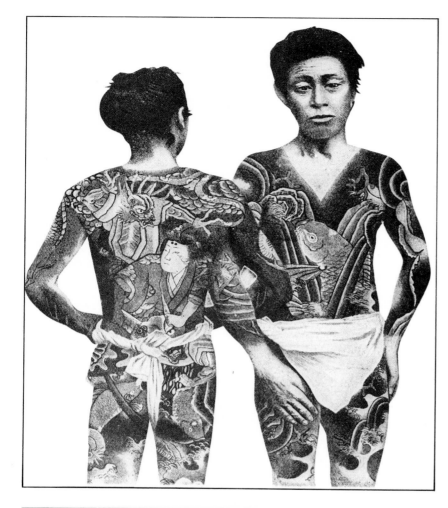

Natural blemishes

There are many natural growths on the skin, many of which can now be dealt with by modern medical techniques. Moles are harmless areas of raised skin, usually pigmented. They can be removed by shaving them flat or by cutting them out with a crescent of skin. Like the horny growths of hard skin known as warts or verrucas, they can also be removed by cryosurgery. In this technique, nitrous oxide at −70°C is applied with a cryoprobe for a few seconds – no anesthetic is needed. This freezes the cells, rapidly killing them. After thawing there is a watery discharge until a crust forms. Healing is complete within 14 days and scarring is minimal – leaving just a pale patch. More than one application may be necessary if the tissue to be removed is particularly thick.

Warts, which are caused by a virus, sometimes also disappear spontaneously. Those that persist can be removed by surgical incision, bloodless removal by freezing with liquid nitrogen or repeated applications of ointments.

Portwine marks are removed by argon laser, which penetrates the upper layer of skin without damaging it, and coagulates and kills the blood vessels causing the mark. These are replaced by transparent tissue and there is no scar.

Tattoos are permanent stains with ink injected under the skin but may be removed by carbon-dioxide or argon laser. Because of the thickness and depth of the tattoo there is always scarring but it is unpigmented.

Corns and calluses

These form in areas where the keratin layer of the skin is thickened. Calluses, uniform in thickness, are always present on the soles, even after prolonged bedrest. These become thicker after regular walking or running. Calluses also form on hands after rough work, and shrink or peel off when such work is stopped.

Corns are cones of keratinous skin. They form after repeated pressure on the sides or tops of toes; they can also form on tops or sides of fingers after work such as lathe-turning. They are tender when touched and may ache spontaneously.

Corns and calluses on hands can be prevented only by ceasing the activity that causes them. Corns on feet can be prevented by wearing comfortable shoes. All can be removed with a nail file or by dissolving with corn plasters.

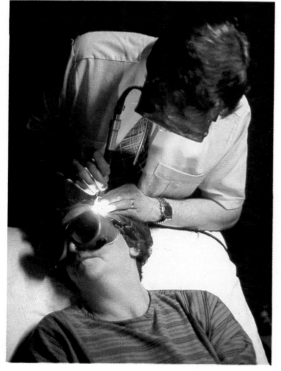

▲ The ancient art form of tattooing was particularly highly developed in Japan and the Pacific.

◄ Argon lasers can be used to remove portwine stains, which result from blood capillaries bursting beneath the skin. These lasers can destroy and seal the blood vessels. They can also be used to remove tattoos, but leave a pale "negative" image on the skin.

◄ A louse, the main parasite of the human hair. Head lice, body lice and pubic lice are distinct species. They are transmitted by close contact. Nits, the eggs of the head louse, stick firmly to the hair and must be removed by a special emulsion; they cannot be removed by regular washing with shampoo.

Digestive and Urinary Disorders

8

Colon disorders...Colitis and diverticulosis...
Appendicitis...Ulcers...Diarrhea and constipation...
Kidney and gall bladder stones...Prostate problems...
PERSPECTIVE...Living with a colostomy

Digestive and urinary tracts

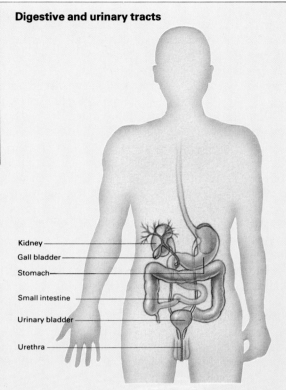

Kidney
Gall bladder
Stomach
Small intestine
Urinary bladder
Urethra

We are in direct contact with the outside world through our skin and its internal continuation, from mouth to rectum, which processes our food. A number of problems result from failures, malfunctions or imbalances in this system, all of them linked – to a greater or lesser extent – to diet.

Diseases of the colon

Colitis is characterized by inflammation of the mucous membrane of the large bowel, which causes bloody diarrhea. It usually strikes in adolescence or soon after. If severe, it can cause anemia, fever, tachycardia and weight-loss; if continuous, it needs surgical treatment. More usually, it is intermittent and the sufferer has only occasional attacks. These may be precipitated by various factors, including oral antibiotics. In addition to mouth ulcers, the side effects of colitis may include body rashes and conjunctivitis.

The incidence of colitis differs geographically and among different population groups. This has led to the idea that it may be diet-related. As with coronary heart disease, the incidence in Japan is substantially lower than in the USA, but among Japanese living in America, it is closer to the US than the Japanese level. Food allergy, notably allergy towards milk proteins, has been suggested as a cause. There is also some evidence that defects of immunity may be involved (♦ page 106), and stressful events can cause sufferers to relapse.

Another disease which usually affects the colon is diverticulosis. This is the presence of one or more pouches, known as diverticula, in the gut wall which may cause pain and a change in bowel routine. The motility of the intestine may contribute to the formation of diverticula. Changes in collagen structure with aging may also play a part. However, the strongest influence could be the fiber content of the diet. In less-developed countries, where the disease is less common than in the West, the diet tends to be much higher in fiber. Similarly, vegetarians have a lower incidence of the disease than meat-eaters.

Diverticulosis can be treated simply by changes in diet and mild drugs to ease the pain and reduce intestinal motility. If the diverticula become inflamed, the condition is called diverticulitis. Diverticulitis arises in less than 10 percent of people with diverticula, when symptoms similar to appendicitis may appear. There is a danger of hemorrhage, and antibiotics and a water-only diet are required until the inflammation subsides. Recurrent diverticulitis may need surgery.

A diverticulum may become inflamed as a result of fecal matter lodging in it. Appendicitis can be caused in the same way. The appendix is a residual tube attached to the beginning of the colon and plays no part in human digestion. Its entrance into the intestine is easily blocked. If this is not diagnosed, the appendix perforates, causing peritonitis (inflammation of the peritoneum), which can be fatal.

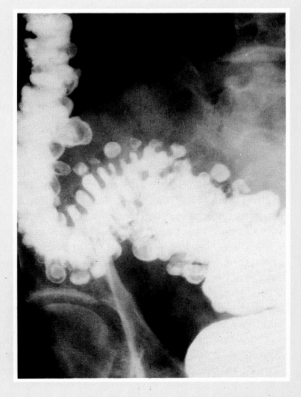

▲ *X-ray taken after a barium meal of diverticula, pouches appearing within the folds of the colon, which often develop after middle age. Diverticulosis is one of the so-called "diseases of civilization", a consequence of eating insufficient fiber, and the resulting unnatural bowel movements and constipation. Diverticula may become inflamed or perforated and lead to massive hemorrhage.*

Kidney stones have become more common in Western countries in this century

Peptic ulcers

Duodenal ulcers, breaks in the mucosal layer of the duodenum, are common. The immediate cause is an imbalance between the mucosal defenses and the amount of acid and pepsin (one of the digestive enzymes) in the duodenum. This is precipitated by factors which may include genetic predisposition, anti-inflammatory drugs such as aspirin, stress smoking and alcohol consumption.

The major symptom of a duodenal ulcer is pain, frequently after eating. If the ulcer perforates, so that the wall of the duodenum actually ruptures, the pain is very severe and the sufferer may collapse. In most cases ulcers heal spontaneously, but relapses are frequent. They can now be treated very successfully with drugs that reduce gastric acid production. Ulcer symptoms are also alleviated by avoiding any food which seems to cause pain – often fatty or spicy foods – and by eating small, frequent meals. Antacids (indigestion remedies) also alleviate pain but may cause constipation (if they contain aluminum salts) or diarrhea (if based on magnesium salts).

Ulcers also occur in the stomach, as a result of acidity and gastric reflux – the return of material from the duodenum into the stomach. Gastric ulcers are generally less severe than duodenal ulcers. Duodenal and gastric ulcers are known collectively as peptic ulcers.

The mouth and lips may also ulcerate, sometimes as a result of viral infections such as herpes. These ulcers may last up to two weeks, during which eating can be painful and difficult. Small mouth ulcers have a number of other causes. The tendency to ulceration seems to run in families and in women there is a relationship between ulcer formation and the menstrual cycle. Ulceration may also be an immune response to antigens in oral mucosa which cross-react with bacterial antigens (♦ page 97). Stress and colitis may also be a cause.

Diarrhea, constipation and stones

The two major gastro-intestinal complaints are diarrhea and constipation. Diarrhea may result from a number of causes including contaminated food or water, excess alcohol, food allergy and laxative abuse. Characterized by watery feces, it usually clears up spontaneously. It can be dangerous, particularly in infants and malnourished people, because of its dehydrating effect. The opposite is constipation – infrequent and difficult defecation, with the production of hard feces. Diet plays a major role, although it can also be caused by drugs, pregnancy and diseases including diabetes and parkinsonism. It is alleviated by a high fiber diet and by laxatives based on plants.

Problems arising in relation to the removal of waste may be directly connected with excretion (as with urinary stones) or have a secondary cause such as prostatic enlargement (♦ page 48). Urinary stone disease – the formation of mineral lumps in the kidneys and urinary tract – is another ailment which has risen in frequency in the developed countries during this century.

Urine contains many different mineral ions, some of which precipitate as solids at low concentrations. The predominant stone substances in the developed countries are calcium oxalate and calcium phosphate. Normal urine contains polymers which interfere with crystal growth, thus preventing stones from growing to a size where they are not naturally expelled in the urine stream. It is when stones become large enough to obstruct the urinary tract that they can cause trouble. This may show up as pains during urination, appendicitis-like pains (renal colic) or an increased incidence of urinary infections.

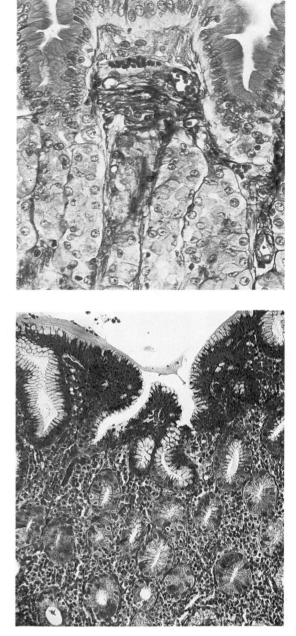

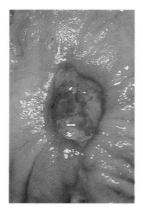

◄ ▲ *Section through the lining of a healthy stomach (top) and a stomach ulcer (above and left). The epithelium layer, here stained blue, becomes thin and broken, allowing the digestive enzymes and acid to attack the body's own tissues. Most ulcers, though not all, are the result of excess acid in the stomach; they may be a side-effect of the body's "Generalized Adaptation Syndrome" to stress.*

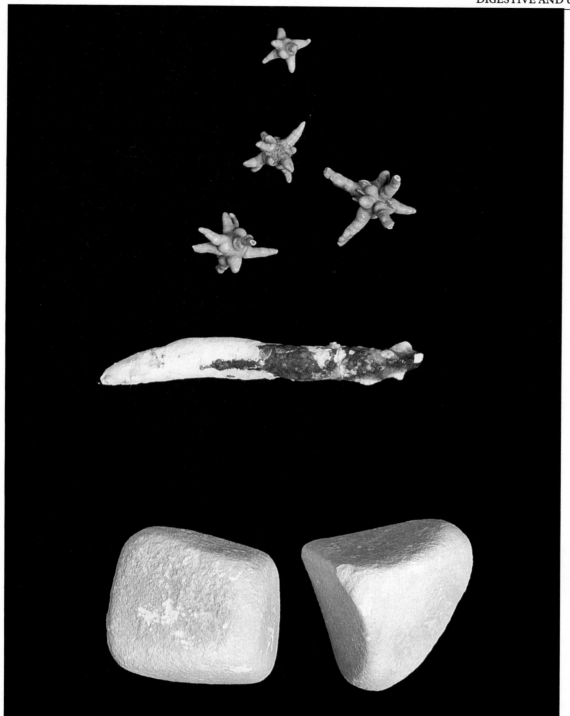

◄ *Stones from the urinary tract, including the knobbly "staghorn" stones from the kidney.*

Ultrasonic probe

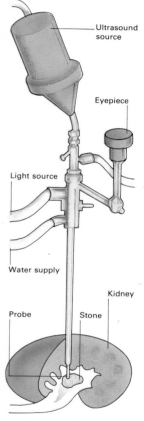

Ultrasound source

Eyepiece

Light source

Water supply

Probe

Stone

Kidney

▲ *Kidney stones can be destroyed using an ultrasound probe inserted into the kidney, allowing the surgeon to view the stone optically, aim the ultrasound source and flush away stone fragments with water.*

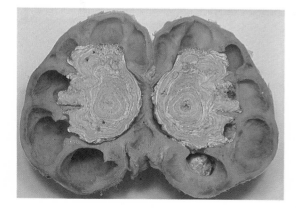

► *Lithotripsy is another new technique for destroying kidney stones. The patient is placed in a bath, above a high-energy sound source contained in an ellipse that focuses the sound-waves on the kidney. These waves destroy the stone and the fragments are excreted. Recovery rates are much faster than with conventional surgery.*

◄ *Kidney stones may virtually fill the calyx, or urine-gathering space in the kidney.*

Lithotripsy

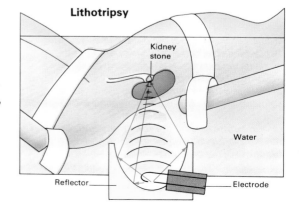

Kidney stone

Water

Reflector

Electrode

See also
Intestinal Infections 49-56
Allergies and Immune Defects 105-8

▲ *A medieval operation on piles. These are benign swellings in blood vessels inside or outside the anus which can cause discomfort and pain. Hemorrhoids rarely have a single cause, though constipation and straining to pass feces may often bring them on. Surgery is sometimes necessary in the most severe cases.*

Colostomy — bypassing the intestines

A colostomy is an artificial anus, which a surgeon can arrange by cutting across the colon and diverting it towards a newly-created opening in the wall of the abdomen.

There are two reasons for carrying out a short-circuiting operation of this sort. Intestinal contents may have to be voided before they pass through a portion of the colon which needs to be allowed to heal after disease and/or surgery. Gunshot injuries and the tearing wounds sometimes received in road accidents are other grounds for adopting this measure. A colostomy done for such reasons is temporary, normal function being resumed and the abdominal hole being closed several weeks or months later. Alternatively, when a large section of the bowel has to be removed because of disease (usually cancer), a permanent colostomy is then created. In either case, the patient uses a colostomy bag, which covers the artificial opening and receives the excreta.

Some intestinal operations are conducted in two parts. The surgeon may arrange a temporary colostomy as the first stage in dealing with a tumor that is blocking the colon. He can then remove the tumor, before closing the colostomy and restoring the normal function of the intestine and rectum. Modern appliances and techniques make it possible for an individual to live both comfortably and hygienically with a colostomy, and to conceal its existence from other people.

Whether or not stone disease needs surgical treatment depends on the nature of the obstruction rather than the size of the stone. The aim of conservative (non-surgical) treatment is to get the patient to pass the stone spontaneously. This can be encouraged by a high fluid intake, sometimes coupled with brief diuretic treatment.

Stones can also develop in the gall bladder, where they cause abdominal pain, often accompanied by nausea and vomiting. Gallstones may affect as many as one in five people worldwide. Again, there is a difference in composition between developed and underdeveloped countries. Cholesterol is a major component of western gallstones, while stones containing calcium ions and bile pigments are more frequent in underdeveloped areas. If the stones are wholly organic, they can be dissolved by chenodeoxycholic acid, but calcified (calcium-containing) stones resist this treatment and usually have to be removed surgically. Both gall and urinary stones have high rates of recurrence.

Urinary tract infections

Although the prostate gland is not directly involved in excretion, its position in the body means that its enlargement may cause excretory disorders. When male hormone production ceases, the prostate gland (which produces a secretion that forms part of semen) degenerates and after the age of 60 enlargement of the fibrous residue is common. This can cause pressure on the urethra, which is surrounded by the prostate, so that the bladder does not empty properly. Stones may precipitate in the stagnant urine remaining and infections or cancer may develop. The condition is alleviated by surgery. The prostate may also become infected (prostatitis) causing gut and back pain.

Urinary tract infection may also be a symptom of polycystic kidney disease, which can cause severe abdominal pain and high blood pressure and eventual deterioration of kidney function. It is an inherited disease in which both kidneys are covered with multiple cysts. A cyst is an abnormal piece of tissue which encloses liquid or semisolid material or gases and can occur in or on many parts of the body, notably the liver. Choledocal cysts are cysts of the bile duct which can contain up to eight liters of material. They also cause abdominal pain and if removed surgically can cause biliary cirrhosis.

Swollen prostate gland

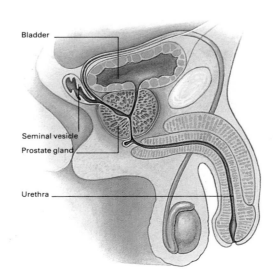

Bladder

Seminal vesicle

Prostate gland

Urethra

◄ *The prostate gland, which provides part of the seminal fluid, tends to become enlarged. This is very common in older men. Since it is situated at the base of the bladder and around the urethra, this swelling can cause disruption to the normal processes of urination. This may result in a sudden inability to urinate, or a gradual failure of the bladder to empty, which may eventually cause kidney problems. In these circumstances it is necessary to remove the prostate.*

Intestinal infection and sanitation...Malnutrition and diarrhea...Cholera, an ancient scourge...Salmonella food poisoning and typhoid fever...Amebic dysentery... Intestinal worms...PERSPECTIVE...The spread of cholera...The agents of gastroenteritis...Recent typhoid fever outbreaks...Food preparation and infection... Modern drugs

The digestive system

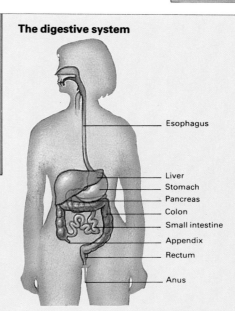

- Esophagus
- Liver
- Stomach
- Pancreas
- Colon
- Small intestine
- Appendix
- Rectum
- Anus

Although we cannot see individual microbes, astronomical numbers surround us from cradle to grave. The vast majority are beneficial, in helping plants to assimilate nitrogen from the air, breaking down dead plant and animal tissues, and recycling elements which are central to the planet's ecology. Many microbes are relatively self-sufficient, finding energy and materials for continued growth in the environment. But some microbes have evolved a parasitic way of life as an easier method of securing the nutrients they require. Known as pathogens, these are recognized by the infectious diseases they cause (♦ page 70). Like other animals, humans acquire such micro-organisms in several different ways – through food and water, by inhalation, sexual intercourse, contamination of a wound, or the attentions of insect "vectors". A few can invade the body by more than one route, but most gain entry through a particular channel and cause their principal damage there.

Diarrheal disease

Intestinal infections comprise one such group. They are caused by microbes ingested with food or water which then proliferate in the gut. The infections are characterized by diarrhea and/or vomiting, perhaps accompanied by abdominal cramps and raised temperature. Eighty percent of all illness in developing countries is linked to water and for this reason the World Health Organization has adopted a target of clean water for all by 1990. Although this percentage includes conditions such as malaria, spread by insects breeding in lakes and streams, it mainly relates to conditions known collectively as "diarrheal disease".

In some regions diarrheal disease is responsible for as much as 40 percent of mortality among infants and young children of up to five years of age. In 1980, intestinal infections alone caused five million deaths – ten every minute of every day – and 750 million disease episodes in Africa, Latin America and Asia (excluding China). Most of the pathogens concerned would seem little more than transient nuisances in the West.

Continual diarrhea promotes malnutrition and impairs defense mechanisms, contributing to a vicious circle in which malnourished children are 50 percent more likely than well-fed ones to succumb to diarrheal disease. Measles in particular forms a horrendous combination with diarrhea, each condition being a common and potentially fatal complication of the other. In 1984 researchers at Moorfields Eye Hospital, London, and Chattisgarh Eye Hospital in India reported a previously unknown link between severe dehydration caused by diarrhea and the development of eye cataracts (♦ page 14). This discovery may account for the puzzlingly high incidence of cataract in a number of developing countries.

Polluted water supplies
In 1854 an English anesthetist John Snow (1813-1858) demanded that the handle be removed from the public water pump in Broad Street, London. A cholera outbreak then raging had caused 500 deaths in ten days in one small area alone. Making house-to-house enquiries, Snow realized that all the victims had collected their drinking water from the same pump. So the handle was disconnected – and a few days later the epidemic abated. Something similar, though on a larger scale, happened in 1971, when cholera swept through West Africa. Although the outbreak seemed indiscriminate, researchers at the Zaria University Hospital, Nigeria, found that the victims' addresses were not randomly distributed throughout the city. Most of the patients came from the old city and the majority of those had been using well rather than tap water. The authorities chlorinated the infected wells, and immediately the epidemic declined.

A cup of cholera
The importance of factors other than specific microbes in causing disease was demonstrated dramatically by the German epidemiologist Max von Pettenkofer (1818-1901) and the Russian pathologist Elie Metchnikoff (1845-1916). Both were unconvinced by claims from the pioneer German bacteriologist Robert Koch (1843-1910) that Vibrio cholerae was the confirmed agent of cholera (♦ page 50). So they drank cultures teeming with this organism, taken from patients with the disease. They developed mild diarrhea and had enormous numbers of the bacteria in their feces – but did not succumb to cholera. Chance probably played a part in the outcome – few if any pathogens cause disease in 100 percent of infected individuals. Nutrition was certainly important – well-fed middle-class doctors are far less vulnerable to a disease such as cholera than are malnourished Asians. Individuals may also have enjoyed inbuilt resistance, of the sort associated with HLA antigens (♦ page 5).

Oral rehydration therapy, developed in the 1970s, has reduced cholera mortality to 1 percent

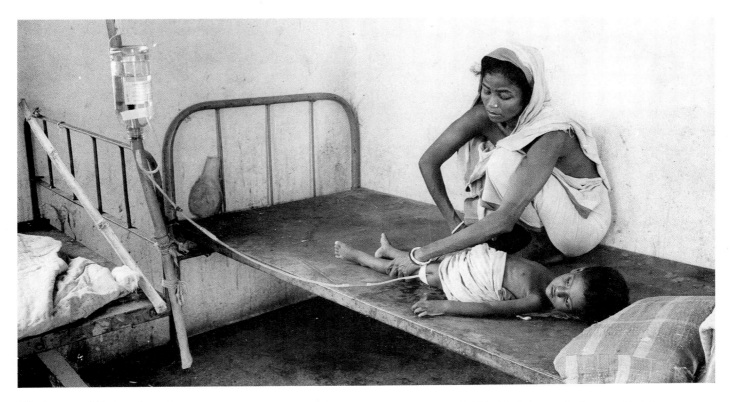

Cholera and its treatment

Pathogens responsible for diarrheal disease include *Vibrio cholerae*, the agent of cholera, plus a wide range of other bacteria and viruses. All are transmitted via food and water contaminated by feces from individuals suffering from the condition, by those of animals, and also by fecal organisms carried by flies. This explains why the problem is so much greater in the Third World than in developed countries with safe water, sewage disposal and food hygiene. The organisms provoke diarrhea by producing toxins (poisons). These make the intestinal tract excrete huge quantities of fluid carrying vital salts.

Dehydration, potentially fatal within a few hours, used to be treated with antibiotics and liquids infused into a vein. But the 1970s saw the advent of oral rehydration therapy (ORT). First employed on a large scale among refugees during the 1971 India-Pakistani war, it reduced mortality from 30 to 1 percent. It is simple to use and (in principle at least) widely available. Patients drink water containing sodium and potassium chloride plus glucose (to help the sick intestine absorb the salts) and sodium bicarbonate (baking soda) to combat acidosis.

Cholera has a very short incubation period between infection and the onset of symptoms – sometimes only a few hours. A comparatively mild illness may ensue, but many victims develop a devastating illness, becoming rapidly dehydrated by vomiting and passing profuse "rice water stools". The bacteria adhere to the microvilli in the intestine. There they generate a toxin which also attaches to cells lining the intestinal wall, activating an enzyme that causes them to excrete water and salts. Losing 15-20 liters of fluid per day, victims develop shrivelled skin and sunken eyes. In addition to ORT, tetracycline reduces fluid loss by reducing the number of infecting organisms. Immunization is short-lived and incomplete, though new, genetically-engineered vaccines promise to give far greater protection. The primary defense will remain good sanitation and hygiene.

▲ *A child with cholera used to be treated by intravenous drip; in poor regions such treatment was prohibitively expensive, and the discovery in 1971 of oral rehydration therapy (ORT) greatly simplified treatment for the disease.*

▼ *Clean water and adequate sanitation is essential to reduce the incidence of intestinal infections in the world.*

Clean Water

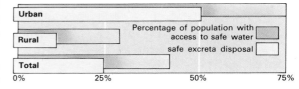

Urban		
Rural	Percentage of population with access to safe water	
	safe excreta disposal	
Total		

0%   25%   50%   75%

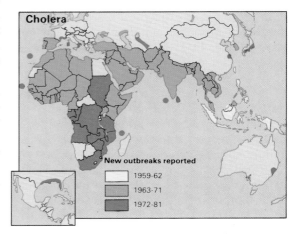

Cholera

New outbreaks reported
- 1959-62
- 1963-71
- 1972-81

▲ *The modern El Tor cholera epidemic originated in South-East Asia in the early 1960s and spread quickly through South Asia and North Africa by 1971. Since 1978 its progress seems to have been halted.*

▲ *A 19th-century illustration of the micro-organisms living in drinking water. The discovery that cholera was a disease contracted from micro-organisms in the water rather than from fumes made possible effective preventive action.*

▼ *"The Grim Reaper rowing his boat down the River Thames", a comment from "Punch" magazine on the cholera epidemic in London in 1858. The epidemic of the 1840s and 1850s led to a wholesale reorganization of the capital's water and sewerage systems.*

The ebbs and flows of cholera

Historically, cholera has occurred as a succession of great global waves. The seventh, most recent, pandemic (worldwide epidemic) began during 1961 in Indonesia. It has since spread to Southeast and Southern Asia, the Middle East, west and east Africa, southern Europe, the Far East and western Pacific, and the USA. Caused by the El Tor strain of "Vibrio cholerae" (after El Tor Quarantine Camp in the Sinai where the strain was first isolated), it has largely displaced the previous, classical cholera in India, where the disease has long been endemic (permanently established). Throughout the world there are now some 80,000 new cases of cholera a year.

Man is the only host for the comma-shaped bacterium. Given that the bacterium can survive in water for long periods, even shellfish can be a source of infection. Sporadic incidents also show that, contrary to expectations, the organism is able to establish itself in developed countries and that outbreaks can occur there, given a relaxation in sanitation. Cholera occurs occasionally along the Texas Gulf coast, for example. In 1981 there were 14 cases on an oil rig there among men who had eaten rice rinsed in canal water containing sewage. In 1973 there were 278 cases and 25 deaths in Naples, thought to be the result of contaminated mussels.

Food preparation and infection

Preventive measures can eliminate dangerous organisms, or prevent them growing, in food and water, and adequate cooking kills those in foodstuffs that may be contaminated. Chlorination destroys residual bacteria, already reduced to low levels by filtration, before water is put into the supply system. Milk is pasteurized by being held at 63°C for half an hour, or "flash" treated at a higher temperature for a shorter time. As with boiling to cleanse polluted water, this obliterates intestinal pathogens but not all bacteria.

Techniques which prevent microbes from proliferating, rather than destroy them, include freezing and refrigeration, pickling, smoking, drying, salting and the inclusion of artificial preservatives. Canned food is sterilized to kill all organisms except the most rugged spore-formers. Tomatoes, rhubarb and other acid-containing foods become sterile when heated to lower temperatures for shorter times than, for example, meat or beans. Meat is invariably slightly contaminated at the slaughter-house and must be kept chilled before being cooked for long enough to destroy any pathogens. Particular care is necessary with poultry, which may carry salmonellae. Shellfish are often heavily infected, although oysters offered for sale raw are usually cleansed in clean chlorinated water for some days beforehand.

Modern Drugs

BODY SYSTEM	MAIN USES	DRUG GROUPS	TYPICAL DRUG	MODE OF ACTION
Central nervous system	Pain	Salicylates	Aspirin	Blocks prostaglandins which cause pain, fever and inflammation
	Severe pain	Opiates	Morphine	Blocks pain receptors in brain
	Anxiety and insomnia	Benzodiapazepines	Diazepam	Blocks brain receptors
	Depression	Monoamine oxidase inhibitors	Isocarboxazid	Blocks mood enzymes
		Tricyclics	Amitriptyline	Uncertain; boosts mood chemicals
	Epilepsy	Barbiturates	Phenobarbitone	Blocks convulsions via brain neurons
		Hydantoins	Phenytoin	As above
	Parkinsonism	Dopaminergic	Levodopa	Affects nerve transmission
Endocrine	Diabetes	Hormone	Insulin	Reduces blood sugar
	Growth failure	Hormone	Growth hormone	Replaces deficient hormone
	Hypothyroidism	Hormone	Thyroxine	Replaces missing hormone
	Hyperthyroidism	Hormone	Radioactive iodine	Destroys part of thyroid
	Contraception	Hormone	Estrogen/progesterone	Prevents ovulation
			Progesterone only	Thickens cervical mucus to prevent sperm reaching egg; may also prevent ovulation
	Menopause	Hormone	Estrogen/progesterone	Restores female hormone balance
Joints	Arthritis	Non-steroidal anti-inflammatory drugs	Many	Reduces pain and inflammation
		Steroids	Prednisolone	As above
			Gold, penicillamine	Tries to halt disease
Skin	Acne	Antiseptics	Many	Helps to clean skin
		Antibiotics	Many	Kills bacteria
		Keratolytics	Many	Peels off skin
		Hormones	Cyproterone acetate	
		Steroids	Methylprednisolone	Reduces inflammation
	Psoriasis	As above	Dithranol	
Digestive tract	Indigestion	Antacids	Many	Neutralizes excess acid production
	Ulcers	H2 receptor blockers	Cimetidine	Prevents excess acid production
	Constipation	Laxatives	Methylcellulose	Increases fecal bulk
			Senna	Stimulates bowel movement
			Liquid paraffin	Softens feces
Cardiovascular	Hypertension	Beta blockers	Propranolol	Blocks heart receptors
		Diuretics	Thiazides	Reduces blood volume and dilates arteries
		ACE inhibitors	Captopril	Blocks kidney enzyme which affects blood pressure
		Calcium blockers	Nifedipine	Blocks calcium movement across arterial wall
Immune system	Allergies	Mast cell stabilizers	Sodium cromoglycate	Prevents overactivity of immune cells to outside allergens
		Bronchodilators	Salbutamol	Relaxes lung passages in asthma
		Corticosteroids	Prednisolone	Suppresses immune cells
	Infections	Antibiotics	Ampicillin, Tetracycline, Sulfonamide, Cephalosporins	Attacks bacteria; drug used depends on causative organism
		Anti-virals	Amantidine, Acyclovir. Idoxuridine	Attacks viruses; drug used depends on virus type
		Vaccines	Many	Protects against infection by boosting immunity
Cells	Cancer	Alkylating agents	Cyclophosphamide	Interferes with cell division
		Anti-metabolites	Methotrexate	Interferes with cell chemical function
		Cytotoxic antibiotics	Doxorubicin	Interferes with cell replication and protein synthesis
		Alkaloids	Vincristine	Halts cell division
General	Colds	Antipyretics	Aspirin	Reduce temperature
	Coughs	Decongestants	Phenylephrine	Unblocks sinuses
		Suppressants	Codeine	Suppresses cough
		Expectorants	Ipecacuanha	No scientific evidence that they work
	Vitamins	Single groups of A,B,C, D and E, or combined		Correct deficiencies where diet is poor, or for young children, pregnant women or elderly

SIDE EFFECTS *	OTHER USES	MARKET SIZE	FUTURE	MISCELLANEOUS
Stomach irritant	Arthritis	Enormous	Stomach problems may reduce use	Better to use soluble aspirin or paracetamol if stomach problems occur
Addiction, constipation, nausea		Stable; only for specific uses	Stable unless non-addictive drugs of same potency developed	
Tolerance, addiction	Epilepsy, major psychotic illness	Enormous	Market likely to decline because of side-effects	Patients should always withdraw slowly from these drugs
Interacts with some foods		Stable		
Dry mouth, sedation		Stable	Use likely to continue unless alternative drugs with fewer side effects developed	
Addiction	Severe insomnia	Decreasing	Declining because of addiction	
Nausea, vomiting		Stable	Stable	Dose has to be tailored carefully to patients
Nausea, insomnia		Stable	May be superseded by more specific drugs	Drug effectiveness decreases with time
Local skin reactions and hypersensitivity		Increasing	Greater use of human insulin to avoid hypersensitivity to animal insulins	
As above		Small	Severe shortages likely to be overcome by use of genetic engineering	
As above		Small		
As above		Small		
Circulatory problems, nausea, weight gain		Large	Stable until safer methods such as vaccines developed	
As above		Smaller		More risk of failure than combined pills but useful for breast feeding women
As above		Growing	Likely to increase	
Indigestion, stomach irritation	Pain	Enormous	Stable until more effective drugs found	
Various, including reduced immunity	Allergies, suppression of transplant rejection	Large		Should be avoided in children because growth is stunted
Severe blood disorders		Small	As above	
		Large		
Overuse of steroids can lead to scarring of the skin				
		Large	Decreasing as some antacids are unnecessary	
Rashes		Enormous	Growing as more cimetidine-like drugs are developed	
Wind, diarrhea		Large	May decrease as people increase their dietary fiber intake	
Nausea, tiredness, vivid dreams, slow heart beat, hypotension	Angina, abnormal heart beat, migraine, acute anxiety	Enormous	May be superseded by ACE inhibitors and calcium blockers	Should never be taken by asthmatics; may have value in preventing heart attacks
Lowers potassium	Reduces edema	Very large	As above	
Nausea, rash, blood disorders	Heart failure	Potentially large	Could take over market if side effects kept down	
Nausea, vomiting, slow heart beat	Heart beat abnormalities, angina	Potentially large	Could have important future role; full potential unknown	
Throat irritation	Rhinitis	Large	Enormous potential with discovery of related chemicals, leukotrienes	
Tremor		Large	Likely to decrease if leukotrienes successful	
Various, including reduced immunity		Large	Likely to decrease for treatment of allergies	
Sensitivity reactions to penicillins		Enormous	Antibiotics becoming increasingly specific but resistance problems mean need for continuing development	
Various		Growing	Enormous potential if more effective drugs developed	
Hypersensitivity		Large	Huge potential if new vaccines can be developed	
Various, from nausea and vomiting to hair loss and major blood disorders		Growing	Enormous potential markets for anti-cancer drugs but unlikely to be a single "cure-all"	
Stomach irritation		Enormous	Continuing large as people seek symptoms relief	
Possible toxicity with large doses of Vitamin A		Enormous	Levelling off and possibly declining because of continuing controversy over supplements for people with balanced diet	

*Side effects are not to be expected in all cases.

Salmonella infections

There are many species of *Salmonella* that cause intestinal infections and diarrhea of varying degrees of severity. These infections are increasingly untreatable because they are caused by strains resistant to antibiotics. In London, scientists at the Central Public Health Laboratory monitored the rise in resistance during the 1970s, and in 1980 announced that all strains of the predominant *Salmonella typhimurium*, causing gastroenteritis, had become insensitive to at least one drug. Some were resistant to six or more antibiotics. The picture is similar in the USA and indeed most parts of the world. Particularly high level of resistance are found in countries, such as those of South America, where people can buy antibiotics across the counter without prescription. It is a paradox of modern medicine that the power of these life-saving drugs is being reduced considerably as a result of excessive, indiscriminate use. That means that correspondingly more emphasis must now be placed on the importance of preventive action via hygiene and adequate cooking – a need underlined by surveys showing that foods such as sausages are often contaminated with salmonellae.

The agent of typhoid fever

Antibiotic resistance is particularly serious in *Salmonella typhi*. This, the most virulent of all species, is the agent of typhoid fever. Historically a scourge of armies, it killed over 8,000 British troops during the Boer War (compared with 7,500 killed in battle). Nowadays, like cholera, typhoid fever occurs mostly in countries with inadequate sanitation. Elsewhere it causes sporadic epidemics, often originating with organisms brought home by holidaymakers. The organism differs from *V. cholerae* in invading cells lining the gut, sometimes migrating further from there. As many as 80 percent of infected people have only mild symptoms, but the rest develop a potentially lethal infection. During the first week, as bacteria penetrate the gut wall and reach the lymphatic vessels, the victim suffers from fever, malaise and general aches and pains. In the second week, there is diarrhea, delerium and a fever of around 40°C as organisms invade the bloodstream and gall bladder. The third week brings either an improvement or complications such as severe bleeding and perforation of the intestine. Although secondary, person-to-person spread is uncommon, about three percent of those who recover become "healthy carriers", harboring the bacteria in their gall bladder and being capable of transmitting them to others. "Typhoid Mary", a cook in the New York area, caused at least six outbreaks between 1901 and 1907 – one of which may have affected 1,300 people.

Before antibiotics were available, typhoid fever killed about 10 percent of patients. The death rate among those given chloramphenicol is now one percent or less. This is why the emergence of chloramphenicol-resistant strains of the typhoid bacillus in Mexico during the early 1970s greatly alarmed bacteriologists. Around 1974, they infected some 100,000 individuals, killing 14,000 of them. Typhoid fever could again be a major danger if such strains were to proliferate around the world. The possibility of *S. typhi* and other salmonellae becoming insensitive to more drugs is increased by the fact that resistance can be transferred between such species, and even between them and both harmful and harmless strains of *E. coli*. As with cholera, vaccines against typhoid fever and the associated paratyphoid fever afford only limited protection and may well be supplanted by more effective versions made by genetic engineering.

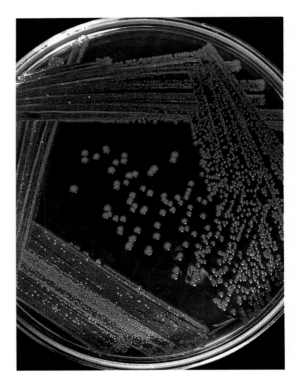

▲ *Salmonella typhi, the agent of typhoid fever, is shown here growing in a laboratory culture. Resistance to the disease may be raised somewhat by vaccination with dead typhoid bacilli. Paratyphoid fever is an infectious diarrheal disease caused by related bacteria, found in temperate and tropical regions. Its symptoms are similar to, though less virulent than, those of typhoid fever.*

Typhoid fever in Aberdeen

Beginning on 12 May 1964, an increasing number of people in Aberdeen, Scotland, went down with what seemed to be gastroenteritis. Four days later one of them was sufficiently ill to be admitted to hospital, where tests revealed Salmonella typhi as the culprit. All the victims were then promptly isolated in hospital and treated for typhoid fever, while public health staff began to seek the source of the outbreak. Enquiries about foods the patients had eaten soon cast suspicions on a dairy, an ice-cream shop and a supermarket. Further cross-comparisons eliminated the first two, and led to the cold meat department of the supermarket, from which three-quarters of the individuals had purchased corned beef. Bacteriologists from the Central Public Health Laboratory in London then confirmed that a six-pound can of this meat, sold in the store, contained S. typhi – and that it was a strain virtually unknown in Great Britain. By tracing the can to its origin, they deduced that the bacterium had entered through a faulty seal while the can was being cooled with sewage-containing water at the manufacturing plant in Argentina. The final toll in the Aberdeen epidemic was 507 cases, and three elderly patients died. Chloramphenicol treatment, seizure of the suspect food, a vigorous campaign to promote public hygiene and the speedy tracing and testing of 4,200 contacts of affected persons, together ensured that those figures were not considerably higher.

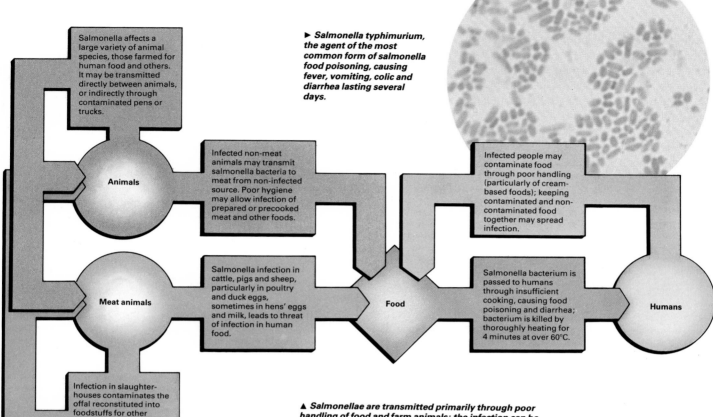

Salmonella affects a large variety of animal species, those farmed for human food and others. It may be transmitted directly between animals, or indirectly through contaminated pens or trucks.

Animals

Infected non-meat animals may transmit salmonella bacteria to meat from non-infected source. Poor hygiene may allow infection of prepared or precooked meat and other foods.

▶ *Salmonella typhimurium, the agent of the most common form of salmonella food poisoning, causing fever, vomiting, colic and diarrhea lasting several days.*

Infected people may contaminate food through poor handling (particularly of cream-based foods); keeping contaminated and non-contaminated food together may spread infection.

Meat animals

Salmonella infection in cattle, pigs and sheep, particularly in poultry and duck eggs, sometimes in hens' eggs and milk, leads to threat of infection in human food.

Food

Salmonella bacterium is passed to humans through insufficient cooking, causing food poisoning and diarrhea; bacterium is killed by thoroughly heating for 4 minutes at over 60°C.

Humans

Infection in slaughter-houses contaminates the offal reconstituted into foodstuffs for other animals, passing on the infection.

▲ *Salmonellae are transmitted primarily through poor handling of food and farm animals; the infection can be passed on from animal to animal; and uncontaminated food can be contaminated by animal or human carriers. Mass use of antibiotics in modern factory farming may, paradoxically, encourage resistant strains to develop, rendering infections unresponsive to treatment.*

Gastroenteritis

In addition to V. cholerae, closely related bacteria such as V. parahaemolyticus, and unrelated ones such as Campylobacter jejeuni also cause considerable amounts of diarrheal disease in the Third World. Other causes are certain strains of Escherichia coli, that usually live without harm in the intestine. Such "wolves in sheeps' clothing" can produce toxins similar to, but milder than, those of cholera. Along with various species of Shigella (responsible for different versions of dysentery) and of Salmonella, these micro-organisms also cause "traveler's diarrhea" and a variety of food poisoning found in developed countries.

Unlike bacteria which produce conditions like botulism (♦ page 114) by making poisons in food before it is eaten, these organisms cause gastroenteritis by colonizing the intestinal tract. The damage they do there is associated with two types of poison. Endotoxins are parts of the bacterial cell wall, which cause fever and shock. Exotoxins, like that of cholera, are excreted by the organisms and provoke diarrhea. Most of these bacteria do not just adhere to the gut wall. They also penetrate the gut lining, particularly in the colon. Salmonellae can invade even deeper tissues.

Rotaviruses, first detected in humans in 1973, are another cause of gastroenteritis in both the developed and developing world, where they are particularly common among young children. They do not produce toxins, but invade and destroy cells lining the small intestine.

The symptoms of enteritis can be combated by substances ranging from kaolin (which absorbs water) to morphine (which reduces the heightened activity of the lower intestine as it seeks to expel its contents). In severe cases – particularly in the very young and the very old – treatment with antibiotics may be required. But these will be ineffective if the illness is caused by a virus or by one of the increasingly common strains of resistant bacteria.

Various species of Salmonella were once thought to be by far the commonest causes of food poisoning in the USA and Europe. Since the early 1970s, however, they have begun to be rivalled by strains of Campylobacter jejeuni. The disease can be very unpleasant, with explosive diarrhea, offensive watery stools and pain so severe as to suggest appendicitis. Although deaths have occurred in elderly people, the infection usually clears up even before a diagnosis can be made. C. jejeuni occurs commonly in pigs and less often in cattle, dogs and cats, but the sources of human outbreaks are seldom pinpointed. A few incidents have been traced to meat, unpasteurized milk and contaminated water. Campylobacters are destroyed by heat at least as readily as other food-poisoning bacteria. Campylobacters are not yet known to manufacture toxins, but researchers in Australia, Great Britain and Holland suggested in 1984 that they may be responsible for peptic ulcers.

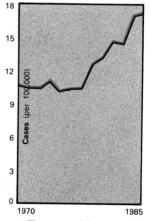

▲ *The cause of the dramatically increased incidence of salmonellosis in the USA is unknown: up to 1977, almost half of those affected were under the age of five, but since that date most sufferers have been in an older age group. Many Salmonella bacteria are now resistant to antibiotics.*

See also
Digestive and Urinary Disorders 45-8
The Body's Defenses 89-96
Diverse Infections 117-24

Parasites and the human host

The human intestinal tract is invaded by several organisms larger than bacteria. One is the ameba *Entamoeba histolytica*. Passed in the stools of people with amebiasis, the amebae are ingested in food or water and take up residence in the large intestine. Digesting cells to provide food, they reproduce and sometimes travel to the liver and elsewhere. Symptoms vary from trivial to severe. At its worst there is profuse diarrhea and considerable pain caused by abscesses in the liver. Amebiasis occurs throughout the world but is particularly common in Southeast Asia, Africa and Mexico. Treatment with drugs such as Terramycin is designed to relieve symptoms and to eliminate the parasites – which is less easily achieved than when using antibiotics to destroy bacteria.

Giardia lamblia is a protozoon which, like *Entamoeba*, occurs in developing countries. But it has also caused major outbreaks of giardiasis in the USSR and smaller ones in the USA during recent years. The parasites are transmitted through water (which, because they resist chlorination, must be filtered to remove them). Using two adhesive disks for attachment, they too colonize the small intestine and occasionally the gall bladder. Infected individuals may be virtually free of symptoms, or suffer recurrent pain and diarrhea, which can lead to weight loss and dehydration. Atabrine is an effective cure. *Giardia* is arguably the first pathogen ever seen by man – the Dutch microscopist Anton van Leeuwenhoek (1632-1723) observed it in his own stools.

The largest residents

Worms are the largest creatures to take up residence in the human gut. The World Health Organization estimates that a quarter of the planet's population is infected by the large roundworm *Ascaris lumbricoides*. It lives in the small intestine, laying eggs which are passed out and swallowed in food or water – sometimes after they have survived for several years in moist soil. The infection (which is easily cured by antihelminthic drugs) often causes no symptoms and comes to light only when the worms travel farther afield than the intestine and appear in the lungs, are vomited up from the stomach or pop out of the nose.

Tapeworms inhabit many millions of human bodies as well as using other animals as intermediary hosts. They are composed of head (with suckers to stick to the intestine), neck and a sequence of segments. They have sex organs and simple digestive and nervous systems. Five to ten meters in length and living for several years, discharging eggs continuously, the beef tapeworm (*Taenia saginata*) does much less damage than might be expected, producing only vague symptoms. The larvae of the pork tapeworm *Taenia solium* (which does not occur in the USA) sometimes causes serious injury in the eyes and brain. Tapeworms, which are acquired initially from uncooked meat, can be removed by Atabrine and purgation, usually being expelled intact.

Whipworms (500 million people affected worldwide) and hookworms (900 million people) are the other main groups of intestinal worms. The latter, which can enter through the skin as well as the gut, are now rare in developed countries, though whipworms still occur there among people with poor environmental hygiene. Threadworms are comparatively common in children's colons in Western countries. They seldom cause anything worse than anal irritation, although they may stimulate appendicitis.

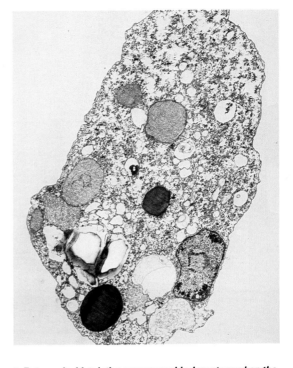

▲ *Entamoeba histolytica causes amebic dysentery when the protozoon penetrates the lining of the colon. In addition to pain and diarrhea, ulcers may develop in the colon, and amebic abcesses occur in the liver. The disease may take months to appear, and people can carry and transmit the disease without showing symptoms themselves. The ameba is destroyed by heat, so boiled water is safe to drink.*

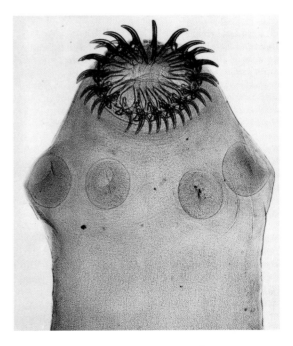

▲ *The head of the pork tapeworm, Taenia solium, carries large suckers as well as rows of hooks to enable it to anchor on the wall of the intestine. Such worms are segmented, and new segments develop continuously near the head. Up to ten segments break away daily, releasing eggs which are discharged in the host's feces, or entering the bloodstream to become established in other tissues.*

Cardiovascular Diseases

Coronary heart disease...Heart attacks...Heart surgery...Treating heart disease with drugs...Arrhythmias...Valve replacements...High blood pressure...Heart disease in the newborn...Other circulatory diseases...PERSPECTIVE...Heart transplants...Lifestyle and blood pressure

The heart

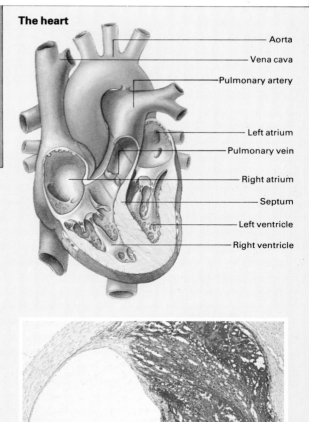

- Aorta
- Vena cava
- Pulmonary artery
- Left atrium
- Pulmonary vein
- Right atrium
- Septum
- Left ventricle
- Right ventricle

The heart is a self-powered pump which drives blood around the body, so that it can oxygenate tissues and carry away waste products such as carbon dioxide. Heart failure occurs when the heart cannot cope with the body's metabolic needs. If the heart stops pumping so that oxygen no longer reaches the brain, death follows.

Cardiovascular diseases are those in which the heart's performance is impaired. Although the proportion of deaths from such diseases has decreased in the USA, Australia and parts of Europe during the 1970s and 1980s, they still cause about half the deaths in Western countries. In half these deaths coronary or ischemic heart disease is the cause. Hypertension (high blood pressure) is the other main cause.

Ischemic (coronary) heart disease – the sort which leads to "heart attacks" – is caused by narrowing or blockage of the coronary arteries which supply oxygenated blood to heart muscle. In a heart attack, (also known as a myocardial infarction), the interruption of this blood supply leads to the death of part of heart muscle tissue. This can cause the normal heartbeat to be replaced by a rapid, uncoordinated beat (fibrillation), which makes the heart's pumping action ineffective. The brain may be starved of oxygen and death often results soon after the start of the attack. If a heart attack victim is still alive two hours later, the chance of survival thereafter is good.

Heart attacks often strike without warning, although after an attack sufferers may recall that they had felt unusual tiredness for several weeks. The symptoms are severe pain in the chest, which can spread to the arms, neck and teeth, accompanied by breathlessness, sweating, nausea and dizziness.

Though a heart attack may occur unexpectedly, heart disease usually shows symptoms, the severity of which indicate the severity of the disease. The coronary arteries narrow gradually as a result of deposition around the artery walls of atheromatous plaques, mixtures of white blood cells, platelets, fibrin and cholesterol. In males, this atherosclerosis may begin during the teens or early twenties. Females have a low incidence of coronary heart disease until after the menopause, when the incidence gradually rises level to the male incidence for the same age group.

The narrowing of the coronary arteries decreases the oxygen supply to the heart muscles. The heart usually copes with this under normal conditions, but when unusual demands are made on it – as a result of exercise, or even walking upstairs in severe cases – chest pain known as angina results. This is often described as a "crushing" pain. Coupled with the chest pains, there is frequently breathlessness. Because the heart is pumping less efficiently, it may fail to drain the lungs properly. Congestion of the lungs with liquid (pulmonary edema) makes breathing more difficult. Severe angina may also be accompanied by sweating and nausea.

▲ *Section through an artery partly blocked with plaque.*

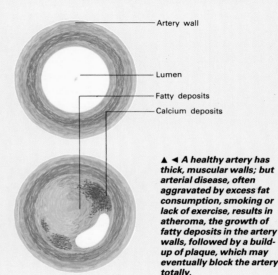

- Artery wall
- Lumen
- Fatty deposits
- Calcium deposits

▲ ◄ *A healthy artery has thick, muscular walls; but arterial disease, often aggravated by excess fat consumption, smoking or lack of exercise, results in atheroma, the growth of fatty deposits in the artery walls, followed by a build-up of plaque, which may eventually block the artery totally.*

Open-heart surgery is one of the great medical achievements of recent decades

If the heart is not working efficiently, one consequence may be swellings in the legs (peripheral edema or dropsy). Liquid passes out of the blood through the capillary walls into the body tissues and accumulates under the influence of gravity; in serious cases, the legs may become swollen up to the thighs. Edema may, however, also have other causes such as kidney or liver disease.

Surgery and coronary heart disease
In extreme circumstances surgery may be needed to treat coronary heart disease. The most common operation is the coronary by-pass. In this operation, pieces of vein from the patient's leg are transplanted into the coronary artery to provide a way around severe constrictions. A person who has suffered a heart attack may have an aneurysm, which can also be removed surgically – often at the same time as a by-pass operation. The aneurysm is a piece of non-functioning ventricle which bulges outward. This can harbor blood clots which may detach and enter the bloodstream. They can then block arteries elsewhere in the body. If this happens in the arteries leading to the brain, the result can be a stroke, which may paralyze large parts of the body by depriving part of the brain of oxygen (♦ page 64), or may even result in death. If such a clot occurs in the pulmonary artery, which takes blood from the heart to the lungs, it is called a pulmonary embolism, and may well threaten the patient's life. An aneurysm may also occur in the aorta, as a result of atheroma. This may swell until it leaks, and immediate surgery is required to strengthen the aorta wall with a woven fabric tube.

Coronary thrombosis

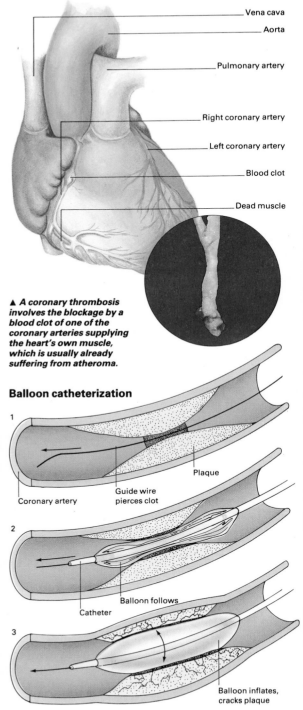

Vena cava

Aorta

Pulmonary artery

Right coronary artery

Left coronary artery

Blood clot

Dead muscle

▲ *A coronary thrombosis involves the blockage by a blood clot of one of the coronary arteries supplying the heart's own muscle, which is usually already suffering from atheroma.*

Balloon catheterization

1

Plaque

Guide wire pierces clot

Coronary artery

2

Balloon follows

Catheter

3

Balloon inflates, cracks plaque

▲ *A modern technique for unblocking coronary arteries involves the insertion of a balloon catheter in the femoral artery in the thigh. A thread is fed through the arterial system into the coronary artery and through the blockage, allowing a balloon to be passed into it. Inflation of the balloon causes the plaque to crack, reopening the artery, even in cases where it had previously been totally blocked.*

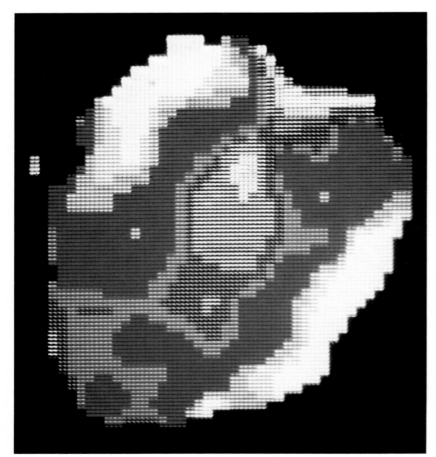

◄ *The condition of the heart can be assessed by computerized scanning after treatment with radio-active isotopes. The image obtained indicates blood flow.*

Heart transplants

Although heart disease may be controlled by drugs and changes in lifestyle, surgical treatment is the only hope of survival in some cases. In the past three decades, heart surgery has made major advances. Many operations are now carried out annually that would have been considered impossible before the Second World War. The most remarkable is heart transplantation.

The first human hearts were transplanted in the late 1960s, following many years of experimenting on animals. At first, the survival rate was low. This led to criticism of the surgeons pioneering the technique, Christiaan Barnard (b. 1922) in South Africa and Norman Shumway (b. 1923) at Stanford University, USA. Today the one-year survival rate for patients under 40 is better than 70 percent.

Heart transplantation is performed only on patients suffering from severe heart failure, particularly those under 55 years old. Donors are usually people aged under 35 who are "brain dead" as a result of an accident, but whose hearts are still beating when they enter the hospital. Donors and recipients are matched by height and weight (so that the size of the hearts is comparable) and the donors must have shown no evidence of heart disease. In addition, donors and recipients must be of the same ABO blood type and one particular HLA characteristic must also be the same. Apart from this, immunological compatibility is not considered important.

When a donor and recipient meet these criteria, the donor's heart is stopped by an overdose of potassium ions. It is then removed, cooled and transported to the recipient. In the Stanford

transplants, which account for nearly half of all those performed, the heart is transplanted within 3·5 hours of removal.

Usually, the recipient is placed on a heart-lung machine and the heart removed by dividing the atria part-way down. The donor heart is attached so that its atria link up with the residual atria of the recipient heart. It is then connected to the arteries.

Heart transplant patients have to take immunosuppressive drugs for the remainder of their lives, to prevent rejection of the new heart. Ninety percent of transplant patients suffer a "rejection episode", a concerted effort by the immune system to destroy the new heart. These episodes are usually overcome by treatment.

Long-term treatment with immunosuppressive drugs can produce side effects. A higher-than-normal incidence of cancers, notably those affecting the lymphatic system, is found in transplant patients. The major effect of such drugs is to reduce the body's ability to deal with infections. More than half the deaths in heart transplant patients are due to infections.

Immune reactions are probably also responsible for accelerated atherosclerosis in heart transplant patients. Attempts by the immune system to reject the foreign heart seem to lead to alterations in the surface of the coronary arteries which help rapid build-up of atheroma. As the new heart is not connected to the nervous system, there is no anginal pain to warn of this. Consequently, heart transplant patients undergo routine checks to assess their cardiac state. If accelerated athero-sclerosis is present, the only satisfactory treatment is a further transplant.

▲ Microscopes are often needed by surgeons when reconnecting tiny blood vessels in heart surgery.

The artificial heart

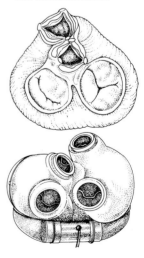

▲ Artificial hearts (here seen from above, and compared to a normal heart from the same angle) were developed in the 1970s, and the first such heart was implanted into a human in 1982. The use of such hearts is beset with difficulties and is highly controversial among cardiac surgeons.

Heart stimulants derived from the foxglove plant are among the oldest drugs still in use

► *Clinical electrocardio-graphy (ECG) was first developed at the turn of the 20th century by the Dutch physicist Willem Einthoven (1860-1927), although earlier studies of the heart's electrical activity had been made by A.D. Waller (1856-1922), seen here. Einthoven recorded ECGs from leads connecting the two arms, and each arm and each leg. He also described the ECG trace and suggested its use as an aid in diagnosing heart disease. Einthoven won the Nobel Prize for Physiology in 1924.*

Drugs and other treatments for heart disease

Edema and angina can often be treated with drugs. Digitoxin and digoxin, poisons (► page 114) derived from the foxglove *Digitalis*, are among the oldest known drugs still in use. They stimulate heart muscle to work more effectively. Many drugs (vasodilators) work by relaxing the veins, so that the back pressure is reduced. Nitroglycerin, better known as an explosive, is a commonly prescribed drug with this effect. Diuretics, drugs which increase urination and so reduce blood volume, can also be used.

More recent are the "beta blockers". The heart beats faster in response to many stimuli such as fear, because of the increase in blood concentration of adrenaline and related substances. These react with sites on the muscle wall called beta receptors. Some molecules, which are known as beta blockers, can obscure the beta receptors without triggering the normal physiological reaction. These have become a very important class of heart drug. They can, however, induce heart failure in some patients, and sudden withdrawal from beta-blocker treatment may precipitate a heart attack.

Palpitations are a symptom of heart disease, although these may have other causes, such as stress. Occasional palpitations occur in the normal heart, and can be induced by excessive consumption of coffee, tea or alcohol, or by heavy smoking. The most common type is the so-called "missed beat"; the heart does not actually miss a beat. The electrical signal which initiates each contraction fires at the wrong moment, making the beat less effective. As a consequence, the next

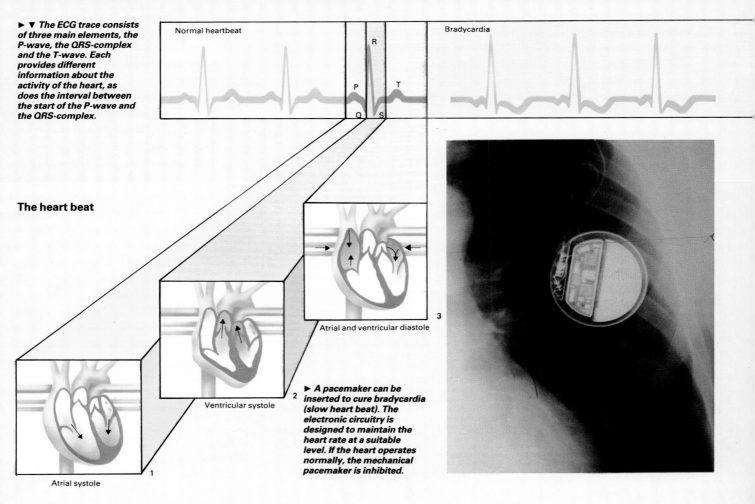

► ▼ *The ECG trace consists of three main elements, the P-wave, the QRS-complex and the T-wave. Each provides different information about the activity of the heart, as does the interval between the start of the P-wave and the QRS-complex.*

Normal heartbeat

R

P   T

Q   S

Bradycardia

The heart beat

Atrial systole
1

Ventricular systole
2

Atrial and ventricular diastole
3

► *A pacemaker can be inserted to cure bradycardia (slow heart beat). The electronic circuitry is designed to maintain the heart rate at a suitable level. If the heart operates normally, the mechanical pacemaker is inhibited.*

beat has to expel a larger than normal volume of blood from the heart and appears as a prominent or thumping beat. Another type of palpitation causes a fluttering feeling in the chest and may be accompanied by lightheadedness and sweating. Known as tachycardia, this is caused by an abnormally fast heart rate.

Persistent arrhythmias (deviations from the normal pattern of the heart beat) can be controlled by drugs or by surgical treatment. Beta-blocking agents and some anesthetics are useful in treatment. In cases of severe bradycardia (palpitations caused by slow heart beat), insertion of a mechanical pacemaker is often the best treatment.

Inefficient operation of the heart can result from damage to its valves. A common cause of this, particularly in less-developed countries, is rheumatic fever. This can cause scarring of the valve tissue so that it becomes stiff and less efficient at closing. As a result, blood may leak backward through the system. In such conditions, the noise of the heart through a stethoscope changes, to give a "murmur".

In some cases, valve segments become partly fused together, so that it cannot open fully. Stenosis, as this is called, reduces the volume of blood passing through the valve at each stroke. One consequence may be the enlargement of the heart as it tries to compensate for this decline in efficiency. Valvular disease can cause a large number of symptoms, notably angina and palpitations.

Valves can be replaced with either natural or synthetic materials. A new valve may be constructed from tissue taken from another part of the patient, or an intact valve from a cadaver or a pig may be used.

Fibrillation

Mitral stenosis

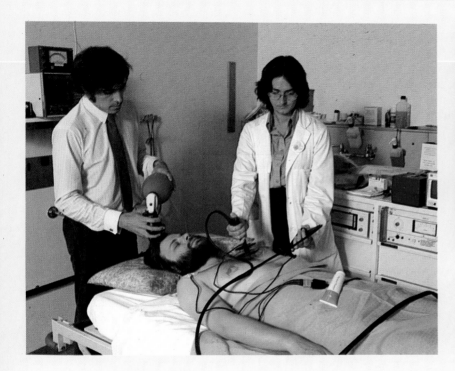

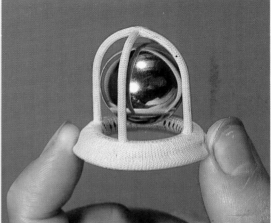

◄ In ventricular fibrillation, the heart's action is uncoordinated and shows up on an ECG as an irregular wave. Normal action can sometimes be restored by delivering an electric shock from a defibrillator, as shown here.

▲ A diseased mitral valve may cause a backflow of blood into the left atrium. It can be replaced by a synthetic substitute of which there are various designs. In the type shown, the base is sewn into the valve position.

◄ *Overweight, lack of exercise, tension, fatty foods, smoking and the intake of alcohol add up to a recipe for potential hypertension with its associated problems later in life, threatening strokes, kidney failure and hastening the onset of atherosclerosis.*

► *The !Kung tribe of Africa do not suffer the usual rise in blood pressure with age. The reasons for this are not clear, but seem to be associated with their low salt intake, the lack of fat on their cattle, their plentiful exercise and, possibly, a lack of mental tension in their way of life.*

High blood pressure

As many as 20 percent of all deaths in the developed world may be partly attributable to high blood pressure (hypertension). This causes excess wear and tear on the cardiovascular system and can damage the heart, kidneys and brain.

Raised blood pressure can be caused by diseases affecting the endocrine glands or kidneys, and by pre-eclampsia (toxemia) in pregnancy (◆ page 76). The oral contraceptive pill raises blood pressure slightly in most women and seriously so in a few cases. Nevertheless, in 95 percent of cases, high blood pressure is "primary" or "essential" hypertension, the cause of which is unknown. An unidentified hormone which affects the loss of sodium from the body may be a cause. Alternatively, calcium imbalance may be responsible.

Grossly overweight individuals frequently have raised blood pressure. This can be reduced by dieting. For most people, drug treatment is the only option. A wide variety of drugs is used, including the vasodilators and diuretics that are also used to treat angina and heart failure (◆ page 60). More recent drugs given for hypertension are the beta-blockers and ACE-inhibitors – the latter prevent the production of angiotensin II, a hormone involved in the raising of blood pressure.

Heart disease and lifestyle

Blood pressure increases normally with age, but when it goes above the norm for the age group, it can be dangerous. The risk of death rises almost proportionally to the increase in pressure. An estimated 10 percent of people in the USA and UK have raised blood pressure, but in only half of them has it been detected.

Although heart attacks may occur without warning, there are factors which predispose people to them. These include raised blood pressure, obesity, smoking and a family history of coronary heart disease. Regular exercise to the point of breathlessness seems to have a protective effect against such attacks.

A number of other correlations have been shown between environmental factors and the incidence of heart disease. Hot climates and hard water are associated with reduced incidences. Alcohol consumption in moderation appears to have a slight protective effect, but alcohol abuse increases the risk. Stressful events, such as a bereavement, seem to increase the likelihood of an attack.

How these factors work and interrelate is not understood. Smoking, for example, appears to predispose people to heart attacks only when other risk factors are present. In Japan the incidence of coronary heart disease is low by Western standards, and smoking behavior seems to have no effect.

Treatment of hypertension improved with the development of new drugs. Special cardiac units in hospitals were introduced, with a view to helping heart attack patients to survive the first few crucial hours after the attack, although the effectiveness of these has been questioned. Finally, developments in cardiac surgery have kept alive people who would undoubtedly have died without the availability of such treatment.

Coronary heart disease

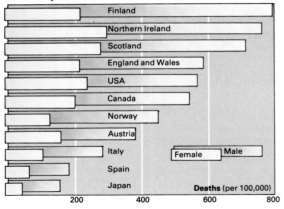

◄ *Coronary heart disease mortality rates show surprising variations; Finland has the highest incidence, even though many of its population take regular exercise. It is likely that a higher than average intake of animal fat is to blame.*

► *In the USA, about 1 million deaths occur annually from heart disease. About two-thirds of these result from coronary heart disease, but the incidence of death from this cause has been falling since the 1950s. The reason for this fall is not certain.*

US mortality from heart disease

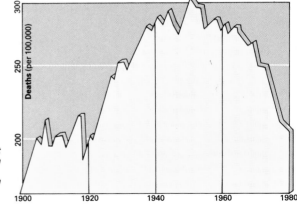

Heart attacks among middle-aged people

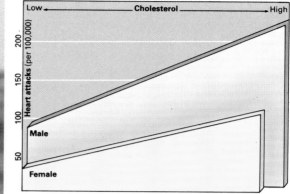

▲ *The amount of cholesterol in the diet has a direct link with the incidence of heart attacks among middle-aged people. Cholesterol is produced by the liver, and plays several metabolic roles including hormone synthesis. If an excess is consumed in the diet, in association with other saturated fats, it seems to promote atherosclerosis.*

Pulse rate when smoking

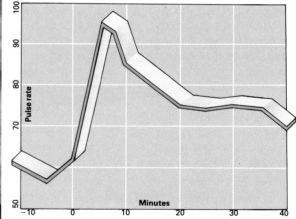

▲ ▼ *Smoking is an important element in hypertension and heart disease. The nicotine from a cigarette remains in the bloodstream for only about half an hour, but in that time stimulates adrenaline production. Tobacco also stimulates inhibitory cells in the spinal cord, thus lowering muscle tone and causing a feeling of relaxation.*

Stopping smoking and heart attack incidence

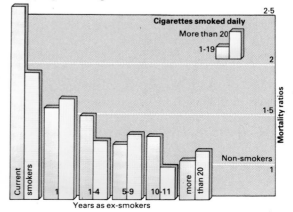

See also
Respiratory Infections 65-72
Hazards and Poisons 109-16

Slightly less than one percent of babies are born with some form of heart disease. In some cases, such as congenital aortic stenosis, the only hope of survival may be surgical operation. In the newly born, the survivial rate is often low.

In some babies, the major arteries leading from the heart are transposed. Effectively, this means that the pulmonary circulation which oxygenates the blood is cut off from the circulation around the rest of the system. In the fetus, oxygen is obtained via the placenta and the lungs do not operate. An arterial duct carries oxygenated blood from the pulmonary artery to the pulmonary veins, thus by-passing the lungs. This duct normally closes a few hours after birth, thus establishing the normal circulatory pattern. In a baby with transposition of the great arteries, closure of the duct leads to oxygen starvation. In recent years, there have been developments in surgical treatment of this disability, but mortality is still high.

In some cases, even when the heart is normal, the arterial duct remains open. This can be a symptomless ailment, but needs eventual surgical treatment. Without treatment, pulmonary hypertension (raised blood pressure in the lung system) leads to death in middle age.

Pulmonary hypertension and early death also occur as a result of other types of heart defect, notably those in which the septum – the wall of the tissue separating the left and right chambers of the heart – has a hole in it. This may occur either between the atria or the ventricles. The ventricular septal defect accounts for a quarter of all congenital heart defects. Between a third and a half of such holes close spontaneously during the first year of life; holes in the septum dividing the atria do not close spontaneously. Neither condition threatens life in young children, so operative correction is usually left until later years.

Other circulatory disorders

Apart from the heart, other parts of the cardiovascular system can become diseased. In anemia, the blood is an inefficient carrier of oxygen. To compensate for this deficiency, the heart has to work harder than normal. This may produce the same symptoms as coronary heart disease – breathlessness, peripheral edema and arrhythmias – although usually the patient is at risk only where there is already a history of heart disease.

Reduced oxygen supply is a problem also with emphysema. In this lung disease, which may be caused by heavy smoking, sufferers are unable to breathe out properly (♦ page 68). Consequently, the lungs are never fully emptied and the amount of fresh (oxygen-carrying) air taken in with each new breath is consequently reduced.

Veins can also cause illness. Notably in the legs, veins may become twisted and distended as a result of faulty operation of the valves that should prevent a backflow of blood. Such "varicose veins" cause swellings and a tendency to cramp. In severe cases, ulceration of the legs may occur.

As a result of increased abdominal pressure, in pregnancy for example, swollen blood vessels may appear in the anal region, where they are better known as hemorrhoids or piles (♦ page 48). Testicular varicose veins, or varicoceles, can be a cause of male sterility.

Thrombophlebitis is an inflammatory disease of the veins which can cause blood clots (also known as thrombi or emboli). These may enter the circulation and lead to stroke, heart attack or pulmonary embolism if they then block an artery.

Fetal circulation

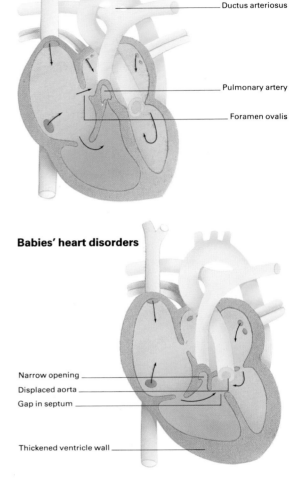

Aorta
Ductus arteriosus
Pulmonary artery
Foramen ovalis

Babies' heart disorders

Narrow opening
Displaced aorta
Gap in septum
Thickened ventricle wall

▲ *The fetal heart has a hole (foramen) between the atria, and a ductus arteriosus linking the pulmonary artery and aorta. In some babies these fail to close at birth, and the aorta opening is misplaced. Corrective surgery may be required.*

Stroke

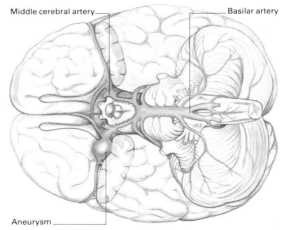

Middle cerebral artery
Basilar artery
Aneurysm

▲ *A "stroke" involves a thrombosis or embolism in cerebral arteries supplying the brain; an aneurysm or weak point in the artery may also cause a hemorrhage in the brain. Both may cause damage to areas of the brain.*

The threat of respiratory disease...Colds and flu... Mutating viruses...Bronchitis...Pneumonia...The appearance of Legionnaires' disease...Tuberculosis, a disease of the past...Whooping cough and diphtheria... PERSPECTIVE...Mind over matter...Monitoring microbes...Vaccination "fever"

The respiratory tract

Muscle
Goblet cell
Mucus
Nasal cavity
Ciliated cell
Alveolus
Trachea
Bronchus

Together with diarrheal disease, acute infections of the respiratory tract are the most important causes of preventable deaths in the world. There are no reliable global figures (because some regions do not provide statistics) but the World Health Organization estimates that such maladies are responsible for over 666,000 fatalities each year in 88 countries, representing a quarter of the world's population. Assuming similar mortality rates in areas not reporting figures, this suggests an annual toll of well over two million. Although the microbes concerned are often never identified, viruses seem to be the primary culprits. They attack different parts of the respiratory passages, producing diseases which include the common cold and influenza plus many less well known infections. Bacteria can often appear as secondary invaders, proliferating in tissues which are already ravaged by viruses.

As with intestinal conditions, the effects are far worse in undernourished people. Respiratory infections kill more that 1,500 babies per 100,000 live births in some countries, including Egypt and Mexico – about 30 times more than in the USA. But such diseases are by no means negligible in the developed world. One study, of 1,000 families in Newcastle upon Tyne, England, showed that respiratory infection constituted half of all illness in pre-school children. There are also strong suspicions that one of the organisms, respiratory syncytial virus (RSV), helps to precipitate some of the sudden deaths which occur among infants in the Western world.

Categorizing respiratory infections

Although physicians divide the respiratory passages into upper, middle and lower portions, micro-organisms do not respect such demarcation. So the labels attached to different diseases are only approximate. Least serious are infections of the upper tract – typically the streaming or blocked nose of the common cold. Infections in the middle tract are of major concern because they can block the airways completely. Named after the tissues most affected, these include tonsillitis, laryngitis and pharyngitis (usually caused by *Haemophilus* bacteria) and bronchitis – infection of the bronchi leading to the lungs – which is often due to adenoviruses plus a mixed invasion by bacteria. The principal diseases of the lower tract are pneumonia and bronchiolitis (affecting the bronchioles in the lung, and typically caused by RSV). Particular viruses may, however, produce a diversity of conditions, even among members of the same family. Commoner during the winter, all such infections are worsened by smoking and to a lesser degree by air pollution (as the 4,000 deaths during London's smog in 1952 testify). They are acquired not only by breathing in droplets expelled during coughs and sneezes but also by transferring to the nose viruses picked up on the hands.

Vaccination "fever"

Influenza is an acute, highly contagious disease caused by a virus infection. Since a number of different viruses can cause the disease (♦ page 66), immunity to one does not prevent susceptibility to another.

In February 1976, virologists isolated an unusual influenza A virus from the body of an American army recruit at Fort Dix who died after collapsing on a night march. Tests indicated that it might be identical with the strain that caused the 1918-19 pandemic – the most devastating worldwide epidemic ever documented, killing over 20 million people. So the US public health authorities decided to immunize the entire population against a predicted epidemic. Appropriate vaccine was manufactured and given to nearly 46 million people before evidence emerged linking it with side effects known as the Guillain-Bare syndrome.

The campaign was halted in December. But by that time, the program had become hotly controversial, with delays in vaccine production, accusations and counter-accusations about its safety, refusals of manufacturers to accept the responsibility for inadvertent damage, and claims that the entire exercise had been too precipitate. Critics felt themselves justified when the Fort Dix virus proved not to be the 1918 pandemic strain after all. But those responsible for the program defended their actions on the reasonable grounds that, had the original suspicions been correct, the population would have been just as vulnerable as their forebears to an epidemic of horrendous scale. The lethal potential of influenza was confirmed in 1979-80 when an A-type virus killed 20 percent of the harbor seal population along the northeast coast of the USA.

The mere prospect of inoculation against influenza can reduce a person's susceptibility to the disease

The common cold

Despite its apparently specific name, the common cold illustrates the difficulty of categorizing respiratory infections. The universal characteristics of the common cold are that virus multiplication is restricted to the nose, nasopharynx and pharynx, and that the condition is much more frequent in children than adults and in households with children than those without. Although rhinoviruses were proclaimed to be the cause when they were first identified in 1960, it is now known that this one complaint can be produced by over 100 different rhinoviruses and by a range of others, including coronaviruses, enteroviruses, influenza C viruses, parainfluenza viruses, and the agent known as *Mycoplasma pneumoniae*. Once this huge variety of pathogens came to light, microbiologists realized that the purpose of their earlier search for a single agent of the common cold – to develop a vaccine – was unachievable.

Attention has since shifted towards drugs which, paralleling the antibiotics employed against bacteria, act on a range of different viruses. Although for most people colds are a trivial nuisance, methods of treating or preventing them are especially needed for those at greater risk because of chest or heart disease. Moreover, about a third of industrial absenteeism is attributable to respiratory infections. There has been some success in using the synthetic drug enviroxime to prevent colds, but the greatest hope lies with interferon. Produced naturally by cells in response to virus infection and serving to prevent the virus replicating itself, interferon was discovered in 1957, but difficulties in purifying it delayed substantial progress until the early 1980s. Then research at Britain's Common Cold Unit and elsewhere indicated that interferon from white blood cells, sprayed into the nose, inhibited the development of colds in volunteers. Several different interferons are now known.

In 1978, an investigation conducted at the Amundsen-Scott South Pole Station clarified a formerly puzzling feature of colds – their sudden appearance in a community without any evidence of viruses being introduced from outside. There were two separate outbreaks during the winter months when the station was totally isolated. On each occasion, researchers found parainfluenza viruses in the victims' throats, but they also found them throughout the winter in people not suffering from colds. The existing belief that people harbor viruses only when they are shedding them during infection, and for a short time afterwards, was demolished by the South Pole study. It proved that viruses can persist for long periods in healthy individuals. As with typhoid fever, there are carriers of the common cold too.

Influenza

Whereas colds recur because many different micro-organisms cause them (on average each person has two or three colds per year), influenza comes in epidemics because it changes genetically, spawning new varieties to which populations have little or no immunity. Produced by influenza virus A or B, it is the only respiratory virus infection whose constitutional effects (fever, lassitude, malaise, and aching limbs and head) overshadow more localized symptoms in the respiratory passages. Bronchitis can follow (♦ page 68), but the most serious complication is pneumonia (♦ page 68) – an acute infection of the lungs. When it results from bacterial invasion, this can usually be cured by antibiotics. Pneumonia caused by the influenza virus itself is more lethal, with virtually no effective drugs available.

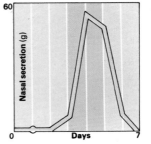

▲ *An air-filtering device marketed at the height of the European flu epidemic of 1919, which killed many millions.*

◄ *Diagram of the duration of a typical common cold. Nasal secretions, at first containing large amounts of infectious viruses, rise quickly but normally pass after a couple of days.*

Mind over matter

Experiments have confirmed that the mind really can affect our receptivity to the common cold. The first was carried out in 1977 at Britain's Common Cold Unit: 48 volunteers were inoculated with rhinoviruses and told they would be expected to develop colds. Half were also warned that after the experiment they would need to have their stomach juices sampled through a tube passed down the nose. Never seriously intended, this was simply a stratagem to make 24 of the volunteers apprehensive about an imminent, possibly unpleasant experience. The outcome was that the colds in this group were significantly more severe, with larger quantities of virus shed in nose-blowings, than the colds suffered by the remainder.

Further evidence of the mind's impact on infection came from research into the effect of immunization against influenza among people working in the UK Post Office. Comparisons of the sickness records of 60,000 workers offered vaccine between 1972 and 1977, and those of a matched group not given the opportunity to be vaccinated, revealed two significant differences. As expected, there were signs that immunization, though far from perfect, did protect some people from influenza. But the figures also showed that the mere offer of vaccination, even though not taken up, reduced peoples' chances of developing the infection. The disparity was evident during winters when influenza was prevalent and when it was not.

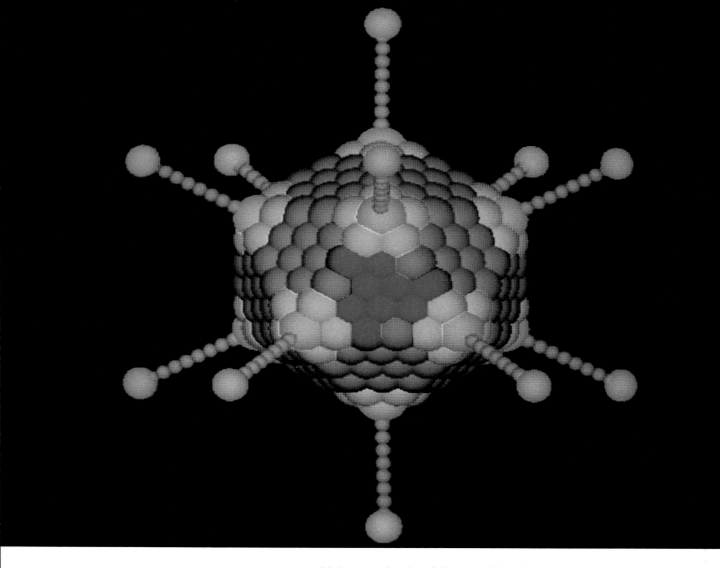

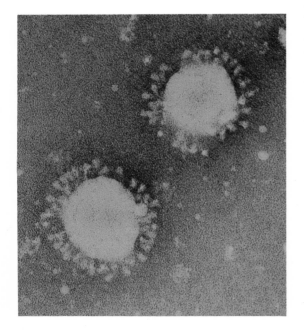

Major pandemics follow sudden changes in the structure of type A virus – as occurred with "Asian flu" during 1957 and "Hong Kong flu" in 1968-9. Both A and B viruses alter gradually to overcome immunity in the population, but only type A viruses change drastically – probably because they can hybridize with flu strains in other animals, such as turkeys, pigs, chickens and horses. It is likely that a virus closely related to swine influenza A was responsible for the pandemic of 1918. More recently, Hong Kong flu virus seems to have acquired one of its eight genes from a duck flu virus.

Influenza virus looks like a medieval mace (above). The eight genes are inside the ball, and the spikes are proteins called hemagglutinin (which helps the virus invade a host cell) and neuraminidase (which allows the viral offspring to break out of the cell after replication). Virologists classify subtypes according to these two proteins, which trigger off antibody production during an infection. When genetic mixing with animal strains produces a major new flu virus, the virus is likely to spread like wildfire in a non-immune population. Vaccine manufacturers need to monitor the emergence of new strains.

Killed and living-but-weakened viruses are used as vaccines, and genetically engineered viruses based on the marriage of human and bird strains are being developed. The alternative approach of seeking protection via drugs has enjoyed some success. Amantadine prevents infection in about 50 percent of people when taken in advance of flu, and reduces its severity if taken within 48 hours of its onset. But amantadine also has side-effects and fails to alleviate the most serious complication – pneumonia.

Diphtheria is hardly amenable to antibiotic treatment but has been defeated by a vaccination program

Bronchitis

Although it can occur as an acute complication of influenza, bronchitis is much more serious in its chronic (permanent) form. It is commoner in Britain than in any other country (presumably because of the climate), and in lower social classes compared with higher. Although many cases are initiated not by infection but by smoking, air pollution, or exposure to coal or other dusts, the affected bronchi lose their resistance and thus suffer recurrent or repeated infection with bacteria and viruses. The airways become obstructed, making breathing difficult, and large amounts of sputum are coughed up. The organisms often found in patients' sputum are pneumococci (bacteria originally identified in pneumonia) and *Haemophilus influenza* (an organism neglected for many years after it was found *not* to cause influenza). Bronchitics are at special risk during flu epidemics. While some can protect themselves by taking antibiotics, others have such poor bronchial defenses that little can be done (other than using oxygen to assist breathing) to relieve the condition.

Pneumonia

As well as an occasional complication of influenza, pneumonia is also a disease in its own right. In pre-antibiotic days, the commonest causes of acute lobar pneumonia (which affects one or more lobes of the lung) were strains of pneumococci. The disease begins suddenly, with violent shaking chills and fever, when pneumococci invade alveolar tissue. The bacteria provoke an outpouring of fluid. But this defensive response actually helps them to multiply and spread to other alveoli. Antibiotics usually arrest the infection at this point. Otherwise pneumococci can spread to the pleural cavity causing the severe pain of pleurisy, the pericardium or layers of membrane around the heart, and even heart valves and the brain. Now known as *Diplococcus pneumoniae* some strains of pneumococci cause the hybrid condition known as broncho-pneumonia, while others live in the respiratory tract without doing any apparent damage.

With the emergence of sulpha drugs during the 1930s and penicillin in the 1940s, the specter of acute pneumonia receded. But the defeat of pneumococci meant that proportionately more cases of the disease were caused by viruses, for which (apart from nursing care) there is little effective treatment. During the 1950s medical authorities became concerned that pneumococcal pneumonia and its complications, especially meningitis (◀ page 18), were still significant causes of death among the elderly and people such as diabetics who were unusually prone to infection. This rekindled interest in vaccines directed against pneumococci, which were licensed for use in the USA during 1977. Such vaccines have undoubtedly saved lives, though considerable controversy surrounds the cost-effectiveness of using them for mass-immunization.

Legionnaires' disease

A particularly severe type of pneumonia is Legionnaires' disease, so-called because the first identified outbreak occurred among delegates to the American Legion Convention in Philadelphia in July 1976, in which 29 out of 182 cases were fatal. Investigations showed that a bacterium, now called *Legionella pneumophila*, was responsible. Since that time, bacteriologists have found the organism to be common in cooling towers, lakes, and other bodies of water, but they are still unsure why such a ubiquitous organism sometimes causes disease.

Lung diseases

▶ *Pleurisy is inflammation of the pleura (membranes surrounding the lungs). Often in children it begins as a viral infection. In older people it is usually linked with pneumonia.*

▲ *Pulmonary tuberculosis is a bacterial infection in which the lung tissue is broken down in various ways. It can be treated by antibiotics, with rest and a good diet.*

▶ *In emphysema, caused by longterm irritation of the lungs, the elasticity in the alveoli walls is lost, and the patient has consciously to exhale. The alveoli pass oxygen to the blood less efficiently.*

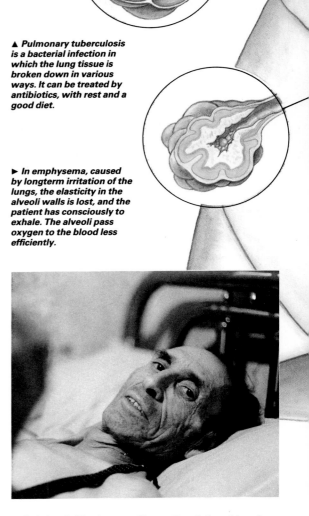

▲ *A victim of silicosis, caused by continually breathing air containing silicon. Macrophages ingest the silica particles, but collect in the air passages in the lungs and form fibrous nodules. The victim becomes short of breath and vulnerable to TB. Encountered in mining and sand-blasting, it is the most serious form of pneumoconiosis, the lung disease produced by inhaling organic, inorganic or chemical irritants.*

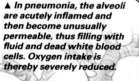

▲ *In pneumonia, the alveoli are acutely inflamed and then become unusually permeable, thus filling with fluid and dead white blood cells. Oxygen intake is thereby severely reduced.*

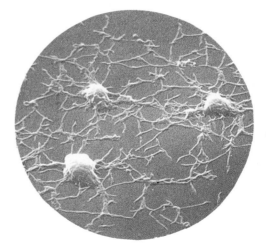

Mycoplasma pneumoniae

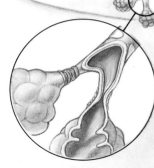

▶ *Bronchitis is an infection of the bronchi, producing excess mucus. Chronic bronchitis lasts·for at least three months of two successive years and is usually caused by smoking.*

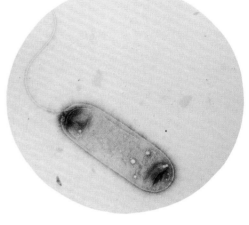

Legionella pneumophila

▲ *In asthma (an allergy rather than an infection) the bronchioles go into spasm and give rise to mucus, reducing the passage of air into the lungs and leading to wheezing.*

Whooping cough

Whooping cough (pertussis) persists because the only available vaccine is not fully effective and because some parents fail to have their children immunized through fear of the slight possibility of brain damage caused by the vaccine. By contrast diphtheria has been virtually obliterated by one of the simplest and earliest vaccines ever introduced.

Whooping cough is a highly infectious disease caused by the bacterium Bordetella pertussis. At first, the bacterium multiplies rapidly on the surface of the trachea and bronchi, making the patient highly infectious but not very ill. Then the explosive cough develops. Ten to 15 coughs may follow in rapid succession before a breath is taken, which is the characteristic "whoop". Exhaustion and sometimes vomiting and convulsions often follow.

Whooping cough, which affects mostly the under-fives, occurs in intermittent epidemics and is perhaps the most serious of the acute specific fevers of childhood. Antibiotics diminish its severity, and immunization at an early age (one to two months) prevents or ameliorates the disease. Pertussis vaccine is usually given as part of a triple immunization with tetanus and diphtheria too.

Diphtheria

At one time, one of the most unpleasant and dangerous of all childhood diseases, diphtheria is caused by Corynebacterium diphtheriae. Growing on mucous membranes in the upper respiratory tract, the bacteria produce a toxin which destroys the tissues and provokes such a massive inflammatory response that a grayish "pseudomembrane" forms over the tonsils, larynx and pharynx. The membrane blocks the airways, suffocating the victim if not promptly removed, while the toxin spreads to other parts of the body, damaging the heart, nerves, kidneys and liver. Deaths from diphtheria are often the result of inflammation of the heart.

Even the most powerful antibiotics have little effect on diphtheria. It can, however, be combatted by neutralizing the toxin that is solely responsible for the disease. Antitoxin, an antibody made by injecting small amounts of toxin into horses, is usually given if diphtheria is suspected. But vaccination with a modified version of the toxin known as toxoid is the measure that has made the disease virtually unknown in the developed countries.

Monitoring Microbes

From microfungi to viruses

By definition microbes are living organisms so tiny that they are visible only under a microscope. The vast majority are beneficial. Although pathogenic (disease-causing) microbes are in the minority, techniques of identifying them are important in diagnosing infections, deciding on appropriate treatment, tracing the sources of epidemics, and monitoring the ways in which many strains change their character and behavior over time.

In general, the larger the microbe, the less sophisticated are the methods needed to identify it. At the top of the size scale are the microscopic relatives of fungi such as mushrooms. These microfungi occur as single cells (yeasts) or hyphae, filamentous threads which produce fruiting bodies complex enough for them to be distinguished under a microscope. Athlete's foot is an example of the many infections caused by fungi.

Next in size are protozoa – the agents of such diseases as malaria. Identifying the different species of malarial parasite involves bleeding the patient every six hours and smearing blood across a microscope slide to monitor the changes in the life cycle of the protozoa. Similar methods can identify parasites such as the trypanosomes of sleeping sickness, which may have to be sought in cerebrospinal fluid. Identifying intestinal protozoa, such as Entamoeba histolytica (♦ page 124), requires a fresh specimen of feces.

Although consisting of single cells comparable with those of animals and plants, bacteria are simpler in appearance than most fungi, protozoa and related parasites. They are crudely classifiable under labels such as cocci (spheres) and bacilli (rod-like), but these groups contain many diverse species. Identification is thus more difficult. Technicians apply sophisticated differential stains to search for specific groups of bacteria recovered from specimens such as urine (urinary tract infections), feces (intestinal infections), pus, and swabs from the respiratory tract. Some organisms – such as tubercle bacilli – may be seen at once, using a light microscope. Most become apparent only after the material has been cultured in nutrient medium. Tests of a bacterium's chemical activities aid identification further. Most discriminating are methods of typing bacteria according to their sensitivity bacteriophages (viruses that invade specific bacteria), and of matching them against antibodies.

Viruses are so small that they are visible only under the electron microscope. They are simply fragments of hereditary material (DNA or RNA) wrapped in protein. In order to multiply they have to invade living cells to take advantage of their reproductive machinery. In the laboratory, bottles containing HeLa or other cells are used for this purpose, as are fertile hens' eggs in some cases. Inoculated and incubated with material on a swab, such cultures produce plaques – clear patches where influenza virus, for example, has attacked the tissue. Like bacteria, particular virus strains can also be identified by antibody tests.

Magnifications

Fungi
Life size

1

×500

Protozoa

2

×12,000

Bacteria

3

×50,000

Viruses

4

1 Athlete's foot occurs when the webs of the toes are invaded by fungi such as species of Trichophyton. Starting with itching and blisters, the skin cracks, making it vunerable to secondary invasion by bacteria. When scrapings from the skin are inoculated onto artificial culture media, the fungus grows profusely, producing a thick felt.

2 Malarial parasites can be seen by smearing a pinprick of blood from the patient on a glass slide, staining it, and examining the smear under a low powered microscope. Repeated samples are needed to identify precise species.

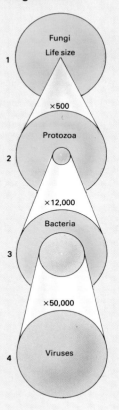

2

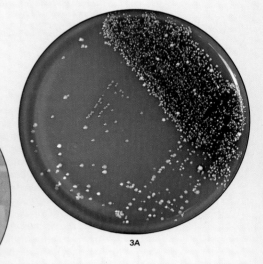

3A

3A The skin's normal population of bacteria can be revealed by swabbing the skin and then wiping the swab across a plate containing nutrient medium. After several hours in an incubator at body temperature, colonies of bacteria become apparent. In this plate of blood agar most of the bacteria have proved to be Staphylococcus aureus. Although usually harmless, some strains can cause boils and other infections if they gain access through a skin abrasion.

3B Examined under the electron microscope, S. aureus is a typical spherical coccus, occuring in grape-like bunches.

1

▲ The most difficult task for a microbiology laboratory is to identify a hitherto unknown microbe responsible for an outbreak of an apparently infectious disease, as when Lassa fever occurred in Nigeria in 1969 and Legionnaires' disease came to light in Philadelphia in 1976. It is also a uniquely dangerous task, because technicians may well have little idea of how the suspect and possibly lethal organism is transmitted. They therefore use conventional techniques, such as inoculating swab material into nutrient media and tissue cultures, but do so in high security facilities precluding even accidental contact with the material.

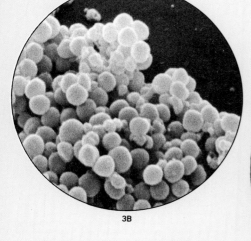

3B

4A

4B

4A   Rotaviruses, seen here under the electron microscope, have been discovered in relatively recent years as important causes of enteritis in young children. Although they look alike, many distinct types can be identified by matching the antigens they carry with corresponding antibodies.

4B   This electron micrograph shows bacteriophages attached to the common bowel bacterium Escherichia coli. Because particular phages attack only particular bacteria, "phage typing" is invaluable as a laboratory tool to identify very precisely bacteria recovered from patients.

Respiratory syncytial virus (RSV)

Not all initially puzzling epidemics turn out to be the work of previously unknown microbes. Thus the outbreak of bronchiolitis, complicated by pneumonia, which killed 121 infants in Naples, Italy, in 1978-9, proved to be a result of RSV infection. RSV is the most important cause of respiratory tract infection among infants and young children. But such was the severity of the Naples outbreak that a novel virus was suspected. In fact, poverty, malnutrition and overcrowding had turned a serious pathogen into a virulent killer.

Pulmonary tuberculosis (TB)

When the pioneer bacteriologist Robert Koch (1843-1910) announced to the Physiological Society of Berlin his discovery of the tubercle bacillus in 1882, there is little doubt that most of his audience had been infected with the organism – yet few if any had developed tuberculosis. *Mycobacterim tuberculosis* is far more likely to cause disease in those debilitated by malnutrition and fatigue. Pulmonary TB, in which the bacteria invade and destroy lung tissue, is the principal type, though TB also attacks bones and other organs. Effective weapons include BCG vaccine and drugs such as streptomycin. Together with improved living conditions, mass radiography to identify early signs, and eradication of the disease in cattle (milk was one source of infection), these have controlled the disease. In the 19th century one person in five died from TB in Britain. Today the death rate is only one per 100,000. But even now tuberculosis kills one person every 30 seconds in the Third World, while elsewhere drug-resistant *M. tuberculosis* persists, particularly among elderly men.

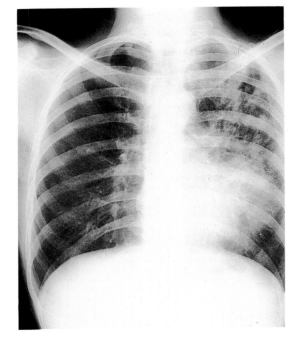

▲ *X-ray of a patient suffering from pulmonary tuberculosis.*

▼ *A tuberculosis sanitorium in England in the 1940s. Such sanitoria were widely built in the late 19th and early 20th centuries. With the advent of mass radiography for early diagnosis and of new drugs, TB became more easily treated and such institutions were no longer needed.*

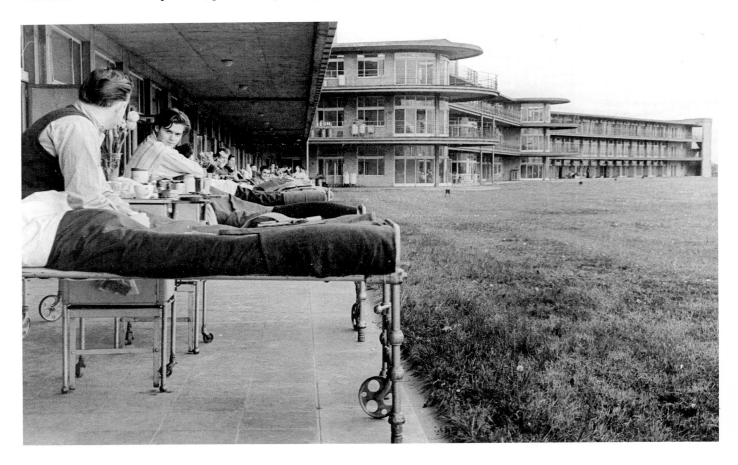

Mechanical and fundamental infertility...Causes of
male infertility...Female fertility problems...Difficulties
in pregnancy...Perinatal problems...PERSPECTIVE...
Test-tube babies and other new techniques...The
rights of the embryo

The male genitals

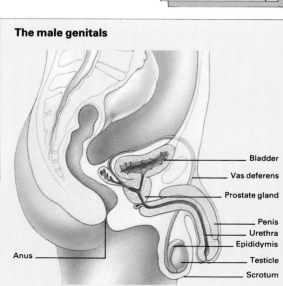

Bladder
Vas deferens
Prostate gland
Penis
Urethra
Epididymis
Anus
Testicle
Scrotum

There is no shortage of babies in the world, but infertility can cause considerable anguish to many people. About one couple in six cannot produce children without help. In recent years, better understanding of embryology has led to an expansion of techniques to overcome infertility. This has raised many complex ethical issues concerning the rights of the embryo and the parents.

As suggested by the physiology of reproduction, the cause of infertility may rest either with the man or the woman. Male malfunctions are responsible in about 40 percent of couples and those of both partners in about 15 percent. As the cause cannot be established in a further 10 percent of cases, infertility may be spread equally between the sexes.

Failure to reproduce may be fundamental or mechanical. In the former case eggs are not produced, and/or sperm are not produced at all, or are produced in insufficient quantity to effect fertilization. A mechanical problem is one in which those elements are produced satisfactorily, but fail to come together, or when the egg is fertilized but does not remain viable. Psychological problems affecting copulation, and more rarely impotence or frigidity of physical origin, can also cause infertility.

Malfunctions of male fertility

Male infertility usually results from a failure to produce sperm (azoospermia), or to produce enough sperm which are normal and sufficiently motile to reach an egg and penetrate it (oligospermia). Infertility of this kind may be caused by hormonal deficiencies, disease, treatment with drugs or the production of antibodies against sperm. These cause the man's defense system to treat his sperm as invaders and destroy them (♦ page 89, 106).

The formation and maturation of sperm are assisted by follicle-stimulating hormone (FSH) and luteinizing hormone (LH). These so-called gonadotrophins are released by the pituitary gland, after stimulation by gonadotrophin-releasing hormone, which is manufactured by the hypothalamus region of the brain to control their release. Consequently, disorders of the pituitary or of the hypothalamus can cause infertility. Such disorders can often be reversed by hormone treatment.

Inflammation of the testes can damage their ability to produce sperm. The common childhood ailment mumps, if caught in adult life, is the best-known example of a disease which can cause such damage. Sperm formation can also be inhibited by some drugs. These include alcohol, barbiturates, cannabis and some antidepressants. Ionizing radiation (radioactivity) and various substances to which industrial workers may be exposed, including some metals and complex organic compounds, may also impair sperm production.

▼ *Seminal fluid can be examined under the microscope to see whether a male is fertile or not. Dilution of the sample, as shown here, enables the technician not only to see whether the sample contains live sperm, but also to assess the number present. Even if live sperm are produced, a man may be effectively sterile if his sperm count is low, since many sperm must be present to allow one to fertilize the ovum.*

► *In a male with a normal sperm count, abnormal sperm, such as this double-headed one, may comprise up to 40 percent of the count without seriously affecting fertility.*

The rights of "test-tube" embryos and babies are still fiercely argued

Drugs may also affect male fertility by reducing the ability of the muscle at the base of the bladder to contract. As a result, sperm are pushed into the bladder instead of being ejaculated. Drugs prescribed from some ailments, including high blood pressure, and some diseases, including diabetes, may also cause impotence, the inability to sustain an erection for long enough to complete intercourse.

Male fertility may also be affected by several other physical conditions. The most common is an enlargement of veins in the spermatic cord (the nerves, arteries, veins, muscle and vas deferens which together form the main supporting structure for the testicles). Such enlarged veins are known as varicoceles, and can be treated surgically. Varicoceles may cause infertility by producing a localized increase in temperature.

Sperm are very sensitive to rises in temperature, and it is known that men whose jobs entail sitting for long periods – truck or taxi drivers for example – tend to have lower sperm counts than average. In some cases relating to the destruction of sperm by heat, male infertility has been cured when the sufferer changed from tight to loose-fitting underpants.

Cryptorchism, in which one or both testicles fail to descend at birth, is a further cause of infertility in which temperature may play a part. This condition usually requires surgical treatment, as does hypospadias, in which the urethra opens on the underside of the penis. This can prevent sperm from being ejaculated sufficiently far into the vagina to achieve fertilization.

The body's immune system sometimes causes infertility by treating the sperm as invading microbes and neutralizing them. This may either happen when the man's own defenses mobilize against his sperm, or when the woman makes antibodies which attack them. Immuno-suppressive drugs are now being used successfully to treat this form of male infertility.

Test-tube babies

In July 1978 the world's first "test-tube baby" was born. She was the result of "in vitro" (literally, in glass) fertilization (IVF), the combining of egg and sperm outside the body. Since that time, many babies have been born to infertile couples as a result of IVF.

IVF involves the removal of a fertile egg from an ovary by laparoscopy (the technique of introducing a fiber-optics tube into the abdomen to enable the surgeon to view the inside of the body without making a large incision). It is then fertilized with sperm obtained by masturbation, and implanted into the mother's womb to develop. This method overcomes infertility only if the partners can both produce viable eggs and sperm.

Fertility drugs may be given to a woman before laparoscopy in order to induce multiple egg production. Then several eggs can be fertilized and placed in the mother, to improve the chances of the pregnancy establishing itself. Or spare eggs may be frozen for use later, if a first attempt fails.

In cases where the male partner is infertile, artificial insemination by donor may be used. If the woman's fertility is unimpaired, sperm donated by a fertile male can be injected into her vagina. If she has fertility problems but produces viable eggs, these may be fertilized in vitro by donor sperm.

If the woman does not ovulate, an egg donated by another woman can be fertilized in vitro by her husband's sperm and then implanted in her. Alternatively, another woman (known as a surrogate mother) can be artificially inseminated and carry the baby. If the woman does ovulate but cannot carry a baby, one of her fertilized eggs may be implanted into another woman's womb (womb-leasing), where it develops normally.

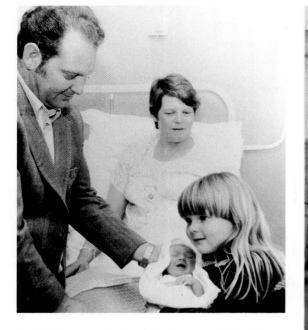

▲ **Louise Brown, the first test-tube baby, with her younger sister, also conceived by IVF.**

► **Gynecologist Patrick Steptoe and embryologist Robert Edwards, who did the first successful IVF.**

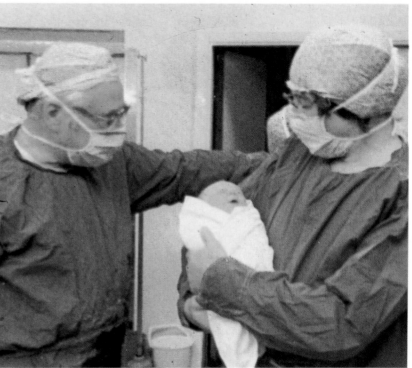

The debate on the rights of embryos

Unless both sperm and egg are contributed by the couple, the baby is not theirs genetically. This raises questions as to what the baby should be told about its parentage when it grows older. In some countries adopted children have the right to know who their genetic parents were. The rights of babies produced by modern techniques to such knowledge have yet to be established.

The rights of the sponsoring parents, and of the woman who gives birth to their child, are also in dispute. If a surrogate mother proves unwilling to part with the child after its birth, should her contract with the sponsoring parents be binding?

When does the embryo itself have rights? Where more than one egg is fertilized but only one implanted, what should happen to the remainder? Until what time during development should it be permissible to use a "spare" embryo for research?

Some causes of female infertility

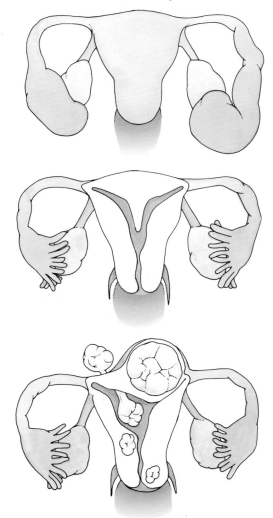

▲ *Top, blocked and swollen tubes (salpingitis) may be caused by infection, and may require surgery. Center, a septum may distort the shape of the uterus; below, fibroids, benign tumors of the uterus, may interfere with pregnancy.*

Malfunctions of female fertility

Female infertility is generally caused by factors similar to those found in men. Hormonal abnormalities can affect not only ovulation, but also the ability of the uterus to retain a fertilized egg. However, in the female, the mechanics of the system may interfere with reproduction in more ways than in the male. After its release from the ovary, an egg has to travel down the Fallopian tube.

The two Fallopian tubes may be damaged so that the egg's passage is hindered. In some cases, the tubes are blocked (sometimes as a result of damage done by an IUD). In others, scar tissue formed after inflammation – resulting for example from gonorrhea or acute appendicitis – prevents the egg's passage without there being an actual blockage. Another tubal problem is endometriosis. The endometrium as specialized tissue produced in the uterus into which the fertilized egg can implant. This adherent tissue sometimes forms in the Fallopian tubes and interferes with the passage of eggs.

During the part of the menstrual cycle when an egg is available for fertilization, watery cervical mucus is produced which helps the sperm to swim into the Fallopian tubes. Sometimes infertility is caused by the failure to produce mucus in sufficient quantity or of satisfactory consistency. Blockage of the tubes and disturbance of the cervical mucus can be overcome, in some cases by drug treatment and in others by surgery.

Eventually, all women cease to produce eggs. The menopause (◀ page 31) usually occurs in middle age, but egg production can become increasingly erratic after about 40 years, even though menstruation is regular. Egg production can also fail prematurely. This causes irreversible sterility, usually in the early 30s. Irregular ovulation, which reduces fertility, can be caused by drugs, disease and psychological stress. In some conditions, such as anorexia nervosa, ovulation may stop completely, although not irreversibly.

◀ ▼ *In laparoscopy, a viewing tube is passed into the woman's abdomen through a small incision in her navel; the technique allows microsurgery, sealing tubes or removing ova, often under only a local anesthetic.*

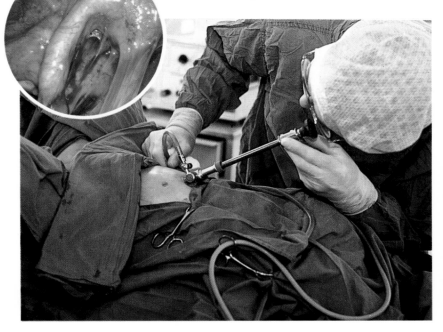

See also
Medicine Before Birth 77-84
Sexual Infections 85-8
Hazards and Poisons 109-16

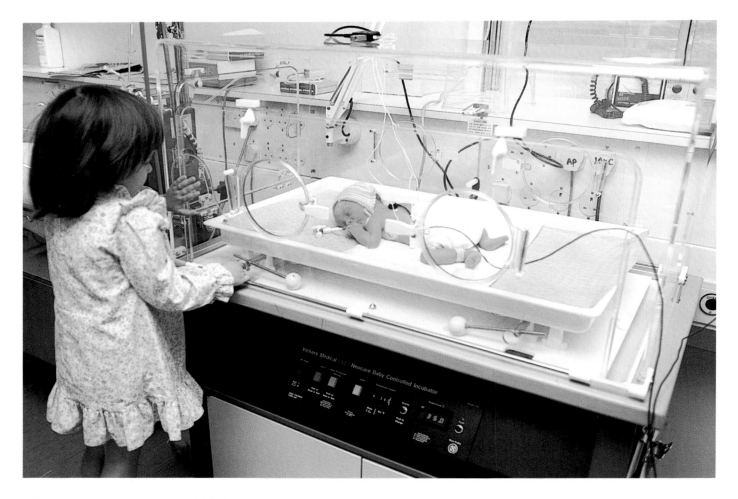

▲ *A premature baby is placed, naked apart from perhaps a bonnet or a diaper, in an incubator, which serves as an artificial womb. It is fed by intravenous infusion or through a nasal tube. The air is kept warm and humid, and the baby may be attached to a ventilator.*

Difficulties in pregnancy and birth

Edema (swelling) during pregnancy, now called pre-eclampsia, occurs in five percent of pregnancies after week 20. Other signs of pre-eclampsia are hypertension and albumin in the urine. If untreated (with bed rest, fluids, intravenous salt solutions and drugs), it leads to eclampsia – fits, and, sometimes, death. It is caused by a partial blockage of arteries feeding the placenta.

Bleeding in the last three months of pregnancy is caused by partial separation of the placenta or implantation of the placenta over or near the cervix. Fetal distress or death may occur if the degree of separation is great. Treatment is bed rest. Birth must be induced – though preferably not before week 35 of pregnancy – if pre-eclampsia or bleeding persist. Labor before week 37 is regarded as premature. If there is bleeding or loss of amniotic fluid the pregnancy cannot last and delivery is necessary; otherwise symptoms can usually be stopped by bed rest and medication, including cortisone to help the baby's lungs mature. Postmaturity – pregnancy lasting more than 42 weeks – is serious because the baby has often defecated and swallowed its own meconium (its first feces). When this happens the uterus shrinks and the fetus is less active.

Premature babies often suffer from respiratory distress syndrome – lack of the chemical released at birth that thins the film of water in the lung alveoli and allows oxygen in and carbon dioxide out. Babies that cannot breathe or have become blue from shortage of oxygen may be given pressurized air from a ventilating machine.

Difficulties in pregnancy

A woman's inability to have a chid may be caused by failure to retain a fetus. There is a 15-20 percent chance of any pregnancy miscarrying. Spontaneous abortion may occur where a fertilized egg has gross genetic abnormalities (♦ page 77). But internal problems in the female can also cause abortion. In the condition known as incompetent cervix, the cervix is insufficiently strong to resist the downwards pressure of the growing fetus and the pregnancy miscarries. As this usually happens without pain to the woman, she may not realize she has been pregnant and may think herself infertile.

A relatively common problem which may interfere with pregnancy is the growth of fibroids, non-cancerous tumors that form in the muscle of the womb. Less common is ectopic pregnancy, in which a fertilized egg embeds outside the uterus, usually staying in the Fallopian tube. Such pregnancies rarely last more than two months, after which time the tube will rupture and death may result without immediate surgery. Such pregnancies are detected after unusual pain and bleeding, and once detected are ended by immediate surgery.

Medicine Before Birth

*Hereditary disorders...Imaging the unborn child...
Down's syndrome...Chromosomal disorders...
Anemias...Hemophilia...Genetic engineering...
PERSPECTIVE...Rhesus babies...Abortion...Poisoning
the fetus...Gene therapy*

Disease is often seen as an attack on the organism from outside; many diseases, however, are built into us from the moment of conception. When two sex cells combine to create a new organism, the collection of chromosomes which this brings together may be faulty in some way.

Assessing the risk

If the embryo's chromosomes are grossly abnormal, it nearly always aborts spontaneously. However, some chromosomal abnormalities, such as Down's syndrome (mongolism), lead to the birth of live but handicapped babies. Increasingly, these problems can be detected before birth. It is also possible to predict that certain people have a higher than average chance of producing an abornomal child before conception. If a couple have already had a child which suffers from a recognized gene-linked abnormality, then "genetic counselling" is advisable to assess the risk of the same abnormality recurring. Similarly, if close relatives have had an abnormal child or suffer from a genetically-linked disease, the risk can also be assessed.

Pregnancy

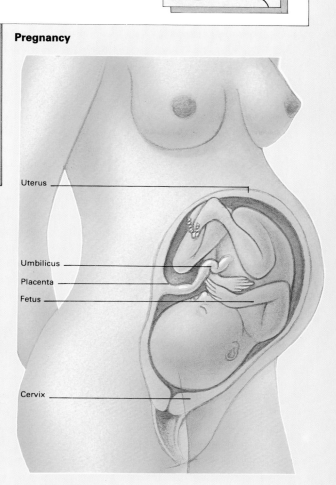

Uterus

Umbilicus

Placenta

Fetus

Cervix

Rhesus babies

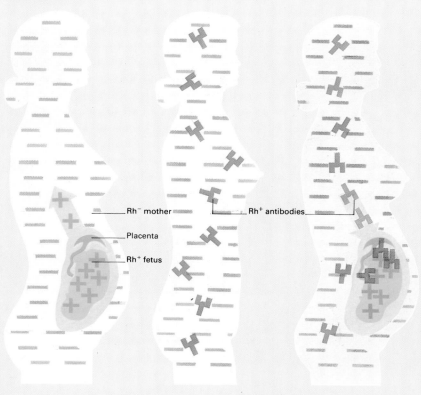

Rh⁻ mother

Rh⁺ antibodies

Placenta

Rh⁺ fetus

Rhesus babies
Blood is characterized by a number of factors. Among these, the rhesus factor is present (Rh⁺) in most of the population, but absent (Rh⁻) in a small percentage.

During birth, there can be interchange of fetal and maternal blood. If an Rh⁻ mother's first baby is Rh+, then the rhesus factor may enter her bloodstream and her immune system (◆ page 89) produces antibodies to it. Circulating antibodies cross the placenta to provide immunity to the newborn against common infections. In a second or subsequent pregnancy, an Rh⁻ mother transfers rhesus-factor antibodies to the fetus. If the fetus is Rh⁺, then these antibodies attack the fetal red blood cells. This may cause only mild anemia, but it can lead to abortion of the fetus.

The problem can be avoided by giving Rh⁻ mothers a large dose of Rh immunoglobulin immediately after the birth of a first Rh⁺ baby. The immunoglobulin reacts with any rhesus factor in the mother's blood before her own immune system has time to respond to it. Using this treatment, it has been possible to reduce sensitization of Rh⁻ mothers more than tenfold. Where sensitization still occurs, the adverse reaction in subsequent Rh⁺ babies is less severe.

◀ So-called Rhesus babies, suffering from erythroblastosis fetalis, occur when a Rh⁻ mother conceives a Rh⁺ child, and her immune system develops antibodies to its blood. Any subsequent Rh⁺ child can be attacked by these antibodies.

Screening techniques

If the risk of having an abnormal baby is above average, screening techniques are used to try to detect abnormalities in the fetus. The most basic is ultrasonography, a study of the developing fetus using ultrasound – electromagnetic waves of a frequency undetectable by the human ear. With this technique, it is possible to tell whether a woman is carrying a single fetus, twins or triplets. It is also possible to detect gross abnormalities such as anencephaly (failure of the brain to develop). Anencephalics mostly die within a few days of birth. Early diagnosis can mean the option of an abortion.

A major advantage of ultrasonography is that it helps to locate the fetus within the amniotic sac and thus makes amniocentesis safer. Amniocentesis is the removal of about 20ml of amniotic fluid by inserting a hypodermic syringe through the mother's abdominal wall. This procedure has immense diagnostic value, mainly because the fluid contains some cells which have been shed by the embryo. As each cell of an individual contains his or her full genetic complement in its nucleus, these can be cultured – much in the way that colonies of micro-organisms are grown – and then examined for genetic abnormalities. In 1968, a case of Down's syndrome in a fetus was diagnosed for the first time in this way.

The fluid itself can also provide useful information. It contains alpha-fetoprotein, the purpose of which is unknown, but which appears to be produced only by fetuses. If the amniotic fluid contains a high amount of this protein, there is a strong likelihood that the fetus suffers a neural tube defect. These defects, including anencephaly and spina bifida, occur when the groove along the back of the embryo, which ultimately becomes the spinal column, fails to close. In some cases, sufficient alpha-fetoprotein escapes from the fetus and crosses the placenta to give detectable levels in the maternal bloodstream. Where it is suspected that a woman may give birth to a baby with a neural tube defect, then her blood is checked for alpha-fetoprotein and she undergoes amniocentesis to confirm the disease.

Amniocentesis usually cannot be carried out before the 16th week of pregnancy because there is insufficient amniotic fluid and free fetal cells before then. The cell culture takes up to four weeks to produce results. Sometimes a second amniocentesis and culturing are necessary to produce a clear result. Consequently, once results are available, there is little time left in which to consider an abortion, as these usually are performed before the 25th week of pregnancy.

A recent advance which may replace amniocentesis is chorion villus biopsy, which can be carried out between 8 and 12 weeks after conception. The chorionic membrane surrounds the amniotic sac and is genetically a part of the fetus. Cells from it can be obtained, either through the mother's abdomen, as with amniocentesis, or via the cervix. Ultrasound is used to guide the instrument to an appropriate point from which to take the cell sample. It is possible to study the genetic makeup of these cells directly, or to culture them. The same types of diagnostic test can be carried out as with amniocentesis. However, there may be a slightly higher risk to the fetus.

Because there is a slight risk with both methods, there is great interest in developing non-invasive techniques. Some fetal cells cross the placenta and enter the maternal bloodstream. If it proves possible to separate these from maternal cells in a blood sample and culture them, even earlier diagnosis of abnormalities may prove possible in the seventh or eighth week of pregnancy.

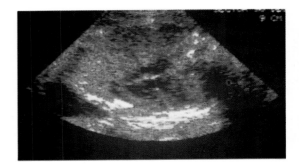

▲ *Echocardiograph of a fetal heart. With this technique, which is a development of ultrasound, it is possible to detect defects in the heart beat and heart structure.*

▲ *Ultrasound scanning of fetuses has become routine in many hospitals. The technique is non-invasive, though some doubts have been raised about the longterm effects.*

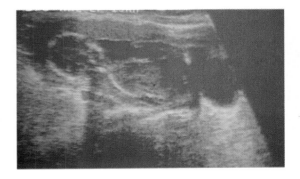

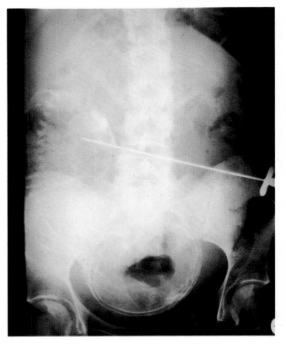

▲ *X-ray of a blood transfusion given to a fetus through the umbilical cord. New imaging techniques have made such operations, and even fetal heart surgery, possible.*

▶ *X-ray of a fetus (colored brown) in its mother's womb, at about eight months, with the head engaged in the pelvic outlet ready for birth, its knees tucked up to its chest.*

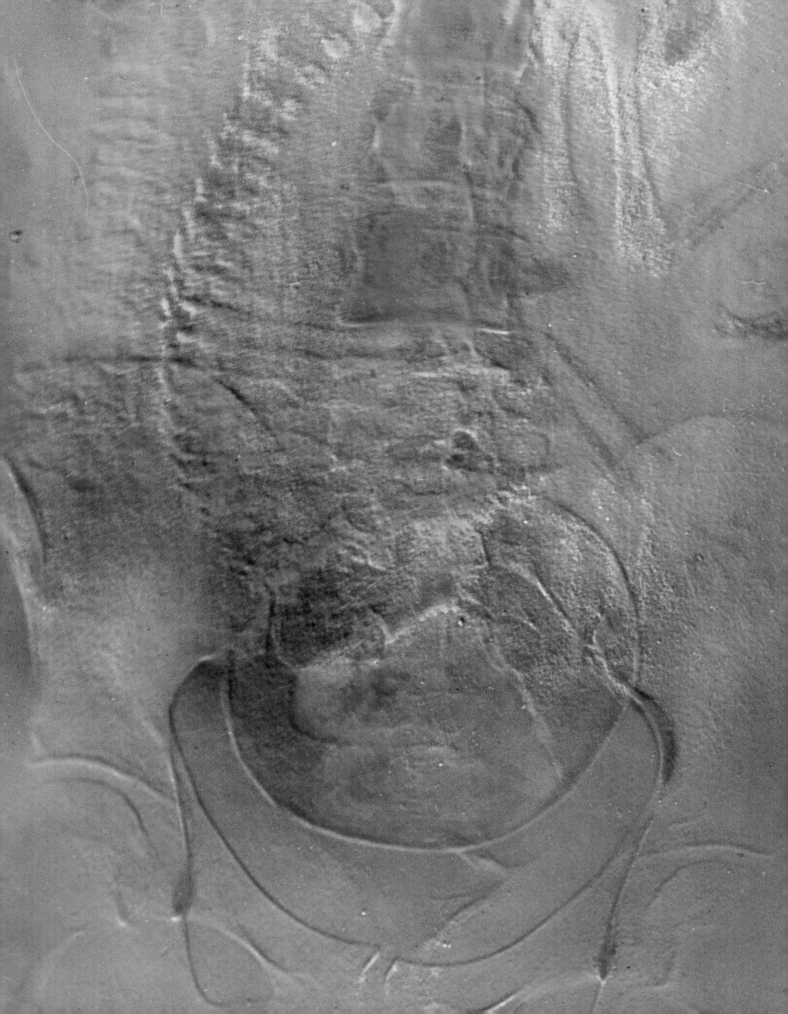

Inheritable diseases – faulty chromosomes

The most common genetic aberration to produce noticeably abnormal babies is Down's syndrome. Whereas a normal cell carries 46 chromosomes in 23 pairs, in Down's syndrome there are three of chromosome 21, giving a total of 47. The disease is characterized by facial features, which led to the name "mongolism", mental retardation and high incidences of diabetes, heart disease and intestinal disorders.

Of the 23 pairs of chromosomes, one is concerned with sexual characteristics. Several illnesses result from an odd number of sex chromosomes. Klinefelter's syndrome, which occurs with a frequency of one in a 1,000 male live births, is the name given to the condition in which there are two X chromosomes and one Y chromosome. This disease is often not diagnosed until puberty, when male secondary sexual characteristics fail to develop. Sufferers are sterile.

Another triple sex-chromosome disease is XYY syndrome, in which there are two male chromosomes. There has been much controversy about this, because some studies have shown a higher-than-average incidence of antisocial behavior among sufferers. The condition occurs with about the same frequency as Klinefelter's syndrome.

Turner's syndrome is a disease of people who have one X chromosome and no Y chromosome; they are usually physically female. Embryos with this aberration often abort spontaneously and the frequency among live births is between one tenth and one quarter of that of Klinefelter's syndrome. There is little development of the female secondary sexual characteristics and sufferers are usually sterile.

Inheritable diseases – faulty genes

Most of the inheritable diseases are caused by a missing or defective gene rather than a whole chromosome. Because the chromosomes and the genes they carry go in pairs, such diseases may be either dominant or recessive. In the first case, inheritance of the gene from either parent is sufficient to establish the disease. Thus, Huntington's chorea, a degenerative neurological disease, is passed on by sufferers to 50 percent of their children. As the disease does not usually show

▲ Twins may result from a single fertilized ovum (identical twins) or from two fertilized ova (dissimilar twins). Exactly how a single egg leads to twins is still not clearly understood. Even less clear is the cause of Siamese twins, identical twins who are partly joined together. The extent of joining differs in this very rare condition. In some cases a vital organ, like the liver, is shared. Where joining is more superficial, Siamese twins can usually be separated surgically. Siamese twins such as Daisy and Violet Hilton, shown here, have lived successfully; Eng and Chang, the "original" Siamese twins from Bangkok, were born in 1811 and lived to the age of 69, having had 21 children.

◄ A girl from the Oysterman tribe of the Botswana-Zimbabwe border, where about 100 people suffer from the lobster-claw syndrome, caused by a faulty gene.

up until middle age, after which it is progressive and incurable, sufferers may have had children before they know they have the disease.

Recessive genetic diseases can be passed on by carriers who have only one affected gene. Hemophilia is caused by a faulty gene which produces an inactive version of a special blood factor (usually Factor VIII) involved in clotting. Sufferers bleed easily and bleeding usually stops only when vessels constrict. Internal hemorrhaging is more common and a major problem, especially in joints such as the knee. The severity of the disease differs between individuals, although sufferers in the same family generally show the same degree of affliction. The faulty gene is located on the X chromosome. A female carrier has one faulty X chromosome and one normal X chromosome and therefore does not suffer from the disease. If she has a male child, then there is a 50 percent chance that it will inherit the faulty X chromosome. As the child inherits a Y chromosome from the father, it has only a faulty X chromosome and therefore is hemophiliac. A female can be a hemophiliac if born to a hemophiliac father and a carrier mother, but this is very rare.

Several other recessive genetic conditions, including Duchenne muscular dystrophy and color blindness have been linked to sex chromosome defects. Many other diseases arise through failure of one or more genes on other chromosomes to produce a biologically important substance correctly. In these cases, offspring suffer the disease if they inherit the faulty gene from both parents.

Tay-Sachs disease causes apparently healthy babies to fall ill and die in early childhood. The faulty gene, which fails to produce an enzyme called hexosaminidase A, is found in nearly five percent of Ashkenazic Jews, (that is Jews who migrated to Eastern Europe). Carriers can now be detected by a blood test. Cystic fibrosis is another recessive genetic disorder. The frequency of carriers among Caucasions is about the same as Tay-Sachs carriers among Ashkenazic Jews. To date, however, it cannot be detected. Cystic fibrosis is a wasting disease of lungs, sweat glands and digestive organs which usually causes death from infection by the early twenties.

▲ ▲ *Down's syndrome is characterized by the moon-shaped face, and is caused by an extra chromosome 21. One child in every 650 live births suffers from Down's syndrome, but the basic incidence is much higher as two-thirds of the embryos abort spontaneously. The likelihood of a mother giving birth to a Down's syndrome baby increases with age, increasing sharply after the age of 35.*

Abortion

When a fetus has been diagnosed as abnormal, the parents may be given the choice of an induced abortion. Abortions also may be performed where the mother is unsuited to childbearing. The way in which the fetus is removed depends on its age.

Early abortions, during the first three months of pregnancy, are usually performed either by suction curettage or dilatation and curettage. In both cases, the cervix is dilated, usually under local anesthetic. In suction curettage, a vacuum aspirator is inserted into the uterus and the embryo is sucked out. With dilation and curettage a sharp instrument is used to remove the fetal tissue.

For abortions between 13 and 24 weeks, two methods are most often used. In the first, some amniotic fluid is replaced by a salt solution. In the second, a natural substance called a prostaglandin is injected into the amniotic fluid. Both methods result in expulsion of the fetus through normal labor. The saline method is not recommended for mothers suffering from high blood pressure or heart or kidney ailments, and is usually slower than prostaglandin injection. Both methods usually involve hospitalization.

Intersexes

Intersexes are physically intermediate between a true male and a true female, either as mosaics of sexual parts, or male on one side and female on the other. The condition is either obvious at birth or it becomes apparent at puberty. There are two causes – extra chromosomes or a hormonal abnormality during development of the embryo. True hermaphrodites have both ovarian and testicular tissue, often with ambiguous external genitalia. About three quarters are raised as boys, but develop breasts and begin to menstruate during adolescence. Surgical manipulation can produce normal-looking genitals.

There are a number of diseases producing an intersexual state. Individuals with Turner's syndrome have a female appearance but they do not menstruate and are deficient in the female sex hormone estrogen, which is given as treatment. The inherited testicular feminizing syndrome, produces apparent females who have a male set of sex chromosomes. They synthesize the male sex hormone testosterone, but their cells do not respond to it. The testes tend to form malignant tumors and are removed surgically.

One drug was used for over 20 years on 2 million pregnant women before its abnormal side effects were recognized

Many of the inheritable diseases are caused by the failure of a gene coding for a particular enzyme. As a result, poisonous substances build up in the body which can cause permanent damage. Provided that such deficiencies are diagnosed at birth, they can be controlled, often by diet restriction. Preventive treatment can be carried out from birth on those babies automatically tested for the common forms.

The first such disease for which a test was devised is phenylketonuria. This is caused by failure to metabolize the amino-acid phenylalanine correctly. Toxic products form which can cause severe brain damage. Treatment involves substituting natural proteins in the diet with synthetic protein containing no phenylalanine. This diet needs to be maintained for the first few years of life, while brain development continues, after which it can be relaxed.

By contrast, failure to produce the enzyme adenosine deaminase is almost always fatal. This enzyme is concerned with metabolism of adenosine. If adenosine and the closely related deoxyadenosine reach high levels in blood and tissues, lymphocytes are harmed, leading to severe combined immune deficiency (◗ page 108). The sufferer is particularly liable to severe infections.

Inherited blood disorders

Two blood diseases which affect large numbers in different parts of the world are caused by recessively inherited genes. Sickle-cell anemia, much more frequent among Negros than among Caucasians or Asiatics, is caused by a faulty gene coding for part of the globin protein in hemoglobin. The difference between the correct and incorrect proteins is only one amino-acid in a protein made up from 140 of them. This single change causes the molecule to deform into a sickle shape that cannot carry oxygen so efficiently. As a result, body tissues receive an inadequate supply of oxygen. Severity of the disease varies greatly. In mild cases, symptoms show up only at high altitude, if the sufferer is flying in an unpressurized aircraft for example. At the other extreme, the disease can be severely debilitating and sufferers may die from a sudden infection which would only rarely prove fatal in a person with normal hemoglobin.

Thalassemia is the name given to a group of recessively inherited blood disorders prevalent in people from countries bordering the Mediterranean; these are also caused by defective globin synthesis. A hemoglobin molecule contains four protein chains in two identical pairs. In the case of sickle-cell anemia, it is the so-called alpha-chains which are affected. The thalassemias are divided into four major types. In two of these, either no alpha globin chains are produced, or only subnormal amounts. In the other two, it is the other – beta globin – chains which are either not produced or produced subnormally. These effects can be produced by many different changes in the structure of the genes which code for these proteins, ranging from point mutations to deletion of part or all of the gene.

The severity of the thalassemias varies, but they are responsible for many infant deaths. In recent years, treatments have been developed based on recurrent blood transfusions. However, these lead to problems, notably the toxic effects of iron, as the iron in the transfused blood accumulates in the body. Sickle-cell anemia and the thalassemias were both originally most common in those parts of the world where Falciparum malaria (the most lethal type) was prevalent. They have probably survived because the genes carrying them offer some immunity to the malarial parasite.

Gene maps

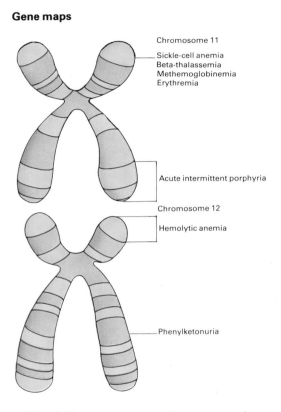

Chromosome 11

Sickle-cell anemia
Beta-thalassemia
Methemoglobinemia
Erythremia

Acute intermittent porphyria

Chromosome 12

Hemolytic anemia

Phenylketonuria

▲ *"Maps" of human chromosomes 11 and 12, showing the locations at which the genetic mutations responsible for various diseases are located.*

▼ *The oxygen-carrying capacity of hemoglobin depends on the shape of the protein (white spheres) around the heme core (red), in turn dependent on its amino-acid composition.*

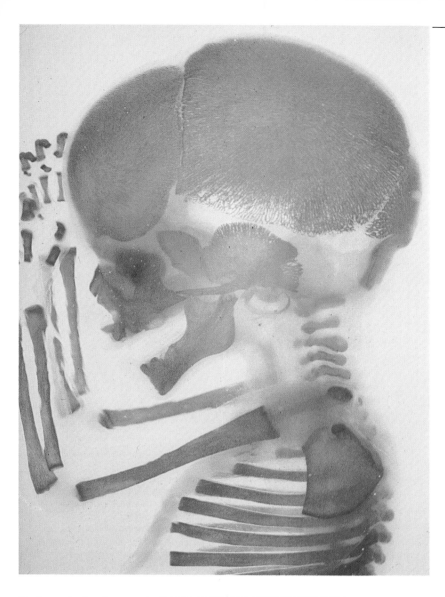

Environmental hazards and abnormal babies

The effect of substances which deform embryos – known as teratogens – is the same for adults, but because embryonic cells are rapidly dividing, poisoning of them may produce very serious consequences.

Substances which interfere specifically with cell division can cause the most severe damage. Thalidomide, a sedative prescribed between 1959 and 1961, is the best known example. Because the generation of particular organs and limbs occurs in a specific sequence, the various types of deformity produced by thalidomide depends on the age of the embryo. The most common affected the arms and legs.

The synthetic hormone diethylstilbestrol (DES) was first used in the late 1940s to help avoid complications in some pregnancies. During the 1970s, genital abnormalities were discovered in a number of children whose mothers had taken DES before the 18th week of pregnancy. Because the abnormalities did not appear until after puberty, the drug was used for 20 years and as many as two million pregnant women may have taken it.

Not all teratogenic effects are produced by man-made poisons. German measles (rubella), if acquired in the first three months of pregnancy, can cause severe fetal abnormalities, as can syphilis, cytomegalovirus infection and toxoplasmosis.

◄ ▼ *The side view of the human fetus shows the development of normal arm bones. These are absent in the X-ray of a victim of the drug thalidomide. This drug, when taken by pregnant women, interfered with fetal cell division at the stage when arms and legs were forming. The consequence was a number of live births of children without these limbs.*

Embryonic development

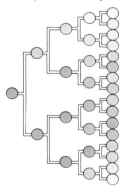

▲ *Starting from a single fertilized egg, a fetus develops rapidly via repeated divisions to become a multicelled organism. Between the 3rd and 13th week, cells differentiate to produce different organs of the body. At this stage, the rapidly dividing cells are particularly susceptible to poisoning which can cause a variety of major malformations.*

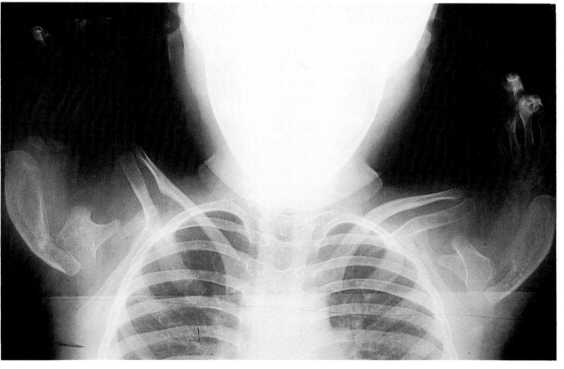

See also
Nervous System Disorders 17-20
Hormonal Imbalance 29-32
Reproductive Defects 73-6

Gene therapy

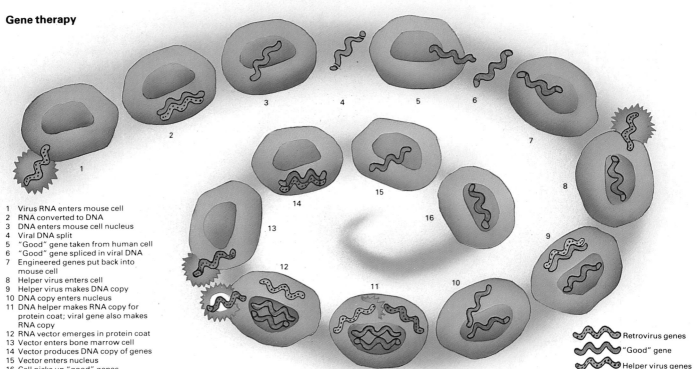

1 Virus RNA enters mouse cell
2 RNA converted to DNA
3 DNA enters mouse cell nucleus
4 Viral DNA split
5 "Good" gene taken from human cell
6 "Good" gene spliced in viral DNA
7 Engineered genes put back into mouse cell
8 Helper virus enters cell
9 Helper virus makes DNA copy
10 DNA copy enters nucleus
11 DNA helper makes RNA copy for protein coat; viral gene also makes RNA copy
12 RNA vector emerges in protein coat
13 Vector enters bone marrow cell
14 Vector produces DNA copy of genes
15 Vector enters nucleus
16 Cell picks up "good" genes

〜〜〜 Retrovirus genes

〜〜〜 "Good" gene

〜〜〜 Helper virus genes

Between one and two percent of babies are born with defects which cannot be attributed to a single faulty gene. These defects often seem to have a genetic component, but the environment is also significant. These multifactorial congenital abnormalities include cleft lip and palate, types of heart disease and neural tube defects. Of the latter, spina bifida has aroused much speculation. At one time, it was thought that a poison associated with blighted potatoes might be exerting a teratogenic effect. Today the high incidence of the condition in manufacturing towns, such as Pittsburgh, USA, and Glasgow, Scotland, makes industrial pollution the possible contributory cause. In addition, the higher risk of a couple with a spina bifida baby having another suggests a genetic link. During 1985 tests based on either DNA "probes" or targetted antibodies were announced for the early detection of conditions such as spina bifida.

The potential of genetic engineering

With the development of genetic engineering techniques, interest has been shown in trying to cure the many kinds of inherited disease by replacing defective genes. Where a single protein is involved, the section of genetic material which codes for it can be isolated relatively easily. The problem is how to insert this material into the cells of sufferers in such a way that it will be reproduced with the cell's own genetic material when the cell divides and, more importantly, will be expressed (will produce protein) at the appropriate time.

Currently, pharmaceutical companies are making some human products, such as insulin, for therapeutic use by culturing bacteria into which the appropriate gene has been engineered. Within the next few years, much of this biotechnological production may be switched into mammalian cell cultures. Developing the technology for that will provide the insights into how similiar insertions might be carried out in living human beings, to overcome their genetic deficiencies.

Gene therapy
In the past, it has been possible to combat damage caused by certain inherited diseases, though without interfering with the defective genes responsible. The ill-effects of phenylketonuria, for example, can be ameliorated by diet, but the gene is still passed on to future generations. In future, however, it may well be feasible to replace certain faulty genes with their normal counterparts. Scientists hope to achieve this feat of genetic engineering by employing a virus to ferry "good" genes into particular body tissues.

As shown in the illustration (above), one chosen vehicle is a retrovirus, so-called because it can make DNA copies of its RNA – the reverse of which occurs in animal cells. Most of the virus genes (including those it requires to make the protein coat which is essential for it to infect another cell) will be removed from such a DNA copy, produced in mouse cells. This will leave room for the "desirable" human gene to be spliced in, yielding a sequence which can then be cloned to generate many copies. These will be added to further mouse cells, together with an RNA "helper" virus which will (again by making DNA copies of its own genes) provide the hybrid sequence with a protein coat. The product should then be a virus which carries the desirable gene and still has the protein coat it must possess if it is to invade human cells – but lacking the protein coat genes it would need to reproduce further. The final projected step is for bone marrow cells to be removed from the patient and be incubated with the tailor-made virus before being reinjected. "Good" genes ferried into these cells by the virus should then enable them to produce the enzyme whose absence caused the disease in the first place.

*Sexually transmitted diseases...Changing incidence...
The difficulties of diagnosis...Sexual infections and
antibiotics...The new threat of genital herpes...Other
infections of the sex organs...PERSPECTIVE...The AIDS
epidemic...The rise and fall of syphilis*

Until the Second World War, "venereal diseases" meant gonorrhea
and syphilis. Since that time, a great many more infections have been
recognized as being acquired through sexual contact. The entire group
now known collectively as sexually transmitted diseases (STD) is
attracting growing concern among health authorities throughout the
world. Although STDs declined in apparent seriousness when antibiotics came into widespread use in mid-century, their prevalence has
increased dramatically since that time – especially in the 15-19 age
group in some countries. Epidemiologists are not sure they know all
the reasons, though greater "promiscuity" and the development of
international tourism are contributory factors. Transfer of micro-
organisms to mucus membranes of the genital tract has also become
more likely as the contraceptive pill has replaced barrier techniques
such as the sheath.

The incidence of particular STDs has been altering too. Forty years
ago most cases of urethritis (infection of the duct leading from the
bladder) were diagnosed as being due to gonorrhea, caused by the
bacterium *Neisseria gonorrhoeae* invading the urethra and producing a
suppurative discharge. In women this can precipitate infection of the
Fallopian tubes, blocking them and causing sterility or ectopic pregnancy. In men it can lead to infection of the epididymis, prostate and
testes. Arthritis and heart disease may occur in both sexes. Gonorrhea
is nearly always acquired during intercourse (the exceptions being eye
infection in babies born to affected mothers, and vaginal infection
transmitted by towels among infants in institutions).

▲ *An Indonesian mask made in the 19th century showing
the facial paralysis that can result from advanced syphilis.
Western sailors introduced sexually transmitted diseases to
the region, where they had previously been unknown.*

▼ *The syphilitic bacterium Treponoma pallidum. It is
transmitted either through direct sexual contact or to the
fetus via the placenta. Syphilis can be easily detected and is
usually treatable by penicillin.*

Female sex organs

Fallopian tube
Ovary
Uterus
Bladder
Urethra
Vagina
Labium
Anus

Male sex organs

Vas deferens
Bladder
Urethra
Penis
Glans
Testicle

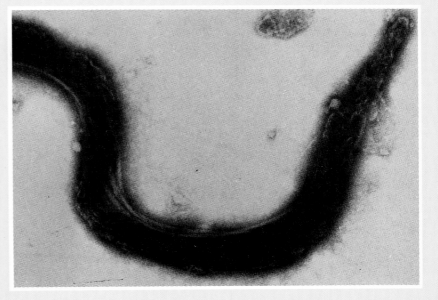

In the 1970s the gonorrhea bacterium became invulnerable to antibiotics

Today, non-specific urethritis (NSU) is as common as that due to gonorrhea worldwide, and twice as common in the West, ranking along with it and syphilis as the trio of most important STDs. About 50 percent of "non-specific" infections are thought to be produced by *Chlamydia trachomatis* – an organism that is related to the trachoma agent (◆ page 117) and is intermediate in size and behavior between bacteria and viruses. The remaining 50 percent are cases in which the cause is uncertain, though *Mycoplasma genitalium*, discovered by David Taylor-Robinson at Britain's Clinical Research Centre in 1983, may play a major role.

The difficulties of diagnosis

Gonorrhea has always proved difficult to control because carriers may show no symptoms but still purvey the disease, and it has become increasingly difficult since the emergence in 1976 of strains of *Neisseria* resistant to penicillin. Common in the Far East and in West Africa, these organisms are being found increasingly in the USA and Europe. The number of patients with such strains doubled each year in Britain between 1977 and 1982, and is still increasing. So, while 150,000 unit shots of penicillin were once considered adequate to obliterate the infection, doses of some 4·8 million units (often accompanied by other drugs) are now necessary. Compounded by a rise in resistance to other antibiotics, the cost of such treatment is growing in parallel. Development of a vaccine has still proved inordinately difficult, but there are hopes for an effective method of immunization in the near future.

NSU due to unknown organisms can also be extremely difficult to treat effectively. But *Chlamydia* (which, like *N. gonorrhoeae*, may also be passed on during birth to infect the baby's eyes) is usually sensitive to tetracyclines. The problem here is identification of the infection. In 1984 one UK specialist estimated that two-thirds of cases were not being diagnosed, leaving thousands of men and women infertile and scores of children with eye disease. There are also strong suspicions that cervicitis (infection of the cervix) often goes undetected. It is hoped that a new spot test for *Chlamydia*, based on highly specific "monoclonal antibodies", will enable all such conditions to be diagnosed and cleared up speedily.

The growing problem of genital herpes

Genital herpes is a major new STD of the past four decades. The characteristic genital sores are caused by a herpes simplex virus (HSV2) related to the one (HSV1) that produces cold sores on the lip (◆ page 120). Although known from much earlier times, the disease increased greatly during the 1970s. So did the frequency with which HSV2 was found in lip sores, and HSV1 in genital sores – a result of more frequent oro-genital contacts. Unlike gonorrhea, NSU and syphilis, genital herpes is incurable. The recurrent and extremely painful blisters can only be relieved by ointments and painkillers before they subside, only to flare up again some time later. As well as interfering with sex life, herpes infection may have very serious complications. At least half the babies born to women with active genital herpes at the time of delivery contract the disease, and half of these will die or suffer permanent neurological damage. There are also suspicions of a link with cervical cancer, though this is not proven. Vaccine trials now under way may provide evidence that the infection is preventable.

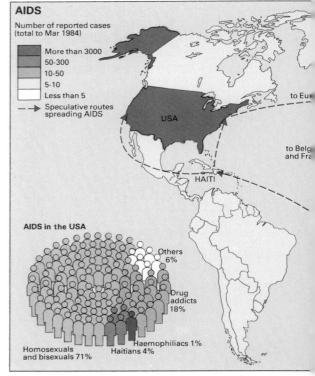

AIDS

Number of reported cases
(total to Mar 1984)

More than 3000
50-300
10-50
5-10
Less than 5
– – ► Speculative routes
spreading AIDS

to Eu

USA

to Belg
and Fra

HAITI

AIDS in the USA

Others
6%

Drug
addicts
18%

Haemophiliacs 1%
Homosexuals   Haitians 4%
and bisexuals 71%

◄ *A demonstration by New York homosexuals demanding action to protect them against AIDS. A great deal of research was quickly begun on the disease, but public awareness often remained at the level of hysteria, with sufferers shunned and some people seeing the epidemic as a "gay plague", even though it is not limited to homosexuals.*

The AIDS epidemic

In June 1981 the US Centers for Disease Control announced that five young homosexual men in Los Angeles had died of pneumonia caused by "Pneumocystis carnii". Shortly afterwards, there were reports that another 26 homosexuals had developed a severe form of Kaposi's sarcoma, a cancer until then extremely uncommon in the USA. Soon it became clear that the two incidents were related. Both groups had been victims of an apparently new condition, acquired immune deficiency syndrome (AIDS), which renders victims vulnerable to a wide range of "opportunisitic infections" and to the onset of Kaposi's sarcoma. Sporadic cases had occurred in the past, but the epidemic which began in 1981 was unprecedented. By April 1984 the disease was claiming 2,000 deaths a year. Four main groups were at risk: homosexual or bisexual men, intravenous drug users, hemophiliacs receiving regular transfusions, and Haitians. But the factor most strongly associated with the illness was the number of sexual partners per year (an average of 60 in one survey). This suggested that AIDS was caused by an agent transmitted during intercourse – probably through the bloodstream. Two groups, one led by Dr Robert Gallo at the US National Cancer Institute and the other by Dr Luc Montagnier at the Pasteur Institute in Paris, have since announced the discovery of the virus which causes the disease.

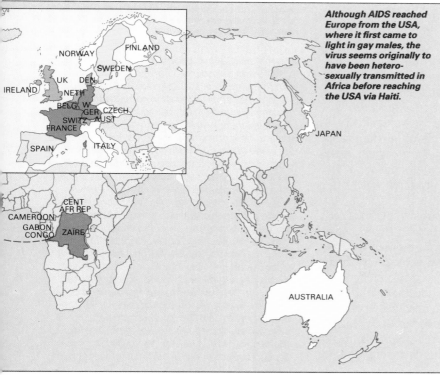

Although AIDS reached Europe from the USA, where it first came to light in gay males, the virus seems originally to have been hetero-sexually transmitted in Africa before reaching the USA via Haiti.

NORWAY
FINLAND
SWEDEN
IRELAND
UK
DEN
NETH
BELG
W GER CZECH
SWITZ AUST
FRANCE
SPAIN
ITALY
JAPAN
CENT AFR REP
CAMEROON
GABON
CONGO ZAIRE
AUSTRALIA

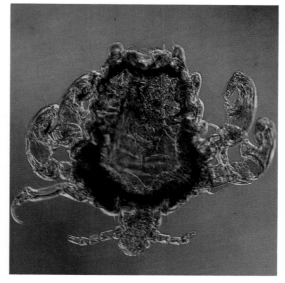

▲ *The crab louse Phthirus pubis is transmitted almost exclusively through intimate physical contact, and not through towels or toilet seats. With front legs capable of grasping just a single hair, it usually resides in the pubic region, but appears occasionally in chest and armpit hair and even eyelashes and thin balding pates. Crab lice are so tiny (1-2 mm long) and well camouflaged that they only reveal themselves after feeding, when they leave bright red feces.*

L'ESPAIGNOL
AFFLIGE
DV MAL
DE NAPLES.

There are 20 or so other STDs. As with gonorrhea, NSU, syphilis and herpes, they are less significant for immediate effects such as urethral discharge than for complications such as infection of the epididymis and Fallopian tubes which can lead to male and female sterility and ectopic pregnancy. Also included in the STD group is trichomoniasis. Caused by the protozoon *Trichomonas vaginalis* living in the vagina and urethra of females, and the urethra and sometimes prostate of males, this generates a watery discharge but is not otherwise harmful. Likewise with the irritating discharge due to vaginal thrush, an infection with *Candida* yeast which is more common than usual among pregnant women, diabetics and women taking certain drugs (including the contraceptive pill). *Gardnerella vaginalis* causes a similarly benign discharge which (despite its odor of rotten fish) often comes to light only during a routine examination.

More than any other group of infectious diseases, STDs act as a monitor of changes in human behavior. So, over the past two decades, microbiologists have found that many bacteria and viruses not previously recognized as being transmitted by sexual activity are being spread in that way. Intestinal pathogens such as salmonellae and giardia are now known to be transmitted among homosexual men by oro-anal contact. Both hepatitis A and B are also particularly common among male homosexuals. They are spread by promiscuous "super-carriers", but there is expert disagreement about the precise routes of transmission. In 1983, the first trials of a hepatitis B vaccine among homosexuals in New York were highly successful.

▲ *Syphilis gave rise to some novel techniques of isolation and disinfection in 17th-century Europe. It spread quickly through Europe from 1500, perhaps brought back from the West Indies by Columbus' sailors.*

The rise and fall of syphilis

Syphilis was unknown to Europe until the end of the 15th century, but quickly reached epidemic proportions. It has declined in comparative importance since the introduction of antibiotics. Like gonorrhea, syphilis is not highly contagious. But untreated, the single chancre which marks the first stage of the disease may be followed within weeks by a secondary stage of fever, rash and possible kidney damage. Years later, after a latent period, some patients develop tertiary syphilis, whose effects range from relatively harmless gummas (lesions of the skin and bones) to paralysis, seizures and other indications of brain infection. Congenital syphilis is a potentially severe, mutilating form of the disease, but infected people can be identified by a simple, routine blood test. One of the bacteria most sensitive to penicillin, T. pallidum has not developed resistance. So the use of this and other antibiotics (plus, as is necessary with all STDs, prompt tracing and treatment of contacts) has made syphilis a less serious danger than before the advent of antibiotics — though there is concern about its global spread among male homosexuals.

The primary defenses against infection...The immune system...The lymphatic system...Macrophages... Lymphocytes, antigens and antibodies...Destroying the infection...Immunity... Vaccination...PERSPECTIVE... Should tonsils be removed?...Interferon, the body's vital poison...The structure of antibodies...Why does the body tolerate itself?

The body is continually liable to attack from infective organisms or to damage from poisons in the environment. Through evolution, protective mechanisms have developed. Some of these are very general, whereas others are much more specific and involve the activation of a highly elaborate defense mechanism. The physical barrier to invasion provided by skin is enhanced by surface secretions containing fatty acids that generally inhibit microbial growth, and the enzyme lysozyme which damages bacterial cell walls. Similarly, the acidity of the stomach helps to protect it from harmful organisms ingested with food. The lungs are protected by nasal mucus, which both traps and destroys foreign bodies, and by cilia which help to expel particulate matter with their beating motion.

If foreign material does enter the body, additional defenses come into play. Inflammation of local tissues may prevent the invaders from spreading through the body. Some viruses are inactivated by slight increases in temperature, so fever can be a defensive response to such invasions. Blood contains substances which are harmful to bacteria. Transferrin, for example, robs them of the iron they need for growth, while white blood cells (leukocytes) digest foreign matter.

There is also a complex system of "specific immunity", the details of which are not yet fully understood. This is characterized by three factors: specificity, memory and self-tolerance. Whereas a nonspecific response does not alter with time or experience of the invader, a specific response allows the body to memorize the structure of a particular foreign body and to react far more quickly and vigorously to any subsequent attack from it.

The body's main defense system
The specific immune system has three major components, comprising two types of lymphocyte and the macrophage. Macrophages are leukocytes; some circulate in the blood, while others reside in tissues throughout the body. They, like granulocytes, scavenge unwanted material such as old red blood cells. Macrophages also cooperate with the lymphocytes to produce specific immune responses.

The lymphocytes – of which an adult has a trillion (10^{12}), weighing about one kilogram – arise from stem cells in bone marrow. Some are transferred via the bloodstream to the thymus, a gland overlying the heart in the chest. Here they rapidly produce many daughter cells, most of which die. The survivors emerge from the thymus and travel to lymphoid tissue as mature T-lymphocytes (T-cells), able to respond to foreign matter. Lymphocytes of the second kind are produced in the bone marrow and the body's other lymphoid organs, which include the spleen, tonsils, gut lining, appendix and lymph nodes. In birds, this type is produced in an organ called the bursa, from which they were given the name B-lymphocytes.

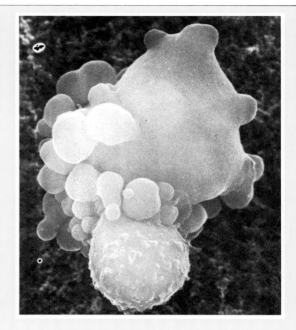

▲ A cancer cell being attacked and destroyed by lymphocytes, the agents of the body's system of defense against invasion from inside or out. The lymphocytes have caused blisters to grow on the cell before finally killing it.

Infected wound

Bacteria

Histamine and prostaglandin

Neutrophils and macrophages

▲ If body cells become infected, they release histamine and prostaglandins to cause inflammation and trap the infection. Blood vessels dilate and allow neutrophils cells to pass through their walls to the tissues, where they and macrophages attempt to destroy the bacteria. If the infection is too virulent, a specific immune response is invoked.

Lymphocytes circulate through the lymphatic system and the blood. Lymph nodes, capsules of tissue which occur at intervals throughout the lymphatic system, filter the lymph and control the direction of its flow. They are also sites where B- and T-cells mature after challenge by an invader. In some infections, a proliferation of lymphocytes causes enlargement of the nodes, the symptom often described as "swollen glands". The spleen plays a similar role, as filter for microbes that have entered the bloodstream, and stimulates lymphocytes into activity.

The B-cells produce immunoglobulins, complex proteins which cover the cell surface and are also released into the blood. A foreign body that reacts with immunoglobulin is called an antigen. Generally, antigens are large molecules, notably proteins and carbohydrates. Small molecules can be antigenic, but usually only in combination with a large molecule; thus, some reactive chemicals are antigenic because they form complexes with the body's own proteins. Similarly, the allergy shown by some people to penicillin derives from its ability to combine with protein and create a new antigen (▶ page 106).

Immunoglobulins – antibodies as they are also called – combine with antigens like a key fitting a lock. Only a small part of each molecule fits together and a single large antigen molecule may have many such sites – called antigenic determinants – on it. Different ones may react with one or more distinct immunoglobulins. Often, several different immunoglobulins will react with several different antigenic determinants, thus producing a large aggregate which the body can attack more readily.

While the immunoglobulin molecules are much the same general shape, each has variable regions which are the antigen-combining sites, so one type of immunoglobulin usually reacts with only one antigenic determinant. In this variability lies two of the strengths of the immune system, its specificity and its memory.

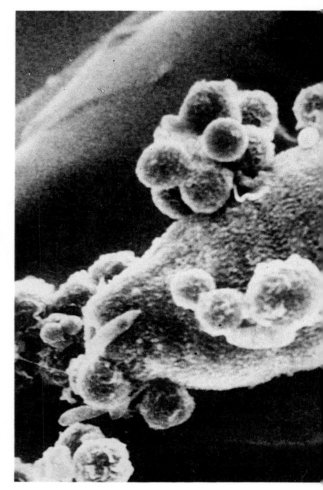

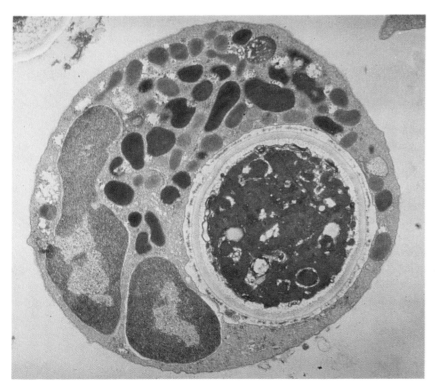

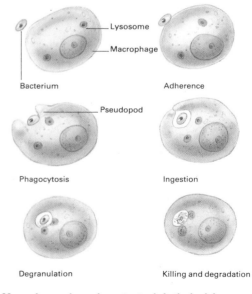

▲ *Macrophages play an important role in the body's defenses, passing through the connective tissue and approaching unwanted tissues or invading organisms. They take the organisms within their cell membranes (phagocytosis) and digest them.*

◀ *A macrophage after ingesting a round yeast molecule.*

Lymph flow

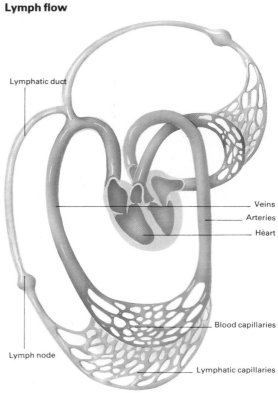

Lymphatic duct

Veins
Arteries
Heart

Blood capillaries

Lymph node

Lymphatic capillaries

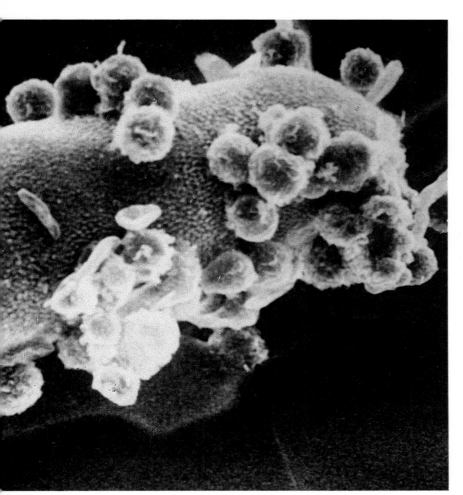

◄ *Electron micrograph of lymphocytes attacking a schistosomiasis (bilharzia) parasite; once activated, the immune system can launch a powerful attack on invading organisms.*

▲ *The lymph flows through the lymph vessels by muscular activity, draining and filtering the body tissue fluid and allowing the lymphocytes to reach the site of invasion quickly.*

Should tonsils be removed?

Until recently, tonsils were a part of the body often removed during childhood. They were considered to be a nuisance, liable to infection, and serving no useful purpose. In fact, tonsils are a major defense against invasion via the oral cavity. There are three types. The ones which used to be removed commonly were the palatine tonsils. The exposed surface of these in the roof of the mouth is pitted and can accumulate debris. This can be a source of infection, which is known as tonsillitis; the swelling may block the pharynx and interfere with breathing and swallowing.

The pharyngeal tonsils, or adenoids, can also produce harmful effects if they become infected, making nasal breathing difficult. The third set of tonsils, the lingual tonsils, are at the back of the tongue and usually cause no trouble.

If tonsils are not completely removed, they may grow again in young children. However, now that their role as a source of lymphocytes in a vulnerable part of the body is known, tonsillectomy is considered undesirable unless there is persistent infection. It can lead to greater susceptibility to some diseases, notably polio and Hodgkin's disease (page 104)*.*

Lymph organs tend to decrease in size and activity as we get older. Consequently, tonsillitis is generally only a childhood disease.

Immunomodulators

In recent years, it has been shown that the immune system uses a variety of chemical messengers – similar in a way to hormones – to communicate between different parts of itself and to activate specific responses. The exact function of many of these immunomodulators, of which there may be 20-30 major ones, is still unclear.

These molecules, all of which are soluble and can therefore travel freely around the lymphatic system, are called lymphokines. Their roles in modulating the immune system are both activating and passivating. Thus, macrophage migration inhibitory factor will prevent overreaction by part of the immune system, while macrophage activating factor has an opposite effect.

In therapeutic terms, it is the role of some of the less well understood lymphokines, such as the interferons and tumor necrosis factor, which may ultimately be important. Self-generated diseases, such as cancer, frequently arise through the failure of the immune system to destroy material that is or has become "non-self".

Attacking these diseases successfully will probably depend on mimicking accurately the immune system response which has failed. Increasingly, it seems likely that a key part of this effective response is the production of a "cocktail" of appropriate immunomodulators.

Lymph node

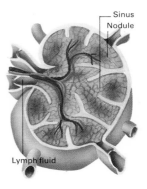

Sinus
Nodule

Lymph fluid

▲ *Lymph nodes, located on lymphatic pathways, are made up of fibrous connective tissue. T- and B-cells are made and congregate in their nodular compartments, as do other phagocytic cells. Lymph nodes tend to be clustered near parts of the body most susceptible to invasion; they filter the lymph fluid of injurious particles and act as the operations center for the fight against any invading organisms.*

The body can remember and recognize 100 million different invading organisms

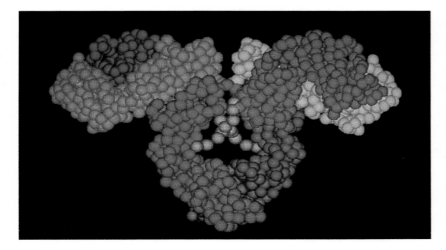

The types of immunoglobulin

Immunoglobulins – the antibodies released from the surfaces of B-cells that react to invaders and act as the crucial memory part of the immune system – are proteins. Five varieties have been identified. The most abundant is immunoglobulin G (IgG). One of its key functions is to pass on immunity to babies, by crossing the placental barrier. Macroglobulins (IgM) are aggregates of five immunoglobulin molecules. Like IgG, IgM can activate the complement system, but it cannot cross the placental barrier.

A first line of defense is provided by IgA, found in tears and saliva and released into the gut and lungs. This helps to inactivate viruses and toxins. Part of its structure makes it adhere to the lining of the gut and respiratory tract. It combines with foreign material and immobilizes it. Bacterial cells are particularly prone to destruction by lysozyme after interaction with IgA. This type of immuno-globulin provides resistance in the gut of the newborn, who obtain it from their mothers' milk.

The other two types of immunoglobulin – IgD and IgE – are less well understood. IgE is implicated in hypersensitivity and allergy, one of its effects being the rapid release of inflammatory substances such as histamine (♦ page 105). It also may have a role in fighting parasitic infections. The function of IgD is not clear. Its main role may be as a B-cell surface receptor, to help to recognize antigens.

Producing the right antibodies

Proteins are manufactured in the body from instructions coded into the genes. The immune system seems able to produce antibodies specific to any foreign matter with which it is challenged, yet it is impracticable to suppose that we have a gene for every possible antigen sequence that we might encounter. Different genes each code for a part of the antibody molecule; these can combine in different ways, thus creating diversity. Further diversity arises from the two variable regions. A third form of diversity is probably supplied by mutation. While most cells contain mechanisms to repair genetic material accurately, lymphocytes may have an error-prone repair mechanism, increasing the number of changes in the genes coding for the variable regions.

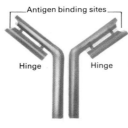

▲ ▲ *An immunoglobulin is a Y-shaped molecule; the binding sites, specific to one antigen, are shaped by the structure of variable regions on the arms.*

▶ *After a B-cell has been matched to the antigen, a "helper" T-cell with the same antigen determinants stimulates the B-cell to divide (4A), making memory cells to await future attacks, and plasma cells which produce huge amounts of the right antibody. This pours into the bloodstream, binds to the antigen and neutralizes it (5A), clumps it to enable macrophages to attack (5B) or stimulates the complement system to kill its cell membranes (5C).*

The structure of immunoglobulins

Basically, all immunoglobulins consist of four protein chains, linked together by disulfide bonds. There are two identical heavy chains and two identical light chains. Both types contain regions which are constant in structure and others which are variable regions. The constant regions of the heavy chain define which of the five types a particular immunoglobulin belongs to, while the variable regions determine which antigen it will react with, and therefore these regions give immunoglobulins their specificity.

It is estimated that we have the capacity to produce 100 million different types of antibody.

When the variable part interacts with an antigen, the shape of the molecule changes. This can help the antibody-antigen complex to attach to a phagocyte or, in the case of IgG and IgM, it can activate the complement system to destroy the antigen.

The blood's secret weapon: complement

The complement system involves eleven different proteins, some of which are latent forms of the natural catalyst molecules called enzymes. The system works in a complex but coordinated manner called a cascade; it has a variety of effects all of which help the destruction of the invader. These include making cells more easily digestible by macrophages; releasing chemical attractants which draw leukocytes to the scene; and disrupting the cell membranes of the foreign organisms, thereby causing the cell to explode.

4A

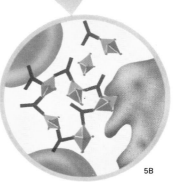

5A

5B

The immune response

▶ *If an invader (antigen) enters (1) the blood stream (2) or body tissues (2A), the first nonspecific response sees it attacked by neutrophils and the complement system. Macrophages may then take it to a lymph node (3), where the antigen is presented to the many T- and B-lymphocytes that are collected there. An appropriate antibody on a B-lymphocyte (or an equivalent site on the T-cell) is matched to the antigen; if none yet exists, a cell with an almost-correct antibody structure is found to mutate and provide an exact fit.*

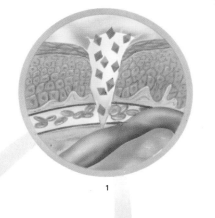

1

◆	Antigen
Y	Antibodies
	Macrophage
	Neutrophil
	Complement
	B-lymphocyte
	T-lymphocyte

2

2A

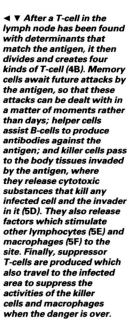

◀ ▼ *After a T-cell in the lymph node has been found with determinants that match the antigen, it then divides and creates four kinds of T-cell (4B). Memory cells await future attacks by the antigen, so that these attacks can be dealt with in a matter of moments rather than days; helper cells assist B-cells to produce antibodies against the antigen; and killer cells pass to the body tissues invaded by the antigen, where they release cytotoxic substances that kill any infected cell and the invader in it (5D). They also release factors which stimulate other lymphocytes (5E) and macrophages (5F) to the site. Finally, suppressor T-cells are produced which also travel to the infected area to suppress the activities of the killer cells and macrophages when the danger is over.*

3

4B

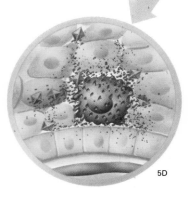

5C

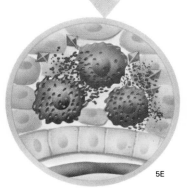

5D

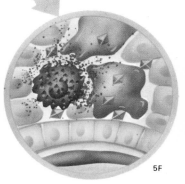

5E

5F

Identical twins can tolerate grafts of each other's body tissues

Memorizing an invader

If a B-lymphocyte reacts with an antigen under suitable conditions, it can become active in one of two ways. It may become a short-lived plasma cell, an immunoglobulin factory which produces much more of the reactive immunoglobulin and releases it into the bloodstream. It may reproduce more B-cells like itself, with the reactive immunoglobulin on their surfaces. Thus, once exposed to a particular antigen, the body contains more B-cells with the right antibody to combine with that antigen, should it ever appear again. This is the basis for immunity against reinfection. If the challenge is not repeated, these "memory cells" gradually die and immunity slowly decreases. Some infections seem to confer little immunity, though this is often because the organism, when next met, has evolved and thus changed its antigenic determinants (as with influenza) or because the disease is caused by many different organisms (as with the common cold).

Specificity is absolute, but different materials can share antigenic determinants. In such cases, if the immune system has reacted to one of the materials, it will subsequently react to the other as if it had been exposed to it already. The sharing of antigenic determinants by the organisms which cause smallpox (♦ page 118) and the related but milder disease, cowpox, led to the scientific discovery of immunization by Edward Jenner (1749-1823). In this case, the organisms involved are closely related, so the cross-reactivity is not surprising. In some cases, the similarity of antigenic determinants is coincidental and may be harmful, as in the case of rheumatic fever (♦ page 106).

Triggering the system

The interaction between T-cells and antigens is a major contributor to the immune response, largely because of chemical substances called lymphokines which are released by an activated T-cell. Some of these signal macrophages to come to the site of invasion, while others stimulate B-cells into activity. Although a B-cell can form an antibody-antigen complex, no immune response will occur unless there is co-operation from a T-cell. Nevertheless, in the case of some foreign matter such as bacterial toxins, formation of the complex may be enough to render it harmless.

The situation is more complex and more effective because there is more than one kind of T-cell. Some "helper" T-cells provoke the immune response, while "suppressor" cells limit it. They recognize antigens through surface receptors, similar to immunoglobulins.

A T-cell will react with an antigen only when it is associated on the surface of a macrophage with a major histocompatibility complex (MHC). These genes produce molecules, present on all cells which an organism recognizes as characteristic of itself. Known as human leukocyte antigens (HLAs), they are tolerated by the organism's immune system. They differ between all individuals except identical siblings, so one person's HLAs will elicit an immune response in someone else. This is why organ and tissue transplants are frequently rejected.

Helper T-cells react to the antigen, particularly if it has been adsorbed on the surface of a macrophage, and consequently stimulate B-cells. For this to happen, the T-cells have to recognize the HLAs on both the macrophage and the B-cells as similar to those on its own surface. Another type of T-cell, which attacks virally-infected body cells, does so only if the infected cell has HLAs in common with it. These cytotoxic T-cells are activated by helper T-cells through the lymphokine gamma-interferon.

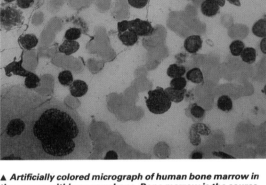

▲ *Artificially colored micrograph of human bone marrow in the spaces within spongy bone. Bone marrow is the source of stem cells, "general purpose" cells from which both B- and T-cells are produced after maturation in the thymus, spleen and other lymph organs.*

Cross-reactivity and double-cross

Cross-reactivity of antigens – the basis of modern immunization, discovered by Jenner – saved lives in Poland in an unusual way during World War II.

Vast numbers of Poles died as a result of the harsh conditions imposed upon them by the German occupation. The insanitary conditions led to outbreaks of typhus, a disease spread by lice. The disease had been kept out of Germany for a quarter of a century, which meant that the natural resistance of the population was low, so the Germans were determined that it should not find its way back. As many Poles were being sent to forced-labor camps in Germany, the Germans instituted typhus testing and refused to take any whose blood gave a positive result.

The test used, known as the Weil-Felix reaction, depends on the ability of typhus antibodies to form clumps with a bacterium called Proteus. This clumping is characteristic of antibody-antigen interaction and works because of cross-reactivity between typhus and Proteus. Two doctors working in southeastern Poland reasoned that an injection of Proteus would induce antibodies which would also give a positive Weil-Felix reaction. They tried this and it worked so successfully that, after repeating the injection on many local inhabitants and submitting blood samples to the Germans, the entire area of about a dozen villages was declared an epidemic zone and remained free of German interference for several years.

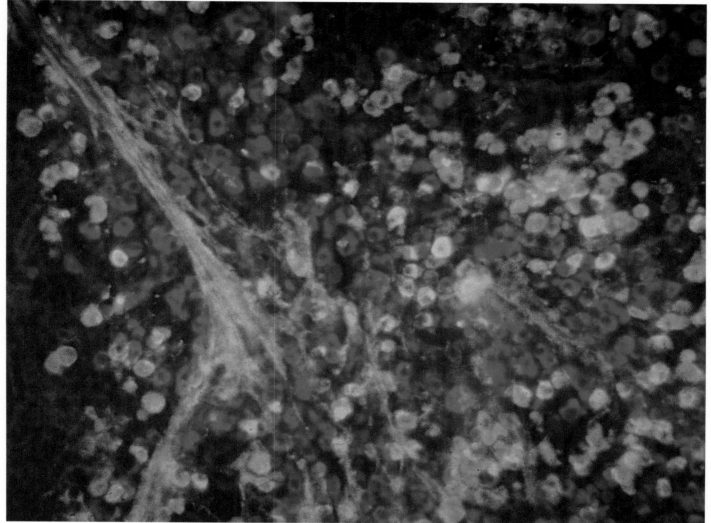

"Self" and "not self"

The Australian immunologist Sir Frank Macfarlane Burnet (1899-1985) noted that the immune system matures at a late stage of embryonic development, by which time most of the substances in the body which could be antigenic already exist. He proposed that any substance present when the immune system develops will be tolerated.

The basis for Burnet's theory was the mutual tolerance shown by some non-identical twin cattle. Identical human twins share immunological tolerance, whereas non-identical twins do not. The difference between humans and cattle in this case is that non-identical cattle twins share the same placenta and mixing of the fetal blood occurs. Consequently, according to this theory, each cow would recognize its non-identical twin as "self", because this mixing predated the development of its immune system.

Sir Peter Medawar (b. 1915), a British biologist interested in skin grafts, set out to test Burnet's theory. He had found that skin grafts between different people were unsuccessful. If one such graft was followed by another between the same donor and recipient, the second graft was rejected more quickly, indicating the development of immunological memory.

He then took two strains of highly interbred mice. Individuals of each strain would accept grafts from each other, but not from the other strain. He injected spleen cells from one into newborn mice of the other strain; these were then found to tolerate skin grafts from both strains. They had developed immunological tolerance.

Although this explains immunological tolerance on one level, it does not explain how it arises or continues. The answer seems to lie with the T-lymphocytes. T-cells can be made tolerant towards antigens, so that they no longer effect an immune response. B-cells still recognize the antigen, but do not become active because of the missing T-cell response. T-cells probably develop their tolerance towards "self" during development in the thymus. In some cases, the protective system breaks down and the immune system treats "self" as foreign, causing auto-immune diseases (page 106).

▲ Micrograph of plasma cells producing antibodies IgM (colored red) and IgG (green). It has been calculated that, during an immune response, each plasma cell makes 2,000 antibody molecules a second for several days.

▶ Sir Peter Medawar and Sir Frank Macfarlane Burnet shared the Nobel Prize in Physiology in 1960 for their research into how an organism's immune system learns how to recognize "self" and differentiate it from "non-self".

Because the immune system's reaction is specific to a particular antigen, exposure to that antigen can be used to produce immunity artificially. This is the basis of vaccination. In the case of a microbial infection, the microbe may be killed without damaging its outer coat. Injection of the dead microbe induces an immune response to the antigenic determinants on it, so that subsequent infection with live microbes of the same species produces a rapid immune response.

The manifold nature of T-cells reflects the multiple functions of the immune system. Not only does the body need to defend itself from outside invasion; it also needs to defend itself from enemies within, such as cells which become cancerous. Characteristically, the surface of cancer cells differs from that of normal cells; in other words, they develop new antigenic determinants or may lack normal ones. The majority of potential cancer cells are destroyed by the immune system before they can gain a hold in the body (◗ page 100).

People who suffer exceptional stress, such as a bereavement, may be more prone to develop cancer than the population at large. From this and related observations, it has been postulated that psychological events can depress the level of activity of the immune system. Some lymphocytes carry receptors which can recognize peptide hormones found in the brain. Some T-cells produce lymphokines, including interferon, in response to them. Ultimately, the immune system must be modulated or influenced by the central nervous system, but how this is effected is not yet understood.

▲ When transfusing blood, the blood groups of donor and recipient must be matched; the blood groups O, A, B and AB indicate the presence or absence of immunogenic substances, which must match.

▼ 18th-century cartoon by James Gillray (1757-1815) satirizing the dangers of inoculation with cowpox vaccine against smallpox.

Cancers

What is cancer?...The universality of cancer...Defining tumors...Viruses and malignancy...Oncogenes... The progress of cancer...Detection and monitoring... Treatment...PERSPECTIVE...Cancer incidence around the world...Smoking and lung cancer...Cancer in Africa... Can cancer be prevented?...Some unorthodox cures.

The body's cells usually regulate their growth and maintenance with exquisite delicacy. They multiply only when required – during childhood, and later to replace those lost through injury, disease and the continual shedding of cells from areas such as the skin and intestinal tract. When this self-control breaks down, the result is a malignant tumor (cancer). What may be a fatal process begins when just one healthy cell becomes cancerous and, free of normal constraints, transmits its abnormality to succeeding cell generations.

A fundamental aberration of cell behavior, cancer is found in all animals except the very simplest. There are even cancer-like growths in plants. For this reason, and because ancient skeletons interred in Egypt have shown deformations suggesting bone cancer, the condition is assumed to have affected all populations at all times.

Defining cancers

There are hundreds of different cancers, in two principal groups. Solid malignant tumors (which should be distinguished from benign, non-invasive ones) include those of the breast and womb in women; the prostate gland in men; and the stomach, lung and colon in both sexes. Systemic cancers are leukemias, affecting the blood-forming organs; and lymphomas, affecting the lymphatic system. Pathologists classify cancers further, according to the type of tissue and cell in which they arise. Carcinomas are based on tissue covering the body's external surfaces (for example, tumors of the skin and breast) or internal surfaces (such as intestinal, prostate and liver cancer). Sarcomas originate in muscle, bone, and other connective tissues. In addition to leukemias and lymphomas, the other principal category contains nerve tumors such as gliomas.

At first, malignant cells may resemble their healthy parents and even conduct some of their normal functions. But as the disease progresses they become increasingly abnormal in behavior and appearance. As well as proliferating out of control (usually rapidly) and invading adjacent tissues, cancers can spread to distant parts of the body. Breaking away from the primary growth, cells travel through the bloodstream, lymphatic vessels or body cavities, where they establish secondary tumors elsewhere. The whole process is known as metastasis.

Metastatic interference with essential organs and a draining of the body's vital resources are the reasons why cancers are sometimes fatal. But the disease can often be treated successfully – by surgery, irradiation, drugs, or any combination of these three. The chances are particularly good when cancer is detected before it has metastasized (which is the reason for regular screening using tests such at the cervical smear). Many patients are cured, and more than one in three survive five years or longer.

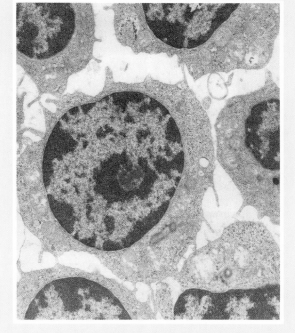

▲ The white blood cells of a patient with leukemia multiply quickly as the bone marrow and other tissues in which they are made become unusually active, and become destroyers, rather than defenders, of the body tissues.

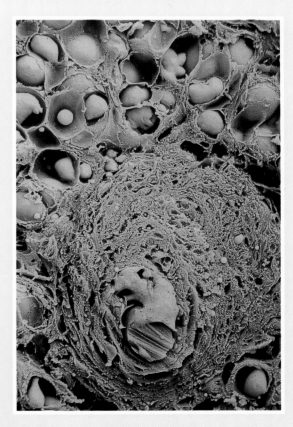

▲ A tumor in an ovary, with the normal tissues severely displaced by the growth; the Graafian follicle, consisting of a mature egg and its surrounding tissue, is visible towards the top of the picture.

The incidence of cancer

Some 5·9 million people develop cancer each year. The organs most commonly affected are the stomach (with 680,000 new cases annually), lung (590,000 new cases), breast (540,000), colon and rectum (510,000), cervix (460,000), mouth and pharynx (340,000), esophagus (300,000) and liver (260,000). About half these cancers, and over half the 4·3 million deaths each year, occur in the Third World: cancer is one of the three major causes of death after the age of five in developed and developing countries alike.

Whereas the mortality rate from stomach cancer is highest in Japan, liver cancer occurs mainly in tropical Africa, Southeast Asia and the western Pacific, with 40 percent of all new cases appearing in China. The picture changes dramatically with time too. In the United States between 1950 and 1980 the number of children under 15 dying of leukemia fell by 50 percent from 1965 onwards. Kidney cancer and other tumors declined by 68 percent. Lung cancer (70 percent of which is attributable to smoking) is becoming less prevalent in many Western countries – but it has been increasing among women, who were later than men in adopting the smoking habit, and is now rising quickly in the Third World.

Carcinogens of many kinds

Such trends reflect differences in the causation of cancers and/or their detection and treatment. Just as cancer itself is a collective term, so there are different factors which initiate malignancy. Thousands of chemicals are now known to be carcinogens: blue asbestos has been incriminated as a cause of the otherwise extremely rare mesothelioma, affecting membranes lining the body cavities. Toxins from the mold "Aspergillus flavus", which promote liver cancer in fish and turkeys, are also thought responsible for some human liver tumors in sub-Saharan Africa, and in part for the high rate of stomach cancer in Japan.

There is evidence linking breast and colon cancer with a high fat uptake, and some other dietary constituents, both natural and synthetic, have been under suspicion. Cancer-causing agents sometimes have a delayed-action effect, so it may be decades before the dangers of presently-used materials come to light. In addition to over 50,000 synthetic chemicals now being marketed, nearly a thousand new ones are introduced each year, some of which may prove to be long-term human carcinogens. In the mid-1960s the high-dose contraceptive pill was shown to cause inflammation of the cervix, which may be a precursor to cervical cancer. The introduction of low-dose pills overcame this problem, although it 1983 it was claimed that long-term users suffered a slightly higher risk of breast and cervical cancer.

Cancer of the esophagus exemplifies the multiple causes which can make the charting of the disease so hard. It is related to both tobacco and alcohol, and is 44 times more common among French people who smoke or drink heavily than those who indulge in moderation. But even higher rates are found in northeastern Iran, where both habits are rare – the cause seems to be shortage of Vitamin A.

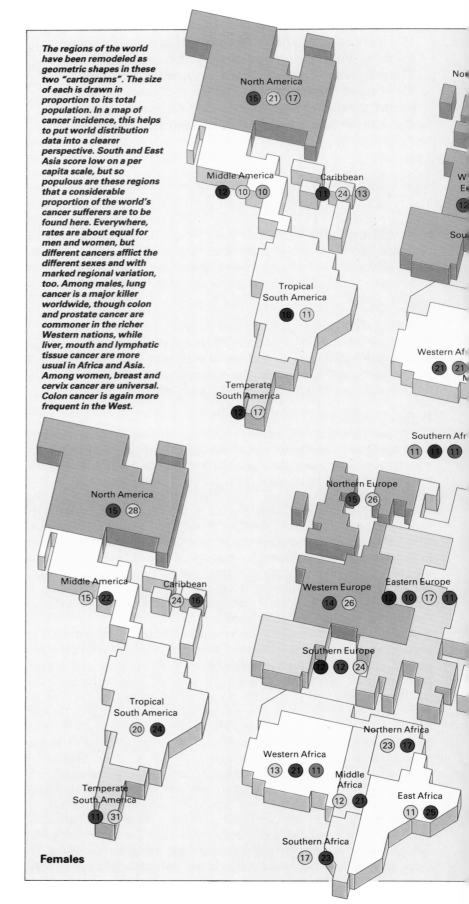

The regions of the world have been remodeled as geometric shapes in these two "cartograms". The size of each is drawn in proportion to its total population. In a map of cancer incidence, this helps to put world distribution data into a clearer perspective. South and East Asia score low on a per capita scale, but so populous are these regions that a considerable proportion of the world's cancer sufferers are to be found here. Everywhere, rates are about equal for men and women, but different cancers afflict the different sexes and with marked regional variation, too. Among males, lung cancer is a major killer worldwide, though colon and prostate cancer are commoner in the richer Western nations, while liver, mouth and lymphatic tissue cancer are more usual in Africa and Asia. Among women, breast and cervix cancer are universal. Colon cancer is again more frequent in the West.

Females

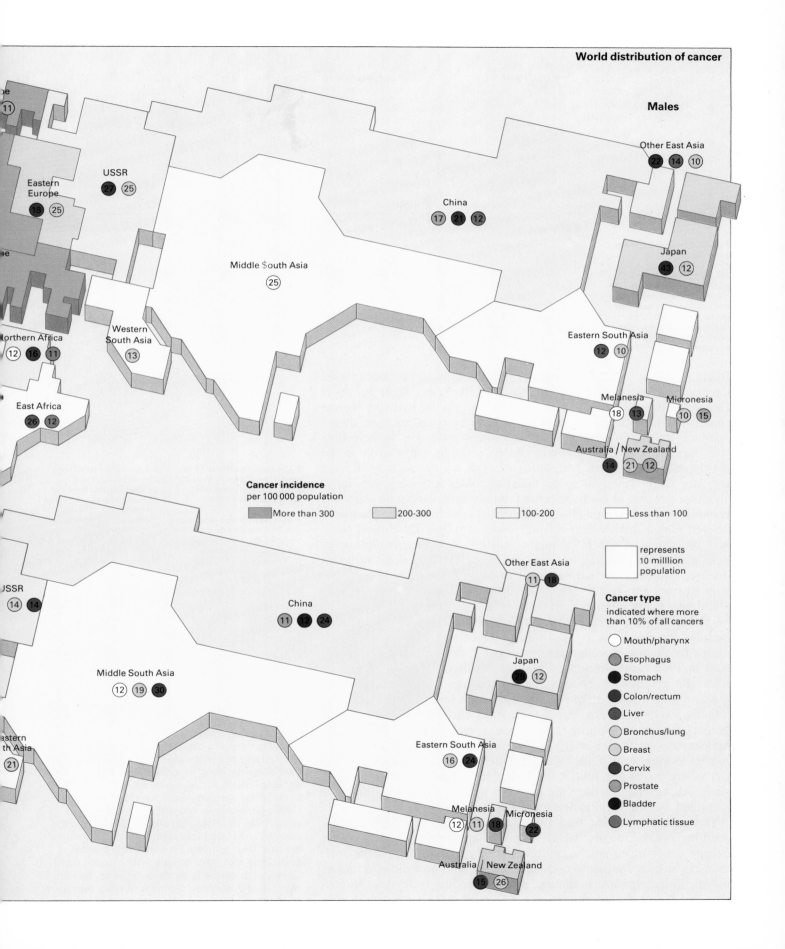

World distribution of cancer

Males

Other East Asia
(22) (14) (10)

USSR
(27) (25)

Eastern
Europe
(18) (25)

China
(17) (21) (12)

Japan
(43) (12)

Middle South Asia
(25)

Northern Africa
(12) (16) (11)

Western
South Asia
(13)

Eastern South Asia
(12) (10)

East Africa
(26) (12)

Melanesia
(18) (13)

Micronesia
(10) (15)

Australia / New Zealand
(14) (21) (12)

Cancer incidence
per 100 000 population

More than 300 | 200-300 | 100-200 | Less than 100

USSR
(14) (14)

Other East Asia
(11) (18)

China
(11) (12) (24)

represents
10 million
population

Cancer type
indicated where more
than 10% of all cancers

Middle South Asia
(12) (19) (30)

Japan
(39) (12)

○ Mouth/pharynx

● Esophagus

● Stomach

● Colon/rectum

● Liver

○ Bronchus/lung

○ Breast

● Cervix

● Prostate

● Bladder

● Lymphatic tissue

Western
South Asia
(21)

Eastern South Asia
(16) (24)

Melanesia
(12) (11) (18)

Micronesia
(22)

Australia / New Zealand
(15) (26)

Carcinogens have to "hit" specific genes in the body's cells to cause cancer

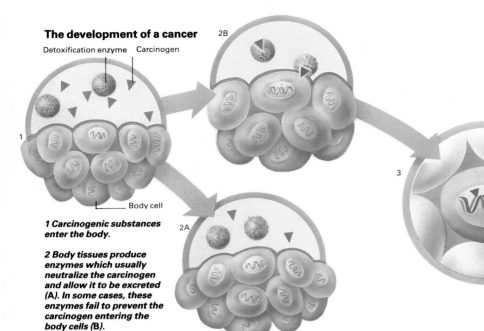

The development of a cancer

Detoxification enzyme   Carcinogen

Body cell

1 Carcinogenic substances enter the body.

2 Body tissues produce enzymes which usually neutralize the carcinogen and allow it to be excreted (A). In some cases, these enzymes fail to prevent the carcinogen entering the body cells (B).

DNA

Because viruses cause many tumors in other animals, biologists have long suspected that they do so in Man too. Ever since Dane Johannes Fibiger received a Nobel Prize in 1926 for proving that tiny worms caused stomach cancer in rats, there have been claims (not always justified) linking infectious organisms with the disease. Epstein-Barr (EB) virus, the agent of glandular fever, certainly plays a role in the development of African lymphoma, though it does so only if some ancillary factor (thought to be malaria) comes into play. Similarly, about 80 percent of liver cancer is strongly associated with the virus responsible for hepatitis B – prevalence of which partly explains the uneven global distribution of this cancer. In 1981 Dr Robert Gallo and colleagues at the US National Institutes of Health discovered what they called human T-cell leukemia virus in two patients with that disease. Unlike many similar finds in the past, further reserch has strengthened the link between this virus and cancer.

As with many other diseases whose relationship to HLA antigens has been uncovered recently, heredity also plays a role in cancer. Familial susceptibility is now known to be based on genes which makes us slightly more vulnerable to particular sorts of malignancy. And in 1960 came the first of a group of discoveries linking cancer with abnormalities in patients' chromosomes. Bone-marrow cells from an individual with chronic myelogenous leukemia proved to be missing a segment from one of their small chromosomes. About ten years later, new staining techniques revealed exactly what had happened – part of the DNA from chromosome number 22 had moved to number 9. Called the "Philadelphia chromosome" after the city where it was first found, this defect has been followed by several similar discoveries, raising the prospect that people at risk might be identified before their cancers develop.

During the early and mid 1980s, came a series of even more far-reaching breakthroughs, which began to answer two riddles. Why, despite exposure to potent carcinogens or radiation did people such as heavy smokers sometimes escape cancer? And how did aberrations like the Philadelphia chromosome actually produce the disease? Scientists had long believed that known causes of malignancy were really

3 The carcinogen may bind with several sites in the cell, notably with a particular site on the cell's DNA.

4 Normally the cell repairs the DNA without further problem (A); sometimes the cell reproduces and duplicates the DNA, thus creating a mutant gene (B).

5 A promotor substance may encourage the replication of the cells with the mutant gene over normal body cells; the carcinogen enters the body for a second time and again binds with the DNA causing a second mutation. It is this second mutation that makes the cell a cancer cell.

Can cancer be prevented?

Arguments about the degree to which cancer is preventable have become polarized in recent years. Some experts argue that because migrant populations tend to lose the cancer patterns characteristic of their native lands and acquire those of their new homes, most tumors are environmental in origin and thus avoidable. Opponents say that comparatively few causes of tumors are known for certain (although the elimination of smoking would certainly reduce lung cancer dramatically). Likewise, some dietary guidelines are uncontentious (such as reductions in smoked and pickled foods, linked with increased risks of stomach and esophagal cancer); others are debatable (such as curbs in fat consumption to diminish the dangers of colon and breast cancer). Others (for example, megadoses of vitamins to combat cancer in general) are challenged by most experts. The sharp increase in cervical cancer over the past three generations, paralleling greater sexual freedom, has encouraged the notion that "lifestyle" is the key to cancer avoidance. This is repudiated by those who see involuntary exposure to environmental carcinogens as more significant.

secondary agents, which initiated cancer only after scoring a certain number of hits on target genes. This hypothesis would explain the element of chance in the process, but was founded on little real evidence. The watershed in understanding began with the uncovering of "oncogenes". These are the genes which chemicals need to hit in order to produce tumors, and they are also those disrupted by chromosome abnormalities related to cancer. Suddenly, the once-confusing mosaic of cancer research began to be unified.

The key experiment, by Geoffrey Cooper at Harvard University and Robert Weinberg at the Massachusetts Institute of Technology, was to chop up human tumor-cell DNA into gene-sized fragments and feed them to normal mouse cells, which then became cancerous. When reisolated and identified, the oncogenes responsible proved familiar, having been extracted earlier from tumor viruses in animals. It seems that they were appropriated originally by the viruses from cells they infected. The specific difference between an oncogene and its normal counterpart has since been discerned by Weinberg and Mariano Barbacid at the US National Cancer Institute. They found that an oncogene was abnormal in the coding of just one of the units in its DNA. The result is that it produces a correspondingly abnormal protein, which presumably accounts for the conversion of a healthy cell into a malignant one. Researchers have since identified the same oncogene in lung and gut tumors that Weinberg and Barbacid found in bladder tumors. From studies on the rare childhood disease retinoblastoma, which develops when a particular gene stops working, it also seems that there may be other cancer-suppressing genes.

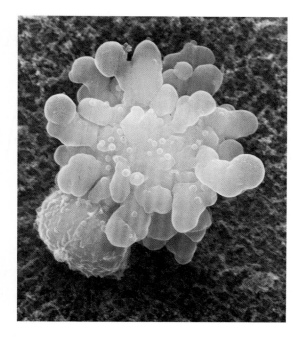

▲ *A cancer cell in the process of being destroyed by a white blood cell, at one of several stages at which the body may invoke its defenses to protect itself against the onset of cancer.*

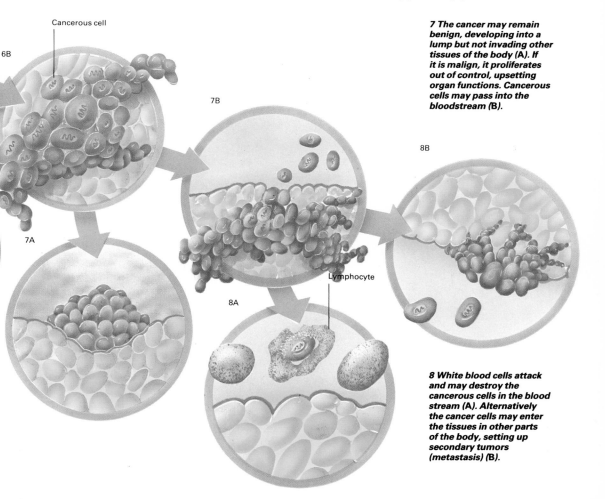

6 The normal cells release an inhibitor substance preventing the action of the promotor molecule and limiting the replication of the genes with mutated DNA (A). Otherwise they replicate wildly, causing a cancer to grow (B).

7 The cancer may remain benign, developing into a lump but not invading other tissues of the body (A). If it is malign, it proliferates out of control, upsetting organ functions. Cancerous cells may pass into the bloodstream (B).

8 White blood cells attack and may destroy the cancerous cells in the blood stream. Alternatively the cancer cells may enter the tissues in other parts of the body, setting up secondary tumors (metastasis) (B).

Promotor substance

Cancerous cell

Lymphocyte

People who give up smoking reduce the danger of lung cancer – until they begin again

The oncogene investigations, and related work with vaccines based on either cancer viruses or tumor "markers" which characterize malignant cells, could revolutionize cancer prevention over the next decade. The first hope is for immunization against liver cancer using hepatitis B vaccine. For the moment, the major strategies are avoidance of carcinogens and routine screening of high-risk groups for early signs of disease. Figures from Holland in 1984 confirmed a 50-70 percent reduction in mortality from breast cancer in women given regular physical examinations and mammography (an X-ray technique showing tumors not large enough to be felt). The Papanicolaou test, which identifies cancerous and pre-cancerous cells from a woman's cervix, is also effective in revealing a treatable but otherwise potentially fatal disease. At the other extreme, radiography has proved a disappointing tool in identifying lung cancer, which is often too advanced for effective therapy by the time it is detectable. Computer tomography (CT) and nuclear magnetic resonance (NMR) scanning should allow smaller cancers to be picked up earlier, and further improvements may come from using radioactively-labelled monoclonal antibodies to home in on a tumor, betraying its location.

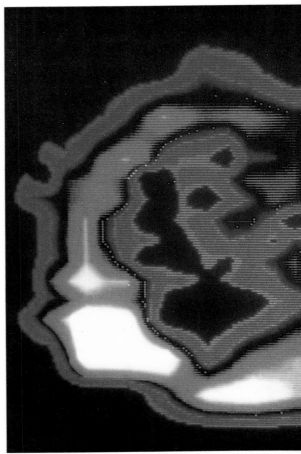

Tumor safaris in Africa

A classic of modern medical sleuthing was the paper by Denis Burkitt, an English surgeon working in Africa, which appeared in the British Journal of Surgery in 1958 and contained the first correct description of a cancer later known as African lymphoma. Burkitt's interest had been aroused by seeing characteristic jaw tumors in African children, often associated with tumors in other parts, which seemed to affect youngsters in a particular age bracket. Although clinicians had long classified these cancers according to the organ affected, Burkitt suspected that they had more in common than a typical primary tumor and its secondaries elsewhere. Intent on studying the natural history of the disease, he organized "tumor safaris" during which he examined hundreds of patients and discerned that the condition did indeed have a common cause and was confined to a warm, moist strip of Africa lying mostly between 10°N and 10°S of the Equator. This led to the idea that an insect might be transmitting a micro-organism responsible for "African lymphoma", and to the subsequent discovery of the Epstein-Barr virus which is now heavily implicated as its cause.

◄ *Percival Pott (1713-1788) produced a pioneering study of cancers in 1775, when he observed the high incidence of a cancer of the scrotal skin among chimney sweeps. He was able to relate this to the particular cause of the contamination: a chemical in the soot affecting the skin of the boys who climbed chimneys.*

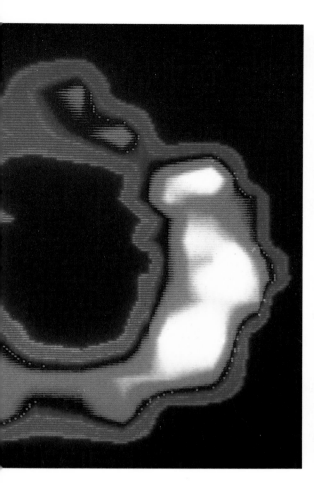

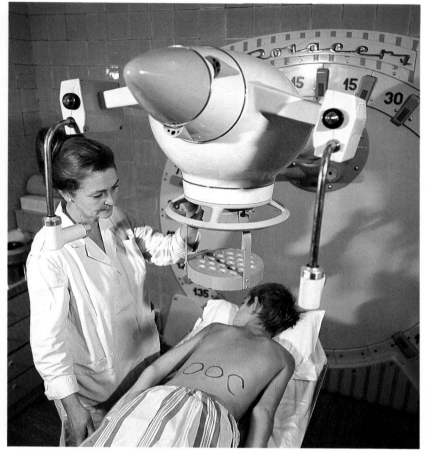

▲ *Oat cell cancer of the lung (shown here in the left lung by NMR) is one of the commonest and deadliest cancers, killing almost all victims within two years. Its name reflects differences between it and other cancer cells under the microscope. The cells secrete hormones, causing some patients to develop Cushing's syndrome.*

Smoking and lung cancer

To establish cause and effect in medicine can be a harder task than it seems, as shown by disputations about the link between smoking and lung cancer. During the first half of this century, physicians noticed that people who smoked cigarettes heavily appeared more likely to develop the disease than those who smoked little or not at all. The common-sense conclusion was clear. But it could have been utterly wrong; perhaps the smoking habit and a propensity to develop lung cancer resulted from a third, inbred factor. If this were true, anti-tobacco propaganda would have been both ill-founded and ineffective. It took meticulous studies by British epidemiologists Richard Doll, Austin Bradford Hill and others during the 1950s before the "obvious" conclusion was accepted. One of their key findings was that smokers who gave up the habit thereby reduced their risk of contracting lung cancer. This evidence, virtually impossible to square with alternative explanations of the association between smoking and disease, clinched the argument, although the tobacco companies continued to argue that no direct link between smoking and lung cancer had ever been demonstrated.

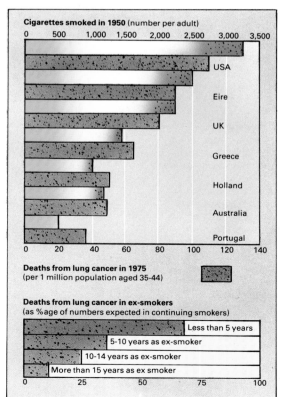

Cigarettes smoked in 1950 (number per adult)

| 0 | 500 | 1,000 | 1,500 | 2,000 | 2,500 | 3,000 | 3,500 |

USA
Eire
UK
Greece
Holland
Australia
Portugal

| 0 | 20 | 40 | 60 | 80 | 100 | 120 | 140 |

Deaths from lung cancer in 1975
(per 1 million population aged 35-44)

Deaths from lung cancer in ex-smokers
(as %age of numbers expected in continuing smokers)

Less than 5 years
5-10 years as ex-smoker
10-14 years as ex-smoker
More than 15 years as ex smoker

| 0 | 25 | 50 | 75 | 100 |

▲ *Screens of X-rays and other forms of radiation, focused onto cancer tissue, are the basis of radio-therapy. Although cells near the tumor may be harmed too, they are usually able to repair the damage. Modern machines allow millions of electron volts to be targeted deep inside the body, without causing the skin reactions associated with earlier, lower voltage treatment. Some cancers, particularly those of varied cell types, are relatively resistant to radiation.*

◄*The link between smoking and lung cancer has been demonstrated statistically, and it is now clear that cigarette smoke contains many different carcinogens. Low-tar cigarettes can reduce the danger of contracting lung cancer, but it remains true that 25 percent of all regular smokers will die killed before their time by the habit.*

See also
The Body's Defenses 89-96
Hazards and Poisons 109-16
Diverse Infections 117-24

Modern methods of treating tumors

The three main weapons in the modern armory for the treatment of cancer are surgery, chemotherapy and radiotherapy. For treatment to be entirely successful it must obliterate all cancer cells if the disease is not to recur. Operations vary in scale, as with the alternatives of mastectomy (removal of the entire breast) or lumpectomy (removal only of the cancerous lump) for breast cancer, and surgery may be augmented by the other therapies. Drugs alone usually produce "remissions", particularly when used in combination. They can completely cure African lymphoma, Hodgkin's disease, choriocarcinoma and certain childhood leukemias, though some cause side-effects such as hair loss because they interfere with normal as well as malignant tissues. Interferon, now made by genetic engineering, could prove a more potent and safer weapon in future. X-ray, neutron and other beams of radiation, which at low levels *cause* cancer, also destroy malignant cells. The latest machines allow huge doses to be directed to deep-seated tumors without destroying the surrounding tissues. Warming patients up to around 42°C while under general anesthetic is another promising therapy, because cancer cells are particularly sensitive to heat.

Improving one's chances of surviving

While disagreements persist about the roles of external and internal factors in producing cancer, few specialists dispute the emerging view that a patient's state of mind can have a decisive effect on the outcome of malignant disease. Steven Greer, at King's College Hospital, London, has found that women treated for breast cancer are more likely to have a favorable outcome if they react to their illness either by showing a fighting spirit or by denying their diagnosis, than if they respond with stoic acceptance or with feelings of helplessness and hopelessness. He believes the mind may affect the body by impairing the immune system – which, as well as manufacturing antibodies to defeat infection, also helps to rid the body of tumor cells. Support for this thesis comes from research in America showing that antibody production is often reduced in efficiency after personal tragedies such as bereavement.

Tumors and chemotherapy

Cure
Childhood lymphoblastic leukemia
Burkitt's lymphoma
Wilm's tumor
Choriocarcinoma
Hodgkin's disease
Testicular teratoma

Palliation
Breast cancer
Many lymphomas
Chronic leukemia
Myeloma

Symptom relief
Squamous cell
  head and neck cancer
Oat-cell lung cancer
Adult leukemia
Ovarian cancer

Little benefit
Lung cancer
Renal cancer
Pancreatic cancer
Colo-rectal cancer
Gastric cancer
Melanoma

► *Chemotherapy, usually involving a combination of several drugs, can prove effective against many forms of cancer, either as the sole treatment or with other forms of therapy.*

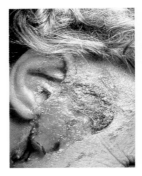
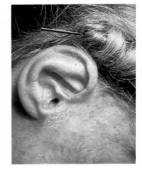

▲ *A squamous-cell carcinoma, before and after radiotherapy. The radiation is aimed to destroy the cancerous tissues.*

Other cures for cancer?

Cancer has been tenuously linked to mind-induced diseases. But more than any other disease, it has been the subject of unorthodox therapeutic claims, with innumerable, plausible but eventually useless remedies on offer.

One which enjoyed considerable fame during the 1970s was laetrile, usually administered in the form of bitter almonds. A combination of folklore, a feeling that in a desperate situation anything is worth trying, and pressure from practitioners of "alternative medicine" aroused sufficient interest among American politicians to persuade over half the states to legalize laetrile therapy. Eventually in a decisive study, 178 cancer patients were given the material and their progress monitored. The results, published in 1982, showed "no substantive benefit in terms of cure, improvement, or stabilization of cancer, improvement of symptoms related to cancer, or extension of life span." But laetrile was found to be dangerous – because its active ingredient releases cyanide.

Acute lymphatic leukemia 0-14 years
4%
50%

Hodgkin's disease 0-14 years
39%
80%

Wilm's tumor 0-14 years
32%
70%

Testicular tumors All ages
50%
85%

Choriocarcinoma
10%
90%

Late 1950s   Mid 1970s   Late 1970s

◄ *The five-year survival rate for cancer patients has improved significantly in the past 30 years thanks to earlier diagnosis and a wider range of effective treatment. Whereas only a tiny percentage of sufferers survived some childhood leukemias in the 1950s, the chances of survival today are 50 percent or more.*

How allergies occur...Wasp and bee stings...
Rheumatoid arthritis...Autoimmune diseases...Immune
deficiences in childhood...AIDS...PERSPECTIVE...Food
allergies... "Total" allergies?

For about one person in every two hundred an insect sting is not a minor inconvenience, but a life-threatening event that produces anaphylactic shock – breathing becomes difficult and irregular, rashes suddenly appear and the subject may collapse and die within minutes. Between 50 and 100 deaths from this cause are reported annually in the USA. Other people – about one in ten – suffer in a more limited way. Their hypersensitivity is localized, generally in areas which produce mucosal fluids – the eyes, nose and throat. Asthma, a disease characterized by constriction of the airways, and hay fever can both be caused by allergens such as pollen and the feces of house dust mites. Both types of response are caused by over-reaction of the specific immune system (◀ page 89).

The same type of over-reaction can also be localized on the skin, causing rashes and swellings. Because of the way in which the immune system works, the first exposure to allergen causes no unpleasant reaction. But it sets in motion the production of antibodies specific to that substance.

Anaphylactic shock and allergic reactions are caused by the class of antibodies known as immunoglobulin E (◀ page 92) bound to a particular type of cell, called a mast cell. When immunoglobulin E reacts with an antigen, it activates the mast cell to release inflammatory substances, such as histamine and leukotrienes, which produce the unpleasant effects associated with allergy. In a normal way these substances are part of the body's defenses against invasion; in the case of an allergic reaction they are released in large amounts in response to miniscule amounts of the allergen.

Allergic-type reactions can occur without involving the immune system. Wasp and bee stings contain substances that act in the same way as those released by mast cells, and so cause irritant swellings even in those whose immune system is not sensitized to antigens in the sting. Jellyfish tentacles and some foods, such as strawberries and fish which is not fresh, contain histamine or closely-related substances. These are known to cause both irritant rashes and asthmatic attacks.

Atopic individuals – those who suffer from allergies – are often allergic to many substances. They can reduce the effects of allergy by avoiding those substances to which they are most sensitive. Prick tests are used to measure susceptibility. In these, a small quantity of a suspected allergen is inserted just beneath the skin and the strength of the subsequent reaction monitored.

Some allergies can be cured by repeated doses of an allergen, in increasing amounts. The course of treatment is usually long and there is a remote danger of anaphylaxis. In other cases, allergies may disappear spontaneously. Some childhood ailments, such as infantile eczema, fall into this category.

The origin of an allergy

▼ An allergic reaction results when the immune system has made antibodies to a certain substance or allergen. These antibodies attach to "mast-cells" in the body tissues: when the allergen returns, even in tiny quantities, the mast cells release histamine, causing inflammation.

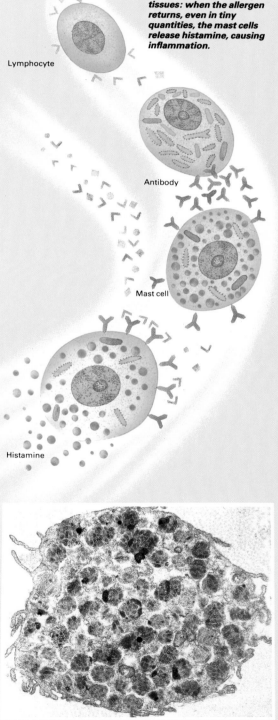

Allergens

Lymphocyte

Antibody

Mast cell

Histamine

▲ A mast cell containing granules of histamine and heparin.

Destructive complexes

The immune system can also cause illness when circulating antibodies form insoluble complexes with antigens. The harm depends on where these complexes are deposited, as neighboring tissues can be damaged by the phagocytic response. In systemic lupus erythematosus (SLE), antibodies to nucleic acids are produced. These frequently form complexes which deposit in the central nervous system and kidneys, which are subsequently damaged.

Antibody-antigen complexes also play a part in rheumatoid arthritis, which usually affects joints but may be found in organs such as heart, lungs and nervous system (◀ page 37). Deposition of the complexes in the synovial membranes leads to inflamed joints as a result of complementary activation by the immunoglobulin G responsible. Both SLE and rheumatoid arthritis are autoimmune diseases, in which the antigens are part of the sufferer's "self" and should be tolerated by his or her immune system but are not. The precise agent of rheumatoid arthritis is still not known, but it has been suggested that a virus, as yet unidentified, is involved.

High concentrations of antigens from an external source can also trigger diseases of this type. Farmer's lung, for example, is produced by breathing in spores from moldy grain; these cause antibody-antigen complexes to deposit in the lung, where the tissue is subsequently damaged. In some other diseases, including leprosy, viral hepatitis and quartan malaria, some of the harmful effects may be caused by immune complex deposition.

Circulating antibodies can also cause tissue damage by reacting with an antigen on a cell surface. Some drugs, including penicillin, may bind to cell-surface protein to create a new antigenic determinant (small molecules that do this are called haptens) which the body does not recognize as self. The result can be destruction of tissues, such as red blood cells. A similar type of immune defect which used to occur commonly was rhesus babies (◀ page 77).

Tissue damage may also result from the activation of T-lymphocytes. Contact dermatitis can occur in various occupations, following exposure to metals (particularly platinum) and other industrial materials. It may be produced also by cosmetics and topically applied drugs. The dermatitic agent acts as a hapten. T-cells are attracted to the site and release lymphokines. These attract phagocytes which release hydrolytic (digestive) enzymes; it is these enzymes that then damage surrounding tissue.

Cases of mistaken identity

Immune disease can arise through mistakes in the immune system's recognition process. A particular type of streptococcal infection, which causes sore throats, occasionally also provokes rheumatic fever which may damage the heart. This occurs because the cell wall of the relevant micro-organism shares antigenic determinants with the surface of the heart muscle. The infection consequently produces large quantities of antibody which contravene the immune system's self-tolerance and attack the heart muscle, most frequently causing scarring of valve tissue. As rheumatic fever develops only if the streptococcal infection is left untreated, the rise of antibiotic treatment in developed countries has led to a reduction in its incidence. Ulcerative colitis (◀ page 45) is thought to be a similar disease. Exposure to intestinal bacteria produces cross-reacting antigens which trigger autoimmune attack on the colonic mucosa.

Asthma

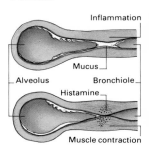

Inflammation

Mucus

Alveolus

Bronchiole

Histamine

Muscle contraction

▲ ► *An inhaler reduces the inflammation of the bronchi which causes asthmatic breathlessness.*

▲ ► *Two of the wide variety of pollens which are frequent causes of the common allergic reaction known as hay fever. Cornflower (above) and hollyhock (right) pollen, here magnified some 1,000 times.*

▲ *House-dust with pollen grains, fibers and soot particles; the feces of dust mites are often allergenic.*

► *The Portuguese man o' war ("Physalia utriculis"), uses histamine as a poison with which to sting its prey.*

Food allergies or food intolerance?

Behavior and physical condition may be affected dramatically by "food allergy". Many studies have tried to show that hyperactivity and emotional disturbance in children are a result too.

"Allergy" strictly refers to ailments involving only an immune response. Food allergies do exist; proteins in cows' milk are probably the most frequent cause. Even in breast-fed babies, such an allergy may show up if the mother drinks milk. True allergies can also develop to carbohydrates and proteins in such foods as fish and cereals.

When tests show no immune reaction to a specific food, but the food nevertheless causes bad effects, it is known as "food intolerance". Migraine attacks can result from specific foods, chocolate for example, containing substances related to psycho-active chemicals in humans. This is a toxic rather than an allergic reaction.

It has been claimed that food intolerance is caused by food processing and artificial additives. Some synthetic colorants can produce an immune response by combining with protein to form new antigenic determinants. However, in many cases, processed foods are likely to be less allergenic than unrefined foods, because processing reduces the number of protein and carbohydrate types.

An extension of the idea that the modern treatment of food makes it harmful, is "total allergy syndrome". Sufferers are said to develop allergy or intolerance to an increasing number of modern materials, as well as to both polluted air and tapwater. Ultimately, they live in increasing isolation from the outside world. The underlying cause remains unidentified. Some immunologists are even sceptical about its reality, arguing that the symptoms are psychological in origin.

◄ **David, an American boy with severe combined immune deficiency (SCID), spent his life in a sterile "bubble" which protected him from bacteria and viruses. Untreated sufferers usually die by the age of 2. Low numbers of T-lymphocytes are produced, and immunoglobulins do not function as antibodies. SCID can be treated with bone marrow grafts.**

Immune deficiencies

In addition to over-reaction, the immune system can cause disease through deficiency. The most common form is deficiency of immunoglobulin A, found in mucosal tissue, which provides a line of defense against invasion. Sufferers are prone to repeated mild respiratory infections. Infantile eczema may also result.

Less frequent, but sometimes more serious, are diseases in which immunoglobulin G levels are low. In some babies they are slow to start, and infections, especially respiratory diseases, increase in the period between the baby using up reserves from its mother and developing its own. Far more serious is X-linked infantile agammaglobulinemia. Immunoglobulin G is very low and all other immunoglobulins are absent. A genetically-determined disease, it affects only males, who usually die from infection as children.

No treatment has yet been devised for the seemingly new immune deficiency disease, acquired immune deficiency syndrome (AIDS), which appeared in the USA in 1979/80 (◀ page 86). It is caused by a virus which attacks T-lymphocytes. Characterized by a drastic loss of natural immunity, it is usually fatal.

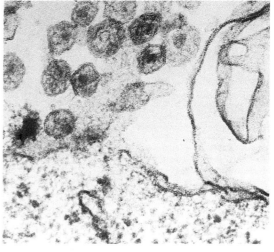

▲ **Acquired immune deficiency syndrome (AIDS) is caused by the virus HTLV-III, (human T-lymphotropic virus III), shown in this electron micrograph.**

The body's internal environment...External threats to internal balance...Poisons and their effects... Homeostasis hazards...Radiation...Natural poisons... The liver and poisons...Alcohol...PERSPECTIVE...Smog... Metal poisons

The human body's complex set of interrelated chemical reactions is viable only within a narrow range of physical conditions. Two of the basics of civilization – clothing and shelter – have developed in order to help us stay within these limits despite variations in the evironment itself. We cannot stand being too hot or too cold, too "hydrated" or too dehydrated; nor can we endure a serious change in the chemical composition of the air we breathe or in the amount of exposure to radiation and electrical charge – both natural and artificial.

Homeostasis is the mechanism that keeps the internal environment of the organism stable, but it cannot always succeed. A rise in external temperature, for example, triggers heat receptors in the skin which cause vasodilation and sweating. The former cools the body provided that the skin's temperature is at least 1°C less than the internal, or core, temperature. If the external temperature is too high for this difference to be maintained, the only available means of cooling the body is sweating, in which the energy used to evaporate water has a cooling effect.

The effects of poisons

A poison is a substance which harms a living organism. Almost any substance, including water, is poisonous if administered in sufficient quantity, though most substances commonly classed as poisons produce a harmful effect in small doses.

If a single dose of a substance causes harm, it is an acute poison. Swallowing less than a quarter of a gram of potassium cyanide will kill most people within a few minutes. On the other hand, chronic poisoning is caused by long exposure to small concentrations of a substance. Liver damage produced by high alcohol consumption over a decade or more is an example of chronic poisoning.

Poisons work in different ways. A common effect is to interfere with the activity of one or more enzymes, which act as catalysts and promote the body's normal metabolism. Many toxic metals bind with an enzyme and alter its molecular structure, preventing it from working. Some enzymes require a particular metal atom for their activity. If this becomes linked to another substance, such as cyanide, or is replaced by a different metal atom, the enzyme can be inactivated. Alternatively, the poison may compete with the enzyme's natural substrate (the substance which it changes), and thus disrupt a metabolic process. Carbon monoxide (CO), on the other hand, competes with oxygen for binding sites on the hemoglobin molecule, thus preventing the oxygen reaching the body tissues. Other poisons attack and interfere with particular cells – digitalis (◀ page 60) makes the heart muscle work faster, neurotoxins interfere with nerve impulse transmission and cytotoxins (◀ page 104) kill cells which are dividing by interfering with nucleic acid synthesis.

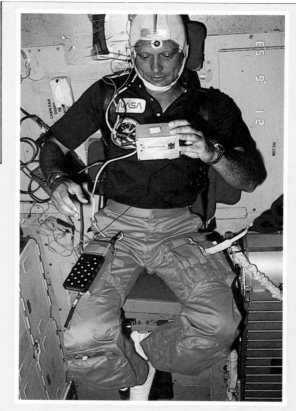

▲ *In addition to motion sickness, the harmful effects of weightlessness suffered by astronauts include loss of strength in muscles, breakdown of red blood cells, a shift of blood from legs to the head, and loss of calcium from bones.*

Skin temperature

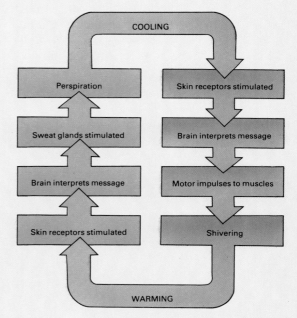

COOLING

Perspiration	Skin receptors stimulated
Sweat glands stimulated	Brain interprets message
Brain interprets message	Motor impulses to muscles
Skin receptors stimulated	Shivering

WARMING

▲ *The body maintains its temperature by protective action whenever the skin temperature rises or falls beyond acceptable limits. If the environment is too extreme for these mechanisms to cope, internal distress results.*

The body is finely tuned to respond to external threats to its internal balance

◄ Usually, it takes many hours exposure to heat before the core temperature rises to a dangerous level. This induces heat stroke. Characterized by mental confusion, heat stroke can also be brought on by exercise in temperatures near normal body heat. Heat may also cause salt loss and dehydration.

The body tends to be more tolerant of cold than of heat, depending on how fat a person is. A drop in skin temperature of more than 4°C below normal induces vasoconstriction and shivering. These prevent further heat loss, and the muscle activity of shivering generates more heat. Fat people can tolerate a skin temperature as low as 12°C. If the core temperature drops by only 2°C, however, the body can no longer warm itself by internal activity and hypothermia results.

As the core temperature drops, hemoglobin becomes less efficient at releasing oxygen. This can cause cardiac arrhythmias (◀ page 60) and cerebral disturbances. Hypothermia can occur as a result of living in cold surroundings, coupled with some other factor such as alcohol or barbiturate consumption, or malnutrition.

A combination of cold and pressure (from tight clothing, for instance) can cause minor damage in the form of chilblains. Extended cooling of parts of the body below 12°C can lead to more permanent damage even if no freezing occurs. Frostbite only develops if the cell fluid freezes, though it is only a portion of the fluid that usually freezes.

Temperature control is essential in the maintenance of homeostasis. The body is heated by vasoconstriction, adrenal and thyroid hormones which boost the metabolic activity of the cells, and activity of the skeletal muscles, and cooled by vasodilation and sweating. Core temperatures above or below normal may disrupt cell proteins, and affect the body's fluid electrolyte balance. As well as heat stroke, a condition in which brain cells may be quickly destroyed, overheating may lead to heat exhaustion, in which there is heavy perspiration but the heart beat is weakened.

The metabolic balance of the body comprises the chemical reactions of both breaking down food (catabolism) and reconstituting the elements into the proteins required by the body (anabolism). The body requires a balance of protein, glucose and lipids in the bloodstream, and these are affected by the food intake and hormones, such as insulin, which affect the deposition of fat and activity of the liver. Metabolic activity affects the temperature balance of the body, burning excess glucose as fuel, and allowing the body to create layers of fat to protect against cold.

◄ The body may be poisoned by tiny quantities of some materials, or by gross overconsumption of a single food that, in normal quantities, might be nutritious. In extreme circumstances, the stomach rejects the food by vomiting; otherwise absorbed nutrients are oxidized, stored or converted, assuming vitamins and enzymes are available. The rise of obesity, diabetes and other dietary "diseases of civilization" are the result of the longterm failure of the body to maintain metabolic homeostasis. Other metabolic imbalances include phenylketonuria (◀ page 80), cystic fibrosis (in which vitamin absorption is inadequate), coeliac disease and protein-energy malnutrition.

► Divers surfacing too quickly may suffer from decompression sickness or bends – nitrogen bubbles form in the bloodstream, cutting the oxygen supply to the body tissues. Similarly, climbers at very high altitudes without extra oxygen deprive their body tissues of the gas and raise acid levels.

The acid-base balance of the body is related to the level of hydrogen ions in the extracellular fluid. This in turn is related to the level of carbon dioxide in the blood, since an increase in CO_2 levels raises the acidity of the blood. Detectors in the carotid artery are linked to the inspiratory center of the brain, thus ensuring the body breathes in fresh oxygen when it is underventilated; hyperventilation makes the body more alkaline. The kidney is responsible for the maintenance of the acid-base balance, by excreting uric acid from the blood. The stomach's acid level may also affect blood acid level.

The fluid-electrolyte balance between the intracellular and extracellular fluids is crucial to ensuring that the cells do not become waterlogged or dried up. Two-thirds of the body's fluid is in the cells, and this moves through the membranes by osmosis. The concentration of salts and other solutes – mostly in the form of electrolytes – is therefore critical. The balance is affected by the level of excretion of fluids in urine or sweat, and by the freezing of the intracellular fluid; this may cause frostbite by raising the salt concentration in the remaining fluid, and thus damaging cell proteins.

Death by drowning occurs less quickly in cold rather than warm water; cooling slows body chemistry, so survival times increase. Children have been resuscitated as long as 30 minutes after drowning in cold water and ceasing to breathe, without suffering brain damage. Cell liquids cannot freeze, if immersed in very cold fresh water, as the salts in the cell make its freezing point lower than that of pure water. The concentration of salt in the sea, however, is greater than in the body, so seawater remains liquid at a lower temperature than the cell liquids.

Cardiac arrest is a major cause of death by electrocution. Many bodily processes depend on ionic impulses, and these can be disrupted by electric shock. The extent of disruption depends on many factors, including the voltage and amperage of the shock, the site of contact and the resistance of the skin. The effects are not always immediate. In some people who have survived electric shocks to the head or neck, cataracts of the eye have developed up to three years afterwards. Because the skin has a higher electrical resistance than soft tissues, a shock may cause damage even when the skin appears to be intact.

► Inhalation of seawater leads to uptake of calcium and magnesium ions by the bloodstream; these then cause cardiac arrest. Fresh-water inhalation causes hemolysis; it also upsets the fluid-electrolyte balance and affects the potassium ion balance in the blood-stream. This can induce fibrillation and death.

We are continually exposed to radiation from naturally-occurring radioactive substances in the environment

▲ *After 10 years, a resident returns to the Marshall Islands – site of US atomic tests.*

Radiation from Sun, Earth and nuclear technology

Non-ionizing radiation includes ultraviolet rays, a component of sunlight which can release energy on the skin and cause sunburn (◀ page 42). The effects of this are well documented. Other forms of non-ionizing radiation, such as high frequency radiowaves, may also be harmful, but the evidence is unclear and not widely accepted.

Ionizing radiation includes the X-rays, gamma-rays, and the alpha- and beta-particles emitted by radioactive substances. This dissipates its energy by knocking electrons out of molecules, thus converting them to ions. In the case of complex biological molecules, this can destroy their function.

There has been much debate in recent years about the safe level of ionizing radiation; this debate has mostly been conducted in connection with the development of nuclear power. Even without nuclear power, we are continually exposed to radiation from space and from naturally-occurring radioactive substances in the environment. In some places, such as parts of Scotland, the major exposure comes from living or working in buildings of granite.

The biological effectiveness of absorbed ionizing radiation is measured in Sieverts (Sv), of which ten at once constitute a lethal dose. The International Committee on Radiological Protection has set some 50mSv (milliSieverts) per year as the maximum safe level for radiation workers. Annual average radiation exposure in Britain and the United States is less than 2mSv, of which more than 50 percent is natural background radiation. Medical sources such as X-rays and radio-isotopes account for most of the rest.

The only likelihood of critical exposure to ionizing radiation comes from nuclear accident or war. An acute dose of 1Sv causes some signs of radiation sickness, including nausea and a drop in lymphocyte numbers (◀ page 89). It may also increase the risk of leukemia and solid tumors in the long term. A 10Sv dose of radiation causes vomiting and diarrhea; death is almost inevitable within a month of exposure. A major effect of this size of dose is to damage the lining of the small intestine and the stem cells from which it is normally replaced. As a result, the intestinal wall becomes smooth. Its surface area and, consequently, its ability to absorb nutrients are much reduced. Lesions occur and intestinal contents mix with the bloodstream, leading to infection and loss of body fluids.

▲ *A factory chimney in the Alps: as well as smog, such chimney emissions of sulfur oxides may cause sulfuric acid to form in the clouds, devastating crops when it falls as "acid" rain, often many hundreds of kilometers away.*

▲ *The "peasouper" fogs of London, such as those of 1952 and 1956, became a thing of the past when a Clean Air Act was passed in 1956 and restrictions were placed on the smoke output of domestic fires and factories.*

Smog now and then

In December 1952, London was enveloped in thick
fog. In the week ending 13 December, 2,851 excess
deaths were reported. Subsequently a further 1,224
deaths were attributed to this unusual combination
of air pollution and weather conditions.

At the time, much domestic heating in Britain
was by coal fire and the atmosphere was laden
with particulate material and gaseous pollutants,
including carbon and sulfur oxides. Cold air moving
in from continental Europe trapped the pollution,
which condensed in the atmospheric moisture to
form a mixture of smoke and fog called smog.
The deaths caused by it were mainly in elderly
people who succumbed to respiratory complaints
such as bronchitis.

More recently, a different type of smog has
caused problems in Los Angeles and other US
cities. In this case, the pollution arises from
automobiles and the smog is created by the action
of sunlight on reactive components in their exhaust
gases. A characteristic component of this type of
smog is peroxyacyl nitrate, which causes eye
irritation as well as respiratory problems.

Air pollution may cause or aggravate disease. It
can occur naturally, but is mostly associated with
industrial activity. In addition to large quantities
of particulate matter, volcanic eruptions throw out
poisonous materials, such as sulfur dioxide,
cyanides and fluorides.

► *Several tons of methyl isocyanate escaped into the air
from Union Carbide's pesticide plant in Bhopal, India, on 2
December 1984, killing over 2,200 people and affecting the
lives of 50,000 others, many with serious eye injuries.*

▲ *Poisonous snakes have enlarged, hollow front teeth which puncture the skin and through which venom is injected from a venom sac in the snake's head. It may be possible to ingest snake venom safely, provided the skin is not punctured. This street performer in South Africa puts poisonous snakes in his mouth and completes his act by eating a live puff adder.*

▼ *It is with the larger fungi that we most commonly associate natural poisoning. Many fatalities are caused by mistaking Amanita phalloides, shown here, for the edible field mushroom. This fungus contains very toxic peptides which inhibit an enzyme involved in RNA production, thus destroying the normal functioning of the body cells.*

Natural poisons

Many plants and animals defend themselves against predators by the use of poisons. Thousands of deaths are caused each year by snakebites, with cobras, rattlesnakes, puff adders, carpet vipers and Russell's vipers being among the most freqent attackers.

Snakes attack only if provoked, although in some cases the provocation need only be slight disturbance. The venoms are complex mixtures, but the major active components are usually toxic peptides, non-toxic proteins and enzymes. All three may cause damage by stimulating an immune response (◀ page 89). The toxic peptides often interfere with nerve cell transmission, while the enzymes can damage cells near the site of the bite as well as breaking down some blood components.

Illness can be caused by ingesting toxins from fish. The puffer fish, considered a delicacy in Japan, where it is called fugu, can contain a potent neurotoxin, tetrodotoxin. Paralytic shellfish poisoning is caused by eating shellfish which themselves have eaten toxin-containing micro-organisms.

Neurotoxins are found in some other foods as a result of microbial activity. Botulism is a form of paralysis caused by botulinus toxin, a poison produced by the anaerobic micro-organism, *Clostridium botulinum*. This substance, a protein, is inactivated by heating. Cases of botulinus poisoning usually result from eating smoked, canned or fermented foods which are not heated before consumption. The micro-organism spores are heat-resistant and survive processing, thus allowing growth and toxin formation in the product during storage.

A more commmon and less severe form of food poisoning is caused by staphylococci, notably *S. aureus*. This grows particularly well in protein-rich foods held at room temperature and produces a toxin that causes severe vomiting. It is found where hygiene conditions in food preparation are unsatisfactory. Recovery is usual within two or three days, although the poison can cause death through shock.

Molds growing on plants can also cause food poisoning. Aflatoxin, produced by a mold which grows on ground nuts, may be responsible for the relatively high incidence of liver cancer in parts of Africa where these nuts form a significant part of the diet.

▲ Crop spraying with pesticides or weedkillers may leave traces of poisons in the crop which remain in the food. The insecticide DDT was banned in many countries when it was found to accumulate in the food chain; but many chemicals, even in minute traces, are suspected of acting as carcinogens; others are feared to cause cumulative nervous system damage, particularly in agricultural workers.

◄ One variety of puffer fish is called fugu by the Japanese. Although it is considered a fine food, fugu can seriously damage the nervous system.

Metal poisoning

Many metals can be poisonous, although their effect frequently depends on the way in which they are taken into the body. Some metals bind strongly to foodstuffs which hinder their absorption and reduce their effective toxicity. Similarly, different salts of a metal can have widely varying solubilities which affect their absorption.

Lead is probably the best-studied metal from a toxicological viewpoint. It has been suggested that the decline of the Roman Empire was caused by chronic poisoning from lead water pipes and storage tanks. Recently, concern has centered on the effect of airborne lead from automobile exhausts. In many countries, tetraethyl lead is added to gasoline to improve its performance. In the engine this is converted to an inorganic lead salt which may be inhaled. One toxic effect of lead is to attack the central nervous system. Children may be particularly prone to such attack and suggestions that chronic exposure to low levels of lead cause mental retardation have encouraged governments to restrict the use of lead in gasoline.

The striking difference in toxicity between some metals and their compounds is shown by mercury. This liquid metal is widely used in industry, and some escapes into the environment where micro-organisms can convert it to methylmercury. Like tetraethyl lead, it is an organo-metallic compound, and as such is more readily taken up by biological systems. If ingested, nearly all of it is absorbed by the gastro-intestinal tract, while less than 0·01 percent of metallic mercury is absorbed in this way.

Cadmium is also widely used in industry and has led to occupational poisoning, through inhalation of cadmium fumes. The metal is found in ores which also contain lead and zinc and the three metals are usually purified in a single refinery. Itai-itai ("ouch ouch") disease, characterized by severe arthritic pain, was first diagnosed in Japan in the late 1940s among elderly people who had eaten rice grown in water containing effluent from a smelter. It has since been suggested that people who eat vegetables from cadmium-rich soils for many years may suffer chronic effects, including high blood pressure.

The main organ for detoxification is the liver. If a poison is absorbed via the stomach or intestine, then it passes through the liver. If absorbed via the mouth or injected directly into the bloodstream, it can avoid the liver and may have a greater effect. The liver contains a large number of enzymes that react with foreign substances and make them less toxic. Often this is done by converting them into substances which are more water-soluble and thus more readily excreted.

Equal doses of a poison may affect two people quite differently. This depends in part on the means and rate of absorption of the poison. It can also depend on other substances to which a person is exposed. Carbon tetrachloride, once used as a dry-cleaning fluid, is mildly poisonous. If inhaled it sensitizes heart muscle, making it more reactive towards adrenaline. This effect is increased dramatically if carbon tetrachloride is inhaled after drinking alcohol, when collapse and death may result from small doses. Doctors are increasingly aware of the possibility of such harmful drug interactions and may warn patients to avoid certain combinations. This can often necessitate abstaining from alcohol while undergoing treatment.

Poisoning by alcohol

Ethanol, the active ingredient in alcoholic beverages, is probably responsible for more chronic poisoning than any other chemical substance. Among US white adult males, liver disease is the fourth most common cause of death. More than two-thirds of the cases are alcohol-related.

Alcohol interferes with the normal metabolic processes, mainly through its metabolic product, acetaldehyde. This can cause acute poisoning, the lethal dose being between 300 and 500ml consumed within an hour (equivalent to about 1 liter of gin or whisky). Related chemical substances are more toxic, and alcohol is sometimes used to prevent death from acute overdoses of both methanol and ethylene glycol. A major ingredient of automobile antifreeze, the latter is not poisonous itself – its metabolic products, though, cause harm. These are produced by the same enzyme that normally metabolizes alcohol. If large doses of alcohol are given to a person who has taken a lethal dose of ethylene glycol, the two substances compete for the limited amount of enzyme available. This slows down metabolism of the glycol and prevents the metabolic products from reaching a lethal concentration.

Ethanol dissolves easily in both water and lipids, so that it can be taken up readily by body tissues. In pregnant women, it can cross the placental barrier and poison the developing embryo. Substances with a toxic effect on embryos are called teratogens (◀ page 83).

▲ *Morphine, the principal alkaloid in opium, is a uniquely powerful pain-killer. But its euphoria-inducing qualities have also made it and the related diacetyl morphine (heroin) an increasingly widely-used and dangerous drug of addiction.*

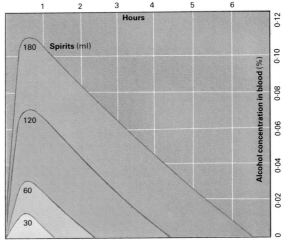

▲ *Alcohol remains in the bloodstream for many hours after drinking. There is some evidence that regular, moderate consumption may help protect against the build-up of fats causing heart disease; in other respects it acts as a poison.*

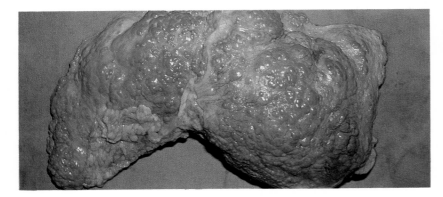

◀ *Chronic alcohol poisoning leads to the depositing of fat in and enlargement of the liver. In cirrhosis, the liver becomes fibrous and nodular, with a "hobnail" appearance. In 20 percent of cirrhoses, cancer of the liver also develops.*

*The sites of infections...Kidney diseases...The
eradication of smallpox...Measles and polio...Skin
infections...Infections caught from animals...Malaria
and yellow fever...Rabies and plague...PERSPECTIVE...
Scarlet fever, fading away?...The threat of meningitis...
Hepatitis...Blood poisoning and toxic shock syndrome...
Opportunistic pathogens*

All the body's tissues are vulnerable to invasion by microbes. Among
well-nourished people with good hygiene, some tissues are attacked
comparatively rarely. Conjunctivitis, for example, is uncommon in
the West – partly because tears, which bathe the conjunctiva (the eye's
transparent layer of skin) and cornea, contain the potent antibacterial
agent lysozyme. Yet one agent of conjunctivitis, trachoma virus, is the
world's commonest cause of blindness. Transmitted by touch and
flies, trachoma is particularly prevalent among the poor of Africa and
the Middle East. There is no satisfactory vaccine, and antibiotics act
only against bacteria as they attack tissue which has already been
infected by the virus.

Infections and sanitation

Two exceptions prove the rule about cleanliness and infection. The
first, poliomyelitis, is much less serious when mediocre living conditions expose children to the virus in their earliest years. Entering the
body by mouth, it multiplies in the throat and intestine, often causing
no ill effects whatever. Occasionally, though, the virus travels to the
spinal cord, where it destroys nerve cells, producing potentially fatal
paralysis. But the chances of this happening became far greater when
improved sanitation in the West began to postpone infection until
later years. This led to the first-ever epidemic (in Sweden in 1887),
then to outbreaks in the USA, and then to identification of the virus
and the development of vaccines. Two vaccines are now used – a live,
weakened poliovirus taken by mouth, developed by Albert Sabin (b.
1906), and a killed virus given by injection, developed by Jonas Salk
(b. 1914). Polio has declined dramatically since their introduction.

Glandular fever caused by Epstein-Barr (EB) virus also passes
unnoticed among children under ten – most of whom, in developing
countries, become infected and develop antibodies against it without
being aware of the fact. The better-known and often lengthy illness
of fever, sore throat and swollen glands is much more likely when infection is delayed until adolescence or adulthood. Often known as the
kissing disease, after one mode of transmission, it can be passed on by
any form of close contact. Time is the only healer. Neither EB nor the
other viruses which cause a minority of cases respond to drugs.

The importance of access

Certain infections are rare the world over simply because the target
tissue is so inaccessible. One is osteomyelitis, caused when a bacterium (usually *Staphylococcus aureus*) travels from an abscess or
wound infection and invades the long bones in a growing child.
Effective treatment requires that large doses of antibiotics are given
promptly and for a long period of time. Permanent deformity can
result if the infection spreads to a joint.

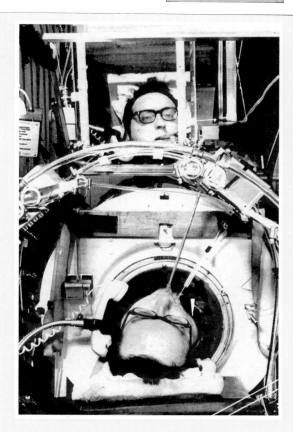

▲ *The iron lung was developed in the 1930s to help patients
whose respiratory muscles had been paralyzed by polio. The
decline of polio since the advent of mass immunization
made it obsolete, but a new use has been found for the
machines in helping patients suffering from nervous
disorders that impede breathing. The lung automatically
expands and contracts the patient's chest.*

▲ *Invented by Willem Kolff in wartime Holland, the artificial
kidney rids the blood of waste products such as urea which
normally filter out through the body's own kidneys to
produce urine. Blood flows between the machine and the
patient's circulation via a permanent "shunt" in the arm or
leg. It passes to a membrane with a vast surface area, across
which the impurities leak away into liquid on the other side.*

The urinary tract is a highly inviting site for colonization by bacteria. Bladder infection (cystitis), with its characteristic burning pain on urination, is commoner in females because of anatomical differences and usually responds to antibiotic therapy. Kidney infection, which is potentially much more serious, can be caused by bacteria migrating from the bladder or other parts of the body (virulent streptococci from a throat infection are particularly dangerous). The resulting damage prevents the kidney from purifying the blood. When untreated or unresponsive to treatment, such infections are one of the major cases of kidney failure. Two solutions are then possible – transplantation of a carefully matched healthy organ, or dialysis in which impurities are removed from the patient's blood as it passes through an artificial kidney (◀ page 117). Some specialists believe that people should be screened regularly for urinary infection – which, though it can be so mild as to be unnoticeable, may lead to irreversible kidney failure.

A killer wiped from the face of the Earth

Smallpox (*variola*) begins with a rash similar to that of chickenpox, but the spots soon become ugly pustules, which may bleed. One of the most severe infections ever known, smallpox killed 60 million people during the 18th century. But an immunization campaign, started by the World Health Organization (WHO) in 1967, ended in Somalia a decade later with the last known natural case. Smallpox is now extinct – the first infection ever to be completely eradicated worldwide. This achievement was possible by using a modern version of the vaccine developed by the English physician Edward Jenner (1749-1823) in the late 18th century. Smallpox itself used to appear in both its devastating, Asiatic form and also as the much milder alastrim. Working in a Gloucestershire village, Jenner decided to investigate the local tradition that farm workers became immune to smallpox if they acquired a similarly mild condition, cowpox, from cattle. Although controversial for decades afterwards, Jenner's inoculation of material from cowpox vesicles into peoples' skin to prevent smallpox was taken up in Britain and abroad, leading to a massive decline in smallpox deaths. WHO field teams were able to eradicate smallpox because immunization is long-lasting, because there is no animal "reservoir" for the virus, and because they could vaccinate large populations very quickly, propelling vaccinia virus directly through the skin with a jet injector.

If another disease is ever to be made extinct, the two most realistic possibilities are polio and measles. Like smallpox, the viruses do not occur in other animals, and similarly effective vaccines are available. Even in developed countries, the rash, fever and respiratory tract infection of measles can be followed by serious, life-threatening complications such as encephalitis or secondary bacterial invasion. But while measles has been virtually eradicated in some North American states, and several other countries are progressing in that direction, the disease remains a killer elsewhere. Its ferocity worsened by malnutrition and accompanying diarrheal illness, measles virus is responsible for 900,000 deaths annually in Africa and other parts of the Third World. Some authorities believe the WHO should embark on a global eradication program. Others feel this is impracticable because the vaccine has to be given in the brief period between infants losing antibodies received from the mothers and becoming vulnerable to infection (unlike vaccinia, which can be administered at birth).

Measles epidemics

► ▼ *Measles is one of the most contagious childhood infections, involving fever, running nose and a rash. Measles occurs in epidemics, the frequency of which apparently corresponds to the density of the population. Since vaccination was introduced in the early 1960s, the disease has declined in the United States.*

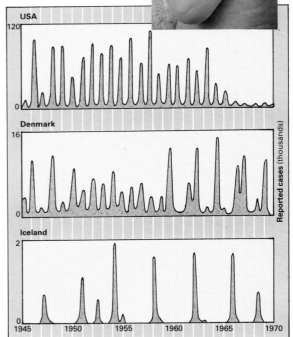

Staphylococci and blood poisoning
One bacterium whose impact on humanity has altered over the decades is Staphylcoccus aureus, an organism well adapted to cause disease by producing toxins and chemicals which allow it to spread by breaking down tissues. Before the antibiotic era, it was feared as a microbe which, having invaded the bloodstream from its primary site such as a carbuncle, boil or infected wound, produced shock, heart damage, and other life-threatening conditions. Some 80 percent of those with such "blood poisoning" died. The advent of sulfa drugs and then penicillin changed this situation dramatically, staphylococci being particularly sensitive to these drugs. But heavy use of antibiotics has led to a worrying increase in the proportion of resistant strains. And during the early 1980s Staph. aureus was incriminated as the agent of a condition among menstruating women: toxic shock syndrome. Characterized by rapid onset of high fever, nausea, vomiting and watery diarrhea, possibly leading to severe illness, this is thought to have been caused by staphylococci proliferating in tampons and producing a toxin absorbed through the membranes of the vagina.

◄ ▼ *Smallpox affected 10 million and killed over 1 million people annually before the eradication campaign which began in 1967. To wipe out the disease it was necessary to inoculate large numbers of people in affected areas after a thorough publicity campaign. Jet injector guns with high-pressure sprays rather than needles meant that it was possible to inoculate up to 1,000 people an hour.*

▲ *Edward Jenner (1749-1823) smearing cowpox pus on the scratched arm of a boy in 1796; until the introduction of mass vaccination, smallpox was primarily a childhood disease: some 30 percent of children died of smallpox before the age of three, and many more were blinded or disfigured by the disease.*

Chickenpox, shingles and mumps

Chickenpox (varicella) is an infection related both to herpes simplex (♦ page 120) and to smallpox. It is clearly identifiable from the crops of spots it causes, first on the trunk and then the face and limbs, when a young child is infected. Usually mild, the disease is highly infectious as these skin eruptions release more virus particles. Far less common is shingles (zoster). This occurs in adults when the same virus, persisting in nerve cells after recovery from chickenpox, becomes reactivated. The skin rash is similar, but the disease is extremely painful because nerves are affected. Although there is no treatment for chickenpox, idoxuridine helps shingles lesions to heal. A chickenpox vaccine has recently been developed, but its use remains controversial because the disease is so mild. But the same vaccine might help prevent the much more disabling condition of shingles too. A similar argument applies to infection of the salivary glands by mumps virus, which also tends to be mainly a childhood infection. Though a vaccine exists, and could forestall the testicular inflammation that follows mumps in 20 percent of men, the disease is rarely dangerous in children.

The dangers of rubella

Rubella (German measles) is not in itself a major health problem. In childhood the rash often goes unnoticed. Even adult victims, who may develop joint pains, usually have only a brief, mild illness. But rubella during pregnancy can cause deafness, heart and other defects in the child. First identified during the Second World War by Australian eye specialist Dr Norman Gregg, who noticed that congenital cataract was common among children of mothers who contracted rubella while pregnant, such teratogenic (fetus-poisoning) effects are the principal reason for immunization. Whereas the 1960s saw an estimated 12·5 million cases of rubella and about 20,000 malformed infants in the USA, the licensing of a vaccine in 1969 prefaced a massive reduction in the disease. Once, young girls were encouraged to attend "rubella parties" at which they allowed themselves to become infected (by droplet transmission from those with the disease), but most countries now have programs to ensure immunization of all girls at 12-14 or all children at an earlier age (thus reducing the possibility of pregnant women being exposed to the virus).

Leprosy still affects over 11 million people, mainly in Africa and Asia

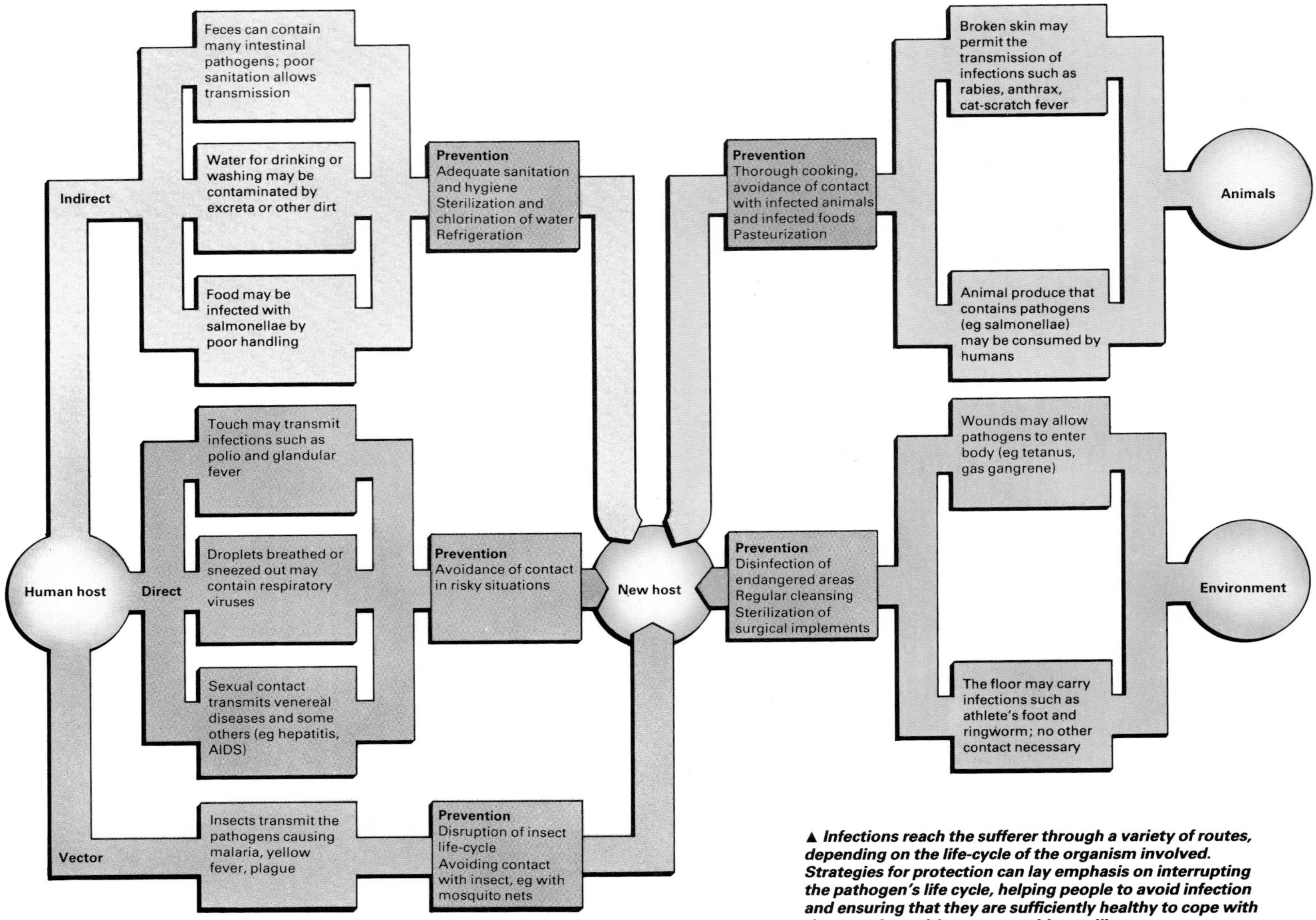
Human host
Indirect
Direct
Vector
Feces can contain many intestinal pathogens; poor sanitation allows transmission
Water for drinking or washing may be contaminated by excreta or other dirt
Food may be infected with salmonellae by poor handling
Touch may transmit infections such as polio and glandular fever
Droplets breathed or sneezed out may contain respiratory viruses
Sexual contact transmits venereal diseases and some others (eg hepatitis, AIDS)
Insects transmit the pathogens causing malaria, yellow fever, plague
Prevention
Adequate sanitation and hygiene
Sterilization and chlorination of water
Refrigeration
Prevention
Avoidance of contact in risky situations
Prevention
Disruption of insect life-cycle
Avoiding contact with insect, eg with mosquito nets
New host
Prevention
Thorough cooking, avoidance of contact with infected animals and infected foods
Pasteurization
Prevention
Disinfection of endangered areas
Regular cleansing
Sterilization of surgical implements
Broken skin may permit the transmission of infections such as rabies, anthrax, cat-scratch fever
Animal produce that contains pathogens (eg salmonellae) may be consumed by humans
Animals
Wounds may allow pathogens to enter body (eg tetanus, gas gangrene)
The floor may carry infections such as athlete's foot and ringworm; no other contact necessary
Environment

▲ *Infections reach the sufferer through a variety of routes, depending on the life-cycle of the organism involved. Strategies for protection can lay emphasis on interrupting the pathogen's life cycle, helping people to avoid infection and ensuring that they are sufficiently healthy to cope with the organism without succumbing to illness.*

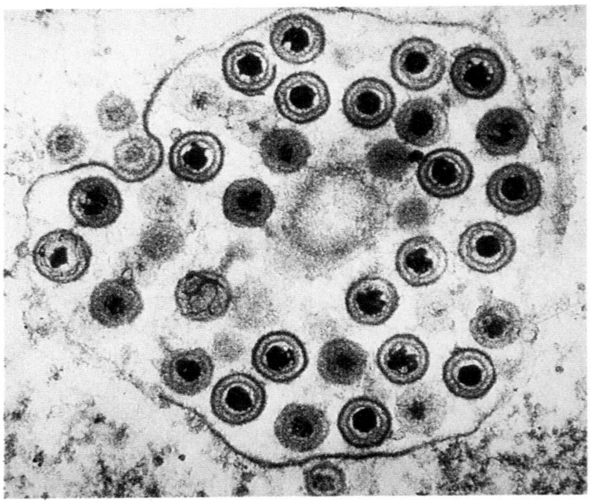

▲ *Herpes simplex, the virus responsible for persistent cold sores on the lips, and closely related to the genital herpes virus. It is thought that the virus is usually acquired during childhood, becomes dormant for many years, and becomes evident after stimulation by sunlight, infection etc. The cold sores may last for two weeks.*

The most disfiguring skin infections

Apart from orifices offered by respiratory, intestinal, reproductive and urinary tracts, the skin is an obvious target for invasion. Like the eyes, it too has defense mechanisms, but these can be breached. One of the commonest occurrences is when a normally harmless skin inhabitant, *Propionibacterium acnes*, proliferates inside sebaceous glands. The inflammation accompanying this invasion, known as acne, affects about 80 percent of adolescent girls and over 90 percent of adolescent boys. Related to excess sebum production resulting from hormonal changes during puberty, acne is usually fairly short-lived.

This is not the case with herpes simplex, probably our commonest virus parasite. Acquired in childhood and often without causing any obvious symptoms, the virus takes up residence as a latent infection – sometimes on the genitals but usually on the lips, where it produces intermittent cold sores.

Although its mode of transmission is still uncertain, leprosy is recognized principally for "granulomas" which appear on the skin. Related to the tubercle bacillus (◀ page 72), the leprosy bacillus produces similar nodules on internal organs but can also cause an anesthetic form of the disease, in which loss of sensitivity heightens the risk of

The decline of the scarlet fever bacterium
Most of us have suffered an occasional sore throat caused by streptococci. Yet scarlet fever, which at one time was a common sequel to such infections, is now very rare. Many of today's doctors are unfamiliar with the vivid red rash – feared because it in turn might be a prelude to the much more alarming rheumatic fever, which damages tissues of the heart. Treatment of serious streptococcal throat infections with antibiotics must be part of the explanation. Improved nutrition and hygiene may have helped. But another reason seems to be that the hemolytic streptococcus itself has become less virulent. Why the bacterium should change in this way is not known. Streptococci which continue to flourish in Asia, Africa and South America retain their virulence.

The new threat of meningitis
While some bacteria have faded in importance, microbiologists have become concerned about two others. Agents of meningitis (inflammation of membranes covering the brain and spinal cord), both are acquired through the respiratory tract. They produce sudden fever, headache and vomiting; are potentially fatal, and attack children in particular. Earlier this century, epidemics of "cerebrospinal, spotted fever" caused by one, Neisseria meningitidis, excited dread, notably in the USA. Today, after epidemics in countries ranging from Latin America to Europe, there is anxiety that the disease may be resurgent. And Haemophilus influenzae – a bacterium once wrongly thought to be the agent of influenza – has become the leading cause of bacterial meningitis.

◀ *The nodular "granulomas" produced in the skin and elsewhere by leprosy bacilli are sometimes accompanied by an anesthetic form of the disease in which victims lose sensation in their hands and feet, leading to injury and mutilation. The incubation period of leprosy can be several years, and drugs take several months to take effect.*

injury to the hands and feet. The disease progresses slowly over many years and is far less infectious than was thought in the days when lepers were synonymous with social outcasts. It still affects 11 million people, mainly in Africa and Asia, but is susceptible to a few drugs. Following the first, long-sought-after successes in growing the bacillus outside the human body – in armadillos – a vaccine was developed in the early 1980s and tests are now underway.

Some of the most disfiguring infections occur when fungi attack the skin, nails or hair. Although producing conditions which are often chronic and resistant to treatment, these fungi rarely affect the victim's general health. The commonest disease is Tinea pedis (athlete's foot), causing blisters between the toes. It is acquired from fragments of skin left behind by other sufferers, and is often contracted in showers and dressing rooms. Tinea corporis (ringworm) produces annular lesions on the non-hairy skin and is picked up by contact with infected children or, very occasionally, cats or dogs. Chemicals such as griseofulvin are effective, but only if used after scrupulous removal of dead and infected tissues. Fungi are also responsible for deeper infections. Many are restricted to certain geographical regions, where most people become infected though few succumb to the full-blown disease.

Opportunistic pathogens
Whereas older textbooks divided micro-organisms into those causing disease (pathogens) and those not doing so, the distinction now appears much less decisive. An individual's constitution and wellbeing may influence the chances of becoming infected with a well-recognized "pathogen", and some microbes are being identified as harmful only when given unusual opportunities. The bacterium Pseudomonas aeruginosa, for example, lives unnoticed in human intestines. But it can produce serious infections if it colonizes burned skin (where its resistance to many antibiotics poses an additional problem). Pseudomonads are also capable of proliferating in preparations such as eye drops and ointments, which can be extremely hazardous if the contamination is overlooked. Such "opportunistic pathogens" have been given further scope in recent decades with the development of substances intended to combat the rejection of transplanted organs by the body's immune system (◀ page 89). These drugs impair the immune response, making patients vulnerable to organisms that are normally harmless, so precautions are necessary to minimize the risk of infection.

Fighting with diseases

During the Crusades, each side tried to spread disease by dumping plague-ridden bodies into enemy camps. More recently, during the Second World War, British scientists tested a possible biological weapon and Japan also tested biological agents on prisoners of war. The 1972 Biological and Toxin Weapons Convention bans offensive work on biological weapons by the superpowers, but it still permits research into defensive measures. The development of vaccines inevitably involves the manufacture of correspondingly virulent bacteria and viruses, however, and there are fears that the spirit of the convention may be being flouted. While allegations of biological attacks by the Soviet Union in Laos and Kampuchea have not been substantiated, Western observers are convinced that the USSR is stockpiling infectious organisms for use in war. The US Department of Defense is also spending heavily on research into genetically-engineered micro-organisms. These could be much more dangerous than those that have evolved naturally.

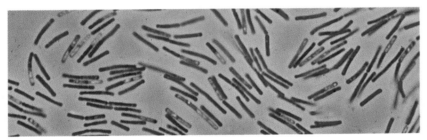

◄ *Bacillus anthracis is the agent of anthrax, a disease that is usually fatal in animals and may be so to humans if the spores are inhaled. The bacillus was first isolated and identified by Robert Koch in 1876; Pasteur then developed an anthrax vaccine which caused the disease to decline in many countries.*

▲ *In World War II the British Government experimented with the anthrax bacillus as a biological weapon. They tested its release on the uninhabited Gruinard Island in Scotland. Many sheep were killed, and it is intended that the island should remain isolated for at least one hundred years.*

Some micro-organisms attack the body only if allowed access through a wound. Best known is *Clostridium tetani*, the tetanus (lockjaw) bacterium. One of several bacteria capable of turning into hardy spores, this tolerates higher temperatures, and survives longer without food, than organisms unable to form spores. Although tetanus spores occur in soil throughout the world, the disease is rare in the West because most people are immunized in infancy (with triple vaccine, against diphtheria and whooping cough as well). Farm workers and others at risk also receive regular booster doses of anti-tetanus vaccine to keep their immunity high. *C. tetani* does not spread through the body. It triggers a potentially fatal illness by producing toxins which attack nerves, inducing convulsive muscular spasms. Penicillin has some effect on the organism, but the main tactic when a non-immune person becomes infected is to inject anti-tetanus antibodies. This confers "passive immunity", in contrast to the active immunity conferred by vaccination. In Third World countries, lack of hygiene during childbirth means that many babies are infected via the umbilical cord and killed by this most easily avoidable of infections.

Other species of clostridia include those responsible for botulism (not strictly an infection but a form of poisoning ◀ page 114) and gas gangrene. So-called because they liberate gases (and foul-smelling substances), the clostridia of gas gangrene gain entry to the body's tissues either through a dirty wound or, in the case of surgical wounds, from the patient's own intestines. Gas gangrene has been a potent threat during warfare – from the trench campaigns of the First World War to the more recent Falklands conflict.

Jaundice and the hepatitis virus

Hepatitis (inflammation of the liver) has emerged as a major public health problem in recent years. Symptoms are nausea, fever, weakness, loss of appetite, sudden distaste for tobacco smoking and (except in the mildest form) jaundice. Although in the earliest days of medicine Hippocrates recognized "epidemic jaundice", knowledge of the viruses responsible dates back only to the late 1960s.

Most serious is hepatitis B. This may persist after its acute and often severe phase to produce cirrhosis (◀ page 116). There is also strong evidence of an association between the disease and primary liver cancer. An estimated 200 million carriers worldwide includes 0·1 percent of the population in Europe and North America, compared with 20 percent in parts of Asia and Africa. Formerly called serum hepatitis because the virus is transmissible via blood and serum, it is now known to be spread by mouth and by sexual contact too; promiscuous male homosexuals are at particularly high risk.

Hepatitis A, acquired through water or food contaminated by feces carrying the virus, is incapacitating but unlike hepatitis B does not cause chronic liver damage. Vaccines against both forms of the disease are now under way – priority being given to those which can be given to groups (which range from dentists and laboratory staff to young male homosexuals) who are in particular danger of contracting hepatitis B.

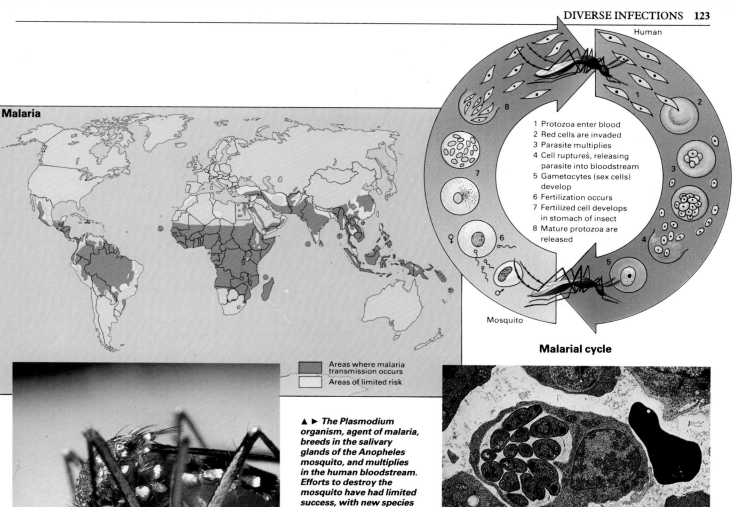

Malaria

Areas where malaria transmission occurs
Areas of limited risk

1 Protozoa enter blood
2 Red cells are invaded
3 Parasite multiplies
4 Cell ruptures, releasing parasite into bloodstream
5 Gametocytes (sex cells) develop
6 Fertilization occurs
7 Fertilized cell develops in stomach of insect
8 Mature protozoa are released

Human

Mosquito

Malarial cycle

▲ ▶ *The Plasmodium organism, agent of malaria, breeds in the salivary glands of the Anopheles mosquito, and multiplies in the human bloodstream. Efforts to destroy the mosquito have had limited success, with new species resistant to insecticide.*

◀ *Aedes aegypti, the agent of yellow fever.*

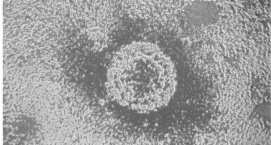

▲ *The virus of hepatitis B, which can remain in the bloodstream of healthy people for prolonged periods, perhaps indefinitely. For this reason people with the virus are never accepted as blood donors.*

Bacillus anthracis, the agent of anthrax, is related to clostridia but requires oxygen for growth whereas clostridia thrive without oxygen. Primarily a disease of sheep, cattle and horses, anthrax is occasionally acquired by humans, either through skin abrasions or by inhalation of the spores. "Hide porter's disease" and "wool sorter's disease" – names given to anthrax in the past – reflect its occupational significance. As a skin infection, it causes blisters which may become purulent; if untreated, blood poisoning may follow. When inhaled, the bacilli trigger a lung infection leading to hemorrages and blood poisoning. An effective vaccine is available, as are several antibiotics.

Anthrax is one of the zoonoses – diseases acquired from animals but which are not usually passed thereafter from person to person. Most are tropical conditions whose parasites spend part of their life cycle in intermediate "vectors". Malaria, caused by protozoa known as plasmodia which have a complex lifestyle in the human bloodstream and liver, and in the stomach and salivary glands of *Anopheles* mosquitoes, is the most widespread disease of this sort, with 400 million cases worldwide. Next come filariasis, whose thread-like worms, carried by various species of mosquitoes, affect 250 million people; schistosomiasis (bilharzia), with 200 million cases, caused by flat worms transmitted by water snails; and onchocerciasis (river blindness), another threadworm infestation, purveyed by a blood-sucking black fly and affecting 40 million people in Africa, central America and the Yemen. Others include sleeping sickness (African trypanosomiasis), caused by protozoa carried by the tsetse fly; Chaga's disease; and yellow fever, spread by *Aedes* mosquitoes.

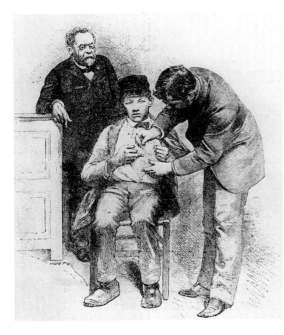

▲ *In July 1885 Joseph Meister became the first person to receive the rabies vaccine developed by Louis Pasteur; Pasteur himself was unsure that the vaccine would work but Meister lived to become caretaker of the Pasteur Institute.*

Some mysterious infections

Although the conquest of infectious disease is one of the great achievements of medical science, puzzles remain. One is that of multiple sclerosis – MS (◊ page 18) – which produces unpredictable defects in the nervous system. MS is probably attributable to a "slow virus" – one causing symptoms which take months or years to appear. The search for the MS agent continues. Another mystery is the cause of a type of encephalitis (inflammation of the brain) which first appeared in China between 1917 and 1927, affecting 65,000 people before spreading to North America and Europe and then disappearing. Several other encephalitides are known – some produced by viruses transmitted by ticks or mosquitoes, some arising as complications of conditions like measles. But the brief history of encephalitis lethargica has never been explained. Virtually unknown since the 1930s, it caused highly variable symptoms – including stupor, coma, fits and visual defects, which suggested that a virus was responsible. As the disease often led to the involuntary movements, paralysis and compulsive behavior of parkinsonism, microbiologists suspect that a slow virus was to blame. Paranoia and psychoses were common among victims, and historians have even speculated that the rise of National Socialism in Germany, with the violent, aggressive behavior and gesticulation of Hitler, may have been due at least in part to this extraordinary historical malady.

▶ *The rat flea, Xenopsylla cheopis, which carried the bacillus of bubonic plague and was responsible for spreading the Black Death and many recurring epidemics throughout the Middle Ages and 17th century. These epidemics spread across the whole of Europe in a few years, carried in ships and bags of wool.*

Offensive tactics are possible against several vector-borne diseases (vaccination to prevent yellow fever, drugs to treat, or better still prevent, malaria). For some recently recognized and highly lethal zoonoses such as Lassa fever (carried by rats), the only measure is to inject antibodies from blood serum donated by victims fortunate enough to recover. The main means of control is to attack the intermediate host though this, in turn, is bedevilled by the increasing resistance of mosquitoes and other vectors to chemical pesiticides.

Rabies, a zoonosis contracted when rabies virus passes into a person's bloodstream following a bite by a rabid dog or other animal, is an acute infection of the central nervous system. Also known as hydrophobia, because victims develop a dread of water, rabies causes vomiting, high fever and seizures, and is invariably fatal if untreated. But because rabies has a long incubation period in man (up to 16 weeks), patients can be helped by both active and passive immunization with pre-formed antibodies. Found in wildlife in many parts of the world (including jackals in India, skunks in the USA and foxes in Europe), rabies has been kept out of countries such as Britain by strictly imposed quarantine on imported animals.

Bubonic plague, the cause of three appalling historic pandemics (worldwide epidemics), begins as a zoonosis, when rat fleas leave their natural host and bite humans. This transfers *Yersinia pestis*, the plague bacillus, which spreads to lymph nodes and proliferates there, producing grotesque nodules called buboes, before colonizing many other organs and killing the victim. Pneumonic plague develops if the lungs are affected, so that bacilli are coughed up, spreading the infection from person to person. Both forms of the disease occured during the second pandemic – the Black Death, which began during the 14th century and killed 25 million people (a quarter of the population) in Europe alone. Now curable by antibiotics, plague remains a public health hazard in many parts of the world.

Index

Credits

Key to abbreviations: SPL Science Photo Library, London. b bottom; bl bottom left; br bottom right; c center; cl center left; cr center right; t top; tl top left; tr top right.

5 BBC Hulton Picture Library, London 6tl Zentralbibliothek, Zürich 6bl BBC Hulton Picture Library br Mansell Collection 7tl Royal Library, Windsor Castle, RL 19003v. Copyright reserved. Reproduced by gracious permission of Her Majesty the Queen 6bl Rembrandt: The Anatomy Lesson / The Bridgeman Art Library, London 6br BBC Hulton Picture Library 8t John Watney, London 8c Mansell Collection 8b Popperfoto, London 9tl Ann Ronan Picture Library 9tr BBC Hulton Picture Library 9br *Illustrite Zeitung*, Leipzig 10t SPL/Guy Gillette 10b SPL/R. Clark, M. Goff 11tl SPL 11tr SPL/Ohio Nuclear Corporation 11bl Frank Spooner Pictures, London 11br SPL/Dr R. Damadian 12 Camerapix Hutchison 13 Equinox Archive 14t SPL/Argentum 14b Rob Judges, Oxford 15t SPL/Argentum 15b Biophoto Associates, Leeds 16 John Watney 17b SPL/Bill Longcore 18-19 Camera Press, London 19b Ken Moreman 20 Network/Barry Lewis, London 21t BBC Hulton Picture Library/Bettman Archive 21b Mary Evans Picture Library 22 Ann Ronan Picture Library 23l Chim/Magnum Archive, Paris 23r Richard and Sally Greenhill 24l Ann Ronan Picture Library 24r Rob Judges, Oxford 25l Mike Abrahams/ Network, London 25r Laurie Sparham/Network 26 Frank Spooner Pictures 27l Laurie Sparham/Network 27t Mike Abrahams/ Network 28t SPL 28b Hogarth: Rake's Progress/Fotomas Index 29 SPL/Science Source 30-31 John Watney 31c Camera Press 31b John Watney 32bl WHO Photo/Best Institute 32c Dr J.J. Bending/Guy's Hospital, London 34 Janet

Hughes/Northwick Park Hospital 35 SPL 36 SPL 37l SPL 37r John Watney 38-39 Gower Medical Publishing 38t Dr J.C. MacLarnon/Nuffield Orthopaedic Hospital, Oxford 38b Zefa Picture Library, London 39c SPL/James Stevenson 39t John Watney 39br Biophoto Associates 39bl Gower Medical Publishing 40t Gibbs Dental Division, London 40b Lawrence Clarke, Witney 41l SPL/Martin Dohrn 41r Mansell Collection 42tl Zefa/J. Röhrich 42tr, cr SPL/John Radcliffe 42cl SPL/Russ Kinne 42 SPL/Hank Morgan 43 Camera Press/Colin Davey 44tl John Watney 44bl SPL/R. Stepney/M. Aumer 44br SPL/Dr Tony Brain 45 C. James Webb, Mitcham 46tr, c SPL/ Manfred Kage 46br Gower Medical Publishing 47t John Watney 47b Ken Moreman 48 BBC Hulton Picture Library 50 WHO/Dr Henrioud 51tl from *Illustrirtes Lexicon der Verfalschungen*, H. Klenske, Leipzig, 1879 51b Mansell Collection 54 SPL/John Durham 55 Biophoto Associates 56t SPL 56b SPL/Gene Cox 57 Biophoto Associates 58 SPL 59 SPL/Jim Stevenson 60-61 BBC Hulton Picture Library 60b John Watney 61bl John Watney 61 Ken Moreman 62 Rob Judges 63 Natural History Picture Agency 66 BBC Hulton Picture Library 67 SPL/Division of Computer Research and Technology, National Institute of Health 67b SPL/Dr S. Patterson 68 WHO Photo/P.Larsen 69t Gower Medical Publishing 69b SPL/Dr E.H. Cook 70-711,2 Biophoto Associates, 3a SPL/John Durham, 3b John Watney, 4a SPL/Dr E.H. Cook 4b SPL/Lee Simon/Sinclair Stammers 71t Michael Salas/Image Bank, London 72t SPL 72b Popperfoto 73 Ken Moreman, inset: Gower Medical Publishing 74l Topham Picture Library 74r Rex Features 75SPL/Dr J. McFarland, inset: Gower Medical Publishing 76 Richard and Sally Greenhill 78t Gower Medical Publishing 78c, b John Watney 79 Frank Spooner Pictures 80l Frank Spooner Pictures

80r BBC Hulton Picture Library 81t Sally and Richard Greenhill 81c SPL 82 Chemical Design Ltd., Oxford 83t, b SPL 85t, b WHO Photo, Geneva 86-87 Frank Spooner Pictures 87b SPL/Eric Gravé 88 WHO Photo 90b SPL/Biology Media 90-91 SPL/Dr D. J. McLaren 92t SPL/ Division of Computer Research and Technology, National Institute of Health 94 SPL/Manfred Kage 95t SPL/Dr A. R. Lawton 95b Associated Press 96t Zefa/Reichelt 96b Fotomas Index 97t SPL/Dr Brian Eyden 97b SPL/Manfred Kage 101 SPL/Andrejs Leipins 102 Mansell Collection 102-103 SPL/Dr R. Damadian 103 Zefa/V.W.S. 104 SPL/Dr Karol Sikor 105 SPL/Dr Rosalind King 106t John Watney 106-107cl, cr, b Biophoto Associates 107 Natural History Picture Agency 108t, b Frank Spooner Pictures 109 Frank Spooner Pictures 110t Topham Picture Library 110 Rex Features 111t, b Frank Spooner Pictures 112tl Topham Picture Library 112br BBC Hulton Picture Library 112-113 Salim Patel 113br Frank Spooner Pictures 114tl, br, Frank Spooner Pictures 114bl Natural History Picture Agency 115 Frank Spooner Pictures 116t BBC Hulton Picture Library 116bl Biophoto Associates 117t Popperfoto 117b Zefa/W. H. Mueller 118 SPL/Lowell Georgia 118tl BBC Hulton Picture Library 119tr Popperfoto 119cr WHO Photo/T. S. Satyan 120bl SPL/Science Source 121 Popperfoto 122tr Popperfoto 122cl SPL/Dr R. King 123cl SPL/Martin Dohrn 123cr SPL/Omikron 123b SPL/E.H. Cook 124t BBC Hulton Picture Library 124b SPL/Dr Tony Brain.

Artists Principal anatomical artwork by Dave Mazierski; other artwork by Lynne Brackley, Kai Choi, Chris Forsey, Alan Hollingbery, Kevin Maddison, Julia Osorno, Mick Saunders, Linda Stevens. **Indexer** Susan Harris. **Typesetting** Peter Furtado / Peter MacDonald, Hampton.